D1713365

THE STUDY OF ORAL INTERPRETATION
THEORY AND COMMENT

Russel R. Windes
Consulting Editor
Queens College of the City University of New York

THE STUDY OF ORAL INTERPRETATION
THEORY AND COMMENT

Edited by
Richard Haas
University of Michigan

David A. Williams
University of Arizona

THE BOBBS-MERRILL COMPANY, INC.

Indianapolis

The Bobbs-Merrill Company, Inc.
4300 West 62nd Street
Indianapolis, Indiana 46268

First Edition
First Printing 1975
Designed by Anita Duncan

Library of Congress Cataloging in Publication Data

Haas, Richard Burton, comp.
  The study of oral interpretation.

  I.   Oral interpretation—Addresses, essays,
lectures.   I.   Williams, David A., joint comp.
II.   Title.
PN4145.H2   808.5   74–13539
ISBN 0–672–61226–7 (pbk.)

CONTENTS

v

PREFACE

Prologue to His Book

—To say
In words the way
The wave, the cloud—
To read aloud
The last wings in the late air,
Interpret the faint character
Of the still flower;
Tell
What mute leaves spell;
Pronounce the dew,
The hushed scent, the silent hue;
To speak, to say
With speech, This way,
See, See, It was this way
The hills, the wind—
To say, Grief was as if. . . .
To say, And love . . . love . . . To say,
Yes, Yes, It was like this,
This way—

Elder Olson, "*Prologue to His Book*," Collected Poems (*Chicago: University of Chicago Press, 1963*), *3. Printed with permission of the author.*

Elder Olson's poem is a statement of a poet's efforts to create that
special feeling which is the poet's "Yes," the poet's knowing that
"it was like this." From our point of view as oral interpreters, the
poem is the poet's plea for a knowledgeable and fully-felt participation with the poem, for an appreciation of the poem which,
through its own saying, "pronounces the dew" without saying it, and
for an activity with those special features of literary art that manifest
themselves only through an active, sympathetic sharing within the
poem. This might sound a bit mystical, even supernatural, and so it
may be. There are moments when anyone dealing with literature
yields to the magic and knows that extra words are useless. But just
as there is a time in oral interpretation for feeling the magic, there
is also a time for *knowing with feeling,* a complete knowing based
on tradition, method, and a multiple critical perspective. The effort
of this book is to offer some "knowing" to enhance the oral interpreter's experiences with literature.

Most of us can recall those moments early in our careers of
interpretation interest when theoretical perspectives appeared too
dominant and "the doing" was more important and rewarding than
"the talking about." We still think so, but with some reservations.
There came a time when "the doing" was unsatisfactory because the
literature eluded us and the theory was in apparent disharmony with
the literature. Many of us proceeded with a self-pleasing revelation
that we had, in some mysterious manner or by virtue of our incredible insight, resolved that interpretation theory was something
for discussion after an oral reading, not a guide for achieving a
critical and humanistic perspective for the preparation of an oral
performance. When, however, theory was found to support and even
to reveal literature and to lay a foundation for our performance of
it, literature gained a stature that was inseparably bound to the act
and the art of oral interpretation.

Finally, we oral interpreters have one common bond—that
special moment when a piece of literature has conquered our inner-
most feelings and we are, for a moment, better than we were, deeper,
richer, and more rewarding to ourselves because we knew "It was
like this, This way." This interest in experiencing the knowing
sensation, "To say In words the way," is the same interest, we trust,

that prompted the contributors of this book to offer their observations to aid the knowing of others. We hope your study and discussion of this book will help you, through oral interpretation, "To say,

>Yes, Yes, It was like this,
>This way—"

CONTRIBUTORS

Wallace A. Bacon
Northwestern University

Janet Bolton
University of Southern California

Elbert R. Bowen
Central Michigan University

Robert S. Breen
Northwestern University

Eric W. Carlson
University of Connecticut

S. H. Clark*

S. S. Curry*

Ralph B. Dennis*

Virginia Floyd
New Mexico School for the Performing Arts

Don Geiger
University of California at Berkeley

Richard Haas
University of Michigan

* deceased

Kemp Malone
Johns Hopkins University

J. T. Marshman*

Alethea S. Mattingly
University of Arizona

William B. McCoard
University of Southern California

Frances L. McCurdy
University of Missouri

W. M. Parrish*

David A. Williams
University of Arizona

ACKNOWLEDGMENTS

Bacon, Wallace A. "The Dangerous Shores: From Elocution to Interpretation," *The Quarterly Journal of Speech* (April 1960), 148–152.

Curry, S. S. "Importance of Studying the History of Elocution and Vocal Training," *Proceedings of the National Association of Elocutionists,* 1895.

Clark, S. H. "The New Elocution," *Proceedings of the Sixth Annual Meeting of the National Association of Elocutionists,* 1897 (published in 1898), 666–684.

Dennis, Ralph B. "One Imperative Plus," *The Quarterly Journal of Speech Education* (June 1922), 218–223.

Marshman, J. T. "The Paradox of Oral Interpretation," *The Quarterly Journal of Speech* (February 1942), 31–36.

Parrish, W. M. "The Concept of 'Naturalness'," *The Quarterly Journal of Speech* (December 1951), 448–454.

———. "Interpreting Emotion in Poetry," *The Southern Speech Journal* (March 1954), 205–213.

McCoard, William B. "How Conversational is the 'Conversational Norm'?" *Western Speech* (May 1952), 199, 200.

Geiger, Don. "Oral Interpretation and the 'New Criticism,'" *The Quarterly Journal of Speech* (December 1950), 508–513.

Carlson, Eric W. "Robert Frost on 'Vocal Imagination, the Merger of Form and Content,' " *American Literature* XXXIII (January 1962), 519–522.

Malone, Kemp. "The Next Decade," *College English* (March 1964), 458–461. Copyright © 1964 by the National Council of Teachers of English. Reprinted by permission of the publisher.

INTRODUCTION

The field of oral interpretation possesses a number of excellent text-books on the act and art of oral interpretation. With only a few exceptions, these books are designed for the beginning student, and while some deservedly have been used for advanced classes, the field is without an advanced-level book dealing with the complexity of theoretical problems facing the discipline. With this book, we have attempted to put together essays reflecting many of the differing theoretical preferences which abound in oral interpretation. The fact that there are differences is a healthy condition of the art, but it is not healthy that these differences have not been discussed frankly in a book. They exist in articles and are discussed at conventions, but these differences are usually translated back to the student second-hand, without the student's opportunity to grapple with these same issues and differences.

This is not a fundamentals book, nor is it a book that deals with the practical aspects of technique and performance. It is intended for the advanced student, the student whose performing skills need improvement, but who needs to develop a theoretical sense upon which to base advanced performing work. Theory can provide a foundation for performance. And although theory, by itself, does not make good oral interpreters, no truly good interpreter can discount the effects that theory has played in the development of his art.

Theory is often forced to compete with performing interests, and the manner by which theory is presented to students is the reason. On the whole, oral performances are evaluated from a theoretical perspective; that is, performances are often required to fit within the theoretical foundations of a particular course. Experience shows that a performance at a festival, which had received plaudits from the original teacher (theory), can be criticized by another teacher (theory) as having missed the point of the literature, was insufficiently clear, overplayed the expressive role of the interpreter, and also might include a number of critical comments open to anyone conversant with a particular theory. A truer approach to the theory of an artistic act might be to allow the theory to describe the artistic activity it encounters, rather than to prescribe guides into which all artistic practices within the art must fit. This is not to belie standards—on the contrary. Without standards, a totally descriptive approach to theory construction would become little more than journalistic reporting. Nor is it recommended that all theories perceive artistic acts in the same way. Oral interpretation is an incredibly eclectic discipline. Eclecticism should contribute to theoretical strength, not divide into schools. At the same time, theoretical agreement is not necessarily advisable, for total agreement can lead to stagnation. Controversy and discussion are fundamental to any healthy theory.

This book does not present a theory; it presents theories. It presents disagreements. It presents discussions. And these are presented to help the student to better construct his own theory, and hopefully a theory that is flexible, eclectic, and always capable of growth. But most of all, we hope these statements, positions, and discussions will be perceived as a potential foundation for enlarging the humanistic benefit to be derived from the oral encounter with literature. We plan to help throughout the book by making observations and offering clarifications, but a number of these essays are quite involved, and honestly, some are quite difficult. Our plan for use of the book should help clarify some of the questions encountered. But before we get to that point, we shall illustrate the kind of theoretical difficulty to be discovered in this volume.

A few sentences back we mentioned, "the humanistic benefit to be derived from the oral encounter with literature." That appears to be an innocent phrase, but in fact, it carries with it certain prejudices concerning the role of oral interpretation. Two words stand out as giving value and direction to the phrase: "humanistic" and "encounter." To believe that oral interpretation helps develop a humanistic growth within the reader is accepted by many, if not by all persons in the field. But not all would agree to the method by which this humanistic growth is attained or the kind of humanistic growth that can be expected. For one thing, the theorist who intends his interpretative activity to unite himself with the text is actually doing something different from the theorist who prefers his interpretation to be an engaging and entertaining performance before an audience. And while another might want both results, and yet another claim that both are possible, a matter of degree enters into the manipulations of the approaches that alter the method and kind of humanism to be expected. The word "encounter" was chosen because it seemed free from too many biases. Rather than "encounter with literature," there are theorists who would prefer "the enactment of the literature," "the sharing of the literature," "the performing of literature for an audience" or "to an audience" or "with an audience." Any of these phrases and terms reveal a preference and a direction to the study of interpretation. Even the word *audience* brings up questions. What should be the interpreter's relationship with his audience? Is the audience the raison d'etre of interpretation? Or is the literature the reason for oral interpretation? Or is the interpreter? Since the interpreter is a member of his own audience, does he need an audience to establish a good oral interpretation? By now, answers are surely apparent to some of these questions we have posed, but what would others in the field say to these and other questions responsible for the differences in the theories of oral interpretation? We hope this book will help in the construction of answers. Here's what the book is.

A few years ago, we read through all the articles about oral interpretation that appeared in the seven regional and national speech journals. Additionally, we read through some of the convention proceedings back to 1892 to get a perspective on how interpretation progressed from the time it was eliminated from college curricula for lacking academic respectability. Occasionally, in our reading, we discovered articles that we thought were of considerable merit, articles that we thought any serious student in interpretation should read. We also found articles that are important for their respective periods, and though they do not necessarily present an acceptable guideline for today, they do reveal what interpretation was like then and illuminate some interesting observations about the more enduring aspects of interpretation theory. For each essay, we have provided a commentary by a modern interpretation theorist. These commentaries take the forms of addenda to previously written essays by the same author, rewritten essays from earlier published works, replies to articles, and discussions of what the contributors think now about what they or others had written before. While we are convinced that the essays chosen for this volume have considerable relevance to the student's theoretical development and performing skill, we recognize that other articles could have been selected. Some of the inclusions relate indirectly to interpretation, but they evoke considerable discussion and sometimes beneficial controversy. When we feel it profitable to group discussions, we will refer to many of the articles not included here. Now it is time to tell how the book is organized and how it is to be used.

The first article is an outstanding essay by Wallace A. Bacon, "The Dangerous Shores: From Elocution to Interpretation." Mr. Bacon reviews the history of interpretation and posits interpretation for 1960. His addendum to this essay, "The Dangerous Shores a Decade Later," appears as the last essay. With these two essays providing a frame of reference for locating interpretation theory, the other essays are presented in a chronological order. There are times when we break the chronology to highlight a particular theoretical premise. The contributors are notable figures in interpretation theory. We requested the contributors to express themselves freely and frankly. In a number of instances, we were delighted that they branched off on the idea they felt most relevant and important at the time. When their interests directed them to issues other than those that we had anticipated, we provided additional comment.

We have some suggestions on how to use the book which we feel will prove effective. First, the book is designed to provoke discussion. The instructor should act not only as an explainer, but also as a resource person, providing additional materials alluded to in the essays. It has been our experience in conducting seminars in twentieth-century oral interpretation theory, critical dimension seminars, and advanced poetry classes that these materials have engendered considerable discussion, discovery of new positions, a strengthening of theoretical understanding, and have contributed to intelligent, artistic performances. We have used the essays and commentaries as material for performances (many of the commentaries were recited aloud), evidence for debates, and sources for the students' own commentaries.

Probably the most exciting way in which this book can be used is to determine whether or not a particular theoretical position and/or approach to oral interpretation does indeed create a performance different from one that follows another theory. Comparative performances can reveal theoretical dimensions in a highly significant manner, as well as help to determine the role of theory in specific performances. In this way, probably better than in any other, a theoretical position may be developed with the realization of its relationship to performance and with the knowledge that a theory may change with every new piece of literature studied.

If we may use "the dangerous shores" metaphor, prepare to set sail! Professor Bacon tells us that the shores are dangerous, "but all the seas between are navigable, and the voyage is wondrous."

R.H.
D.A.W.

THE STUDY OF ORAL INTERPRETATION
THEORY AND COMMENT

WALLACE A. BACON

The Dangerous Shores:
From Elocution to Interpretation

When Thomas Sheridan defined *elocution* in the second of his famous eight lectures delivered in London in 1762, he said that it
was "the just and graceful management of the voice, countenance,
and gesture in speaking."[1] His concern was largely with pronunciation, accent, emphasis, tones, pauses, pitch, and gesture. Of these, he
singled out tones and gesture as the "pleasurable aspects of delivery," related particularly to the emotions; the other elements he
related particularly to the expression of ideas. Tones, he said, are
the auditory aspects of emotion, and gestures are the visible aspects
of emotion; for Sheridan, each passion had its own tone as well
as its peculiar look or gesture. Although he stated very clearly the
great significance of tones and gesture, Sheridan devoted only two
of the eight lectures to these elements. The bulk of his attention
went to the expression of ideas.

Sheridan's position was not in this respect new. The basic significance of meaning was expressed a century earlier by William
Holder[2] and others in their published lectures and writings, by Isaac

*This article is an adaptation of a paper read at the Washington,
1959 convention of SAA.*

[1] *A Course of Lectures on Elocution* (London, 1762).

[2] In *Elements of Speech* (London, 1669), Holder described the
art of speaking as "A sensible Expression and Communication of the

2 *The Study of Oral Interpretation*

Watts in 1720[3] and by John Mason in 1748.[4] In his own time, Sheridan was by no means alone in emphasizing the importance of ideas, for John Walker,[5] William Enfield,[6] Joseph Priestly[7] (to pick three names almost at random) were equally alive to the role of meaning in the whole art of speaking and reading. The eighteenth-century term *elocution* embraced not alone the classical concept of "style of composition," but the whole conveyance of meaning through style of composition *delivered,* and it was neither a "mechanical" nor a "natural" view, but simply a conventional and normative view, which recognized that Sense was the determining element, and that all passions must arise from and be fixed by that element. Giles W. Gray reinforced this point in his article, "What Was Elocution," in the previous issue of *QJS.*

Notions of the Mind by several Discriminations of utterance of voice, used as Signes. . . ." (p. 17). Holder has been too much overlooked by those interested in the history of elocution.

[3] *The Art of Reading and Writing English: Or, The Chief Principles and Rules of Pronouncing our Mother-Tongue* . . . (London, 1720). I have seen only the second edition of this work, dated 1722.

[4] *An Essay on Elocution, or, Pronunciation* . . . (London, 1748). See also *An Essay on the Action Proper for the Pulpit* (London, 1753).

[5] Walker's *Elements of Elocution* (London, 1781), published in a series of editions, became one of the best-known manuals for teaching elocution. It was described as being "the Substance of a Course of Lectures on the Art of Reading, delivered at several Colleges in the University of Oxford," in an advertisement suffixed to Walker's later *The Melody of Speaking Delineated* . . . (London, 1787).

[6] William Enfield's *The Speaker,* a remarkable anthology for its time, went through a series of editions beginning in 1774. To it was prefixed an essay on elocution. Enfield published as a sequel to the work another volume entitled *Exercises in Elocution* (Warrington, 1780).

[7] Priestley discusses language, oratory, criticism, grammar, and liberal education in a series of volumes. I am thinking here primarily of *A Course of Lectures on the Theory of Language and Universal Grammar* (Warrington, 1762).

Much modern discussion of the seventeenth- and eighteenth-century teachers of the art of speaking and reading—for they did not normally distinguish between these arts, but regarded them as nearly identical—has confused our view of these teachers by dividing them artificially into "natural" and "mechanical" schools. To be sure, some were mechanical in their methods of teaching and some few were not. But *all* stressed the significance of meaning in the act of reading and speaking, and none claimed that effects could be obtained or should be obtained apart from the text being read or spoken. Quite properly, teachers of reading and speaking, from classical times to the present, have at least bowed in the direction of the text.

Perhaps, rather than saying that earlier teachers *stressed* the significance of meaning, it ought to be said that they *recognized* it. It is also true that once having recognized it, they often took off speedily on their own vehicles for expressing it, scarcely looking behind them again to see whether it was following them. Nevertheless, meaning has always been at the center of the art of elocution, even when the center became only a point from which to move. It is worth urging the fact simply because teachers of interpretation are sometimes led to say nowadays that the recognition of the significance of meaning is a modern contribution to the study.

But when one has said that the elocutionists recognized the importance of meaning and has said again that teachers today recognize the importance of meaning, he may be saying two things rather than one thing. When Sheridan thought of meaning, he was not thinking of meaning as modern teachers of interpretation think of it. Perhaps one can illustrate the change most sharply by putting against Sheridan's definition of elocution ("the just and graceful management of the voice, countenance, and gesture in speaking") a modern view of interpretation as the study of literature through the medium of oral performance.[8] Both definitions reveal interest in the fundamental contributions of the oral performance. (It is

[8] See the preface to *Literature as Experience* (New York: McGraw-Hill, 1959) by Wallace A. Bacon and Robert S. Breen.

important to underscore the fact that in neither is literary appreciation viewed apart from delivery.) But Sheridan's definition uses the text as a point of departure whereas the other uses the text as a point of return. And this, very simply, seems to be the clear line of change from the eighteenth century to our own time in the teaching of oral reading. The single additional fact to be noted is that interpretation tends (though not absolutely) to restrict its materials to works of imaginative literature, in keeping with its position in the liberal arts-humanities tradition in educational institutions.

The two definitions cited above point to a polarity which can be discussed in terms of a metaphor of the young Troilus in Shakespeare's *Troilus and Cressida*. The poles here are, of course, text on the one hand and delivery on the other.[9] These are, in elocution and in interpretation, the two "dangerous shores" between which, or on which, any ship can founder. The double character of the subject can be stated in a whole series of compounds: scholarship-showmanship, reason-passion, logic-emotion—even, in the eyes of some observers, in the pair dull-exciting. Or in the old pair, naturalmechanical.

All these bifurcations are simply underscoring the dilemma which exists, has always existed, and always will exist in the art of reading; the whole art consists, has always consisted, and always will consist in a union of the two elements. It has not in the long run worked to overlook the basic and determining character of the text being read; neither will it work to overlook the essential significance of the oral performance. Literary appreciation for the silent reader and literary appreciation for the oral performer are in some respects vitally distinct, and teachers of interpretation, as separate

[9] Troilus has another set of poles in mind. As Shakespeare puts it (II.ii.61–65):

> *Troilus.* I take today a wife, and my election
> Is led on in the conduct of my will;
> My will enkindled by mine eyes and ears,
> Two traded pilots 'twixt the dangerous shores
> Of will and judgment. . . .

from teachers of English, must keep their eyes and ears on the distinctions.

It is necessary to underscore this remark. Unless the text in oral performance is both audible and alive, the reader has not learned what oral interpretation is meant to teach him. There are three things involved—not just audibility and life, but the text which is meant to be audible and alive. The thing read is, on the whole, the interpreter's excuse for being.

When the modern student of interpretation talks of the meaning of a literary text as the thing which it is his responsibility to convey, he is not talking simply about lexical meaning, as Sheridan and his contemporaries largely were. His keen interest in and awareness of psychology has made him very sensitive to the interlacing of motives, attitudes, and tensions in literature, and to the ambiguities, ironies, and ambivalences of literary works. The language of literature is a wonderfully complex and efficient thing—wonderfully because its intricacy is a very exciting and compelling fact; indeed, it is almost incredible, sometimes, how sharp a distillation of experience can be bound into words. The fact is as true of Robert Frost as of—whom?—Shakespeare. This is not a matter simply of difficulty of comprehension.

Interpretation today seems to be moving in the direction of the thing read, not in the direction of the person reading. This is not because the person reading is unimportant—it is the function of teachers to educate students—but because it is possible to feel that the best way to educate students is to teach subjects. If it is true to say that works of literature are both pleasurable and valuable to human beings, then it seems also true that the fullest kind of reading of works of literature is the most pleasurable to human beings. And if interpretation is concerned not only with an "awareness" of the poem or story or play, but with the student's own active participation in the text by way of the oral reading, then it is possible to feel that interpretation provides the student with the fullest kind of reading. But the point is that the participation is participation in the life of the text—and such participation can follow only from understanding (deliberate or intuitive) of the text. Understanding (even informed intuition) involves knowledge.

As Lily Bess Campbell[10] suggested in reply to Mark Van Doren, the study of literature often involves more than "a whole heart and a free mind," and there are many teachers of interpretation who are too timid in venturing out into the world of scholarship and criticism for the kind of solid assistance which that world can often supply. The teacher who reads no more than the students in his class—and who does not know where to go to find more to read— will not necessarily find that such reading makes him a full man.

For some people, such close reading of texts as a *full* reading demands will always seem a little dull. Some people will feel sure that such reading must necessarily result in dull performances—but they can very easily be shown to be wrong. It is not a matter of arguing for "scholarship" as opposed to "entertainment," but rather of suggesting that the good reading is exciting because it is really full. And fullness must be judged in terms of the text being per- formed, not simply in terms of reading techniques, though one must grant the importance of techniques and the value of techniques, which must not be sacrificed. It would be a mistake for interpreta- tion to follow certain practices in the teaching of public speaking, in which an interest in something called "content" has led to a corresponding decrease of interest in something called "delivery," to the ultimate disservice of "content." Or to follow certain practices in the teaching of the dramatic arts, where the theatre becomes a theatre-museum. *Both* shores, as Troilus recognized, are dangerous. The approach to both shores is over shallows.

One way of illustrating the recent direction in interpretation is to point to the changes in the titles of courses in curricula in the field, and to the change in the nature of the topics listed in convention programs over the past fifteen years. In curricula ranging from the freshman year through the doctoral program—though the statement is naturally more applicable to some schools than to others—there has been a clear increase in the degree of emphasis placed upon the study of literature. One finds courses devoted to literary forms, to literary periods, to single authors; there are courses

[10] *Shakespeare's "Histories," Mirrors of Elizabethan Policy* (The Huntington Library: San Marino, California, 1947), 3.

in the general aesthetics of literature and interpretation; there are increasing numbers of seminars in interpretation.

It is not unusual to find, on the whole, that the greater interest in the texts being performed has led to a greater interest in performance and to larger audiences for performances. More students read; more people come to listen. The range of things read is wide, the kinds of performance varied. It would be a mistake to equate the value of interpretation with the size of audiences, of course. Little would be gained if, with increased audiences, the quality of performance and literature decreased. Too much interest in the audience is as bad as too exclusive interest in text—another way of looking at the dangerous shores.

The current interest in text has not taken form out of thin air, to be sure. Interest in meaning has always been with us; but besides this, nineteenth century interest in psychology contributed to eighteenth century interest in language and delivery a serious concern with the mechanisms involved in the body's representation of literary texts. Words, attitudes, movements, tones, rhythms—all these are thought of now as forms of gesture, as ways of communicating meaning from the mind and heart outward. S. S. Curry and Charles Wesley Emerson, in this country, explored, as fully as their knowledge of psychology would permit, the mechanisms of conveying meaning *via* the body and the voice. Both men valued meaning, though for them as for the men preceding them meaning was a limited term. In our own century, Solomon Clark, Robert L. Cumnock, Hiram Corson, and others—in our own time, Gertrude Johnson, C. C. Cunningham, and Wayland M. Parrish have carried us further. Frank Rarig related the psychology of the reader to the psychological interests in the literary text and hence performed a uniquely valuable service. There are many others—few are named here and those only from among the teachers officially retired from teaching. The development has been steady if gradual.

But interpretation *today* is interpretation with something of a difference. Psychology, the new criticism (which is no longer new, and no longer reigns), the nature of contemporary literature, and the nature of teachers and students now entering into the study of our subject have all combined to point sharply and incisively to the literary text as the source of all the problems with which students and teachers of interpretation are concerned. How to body forth the whole complex structure which is the work of literature? Many teachers have come more and more to recognize that all other questions spring from this. What the poem or the story or the play means is not something to be extracted or abstracted from the literary structure, but something to be felt and understood fully only within the structure. Enjoyment is the final aim—but enjoyment in a full rather than in a reductive view. The wonderful thing is that such a pleasurable activity is also so finely instructive to us as human beings. If one values teaching the reading of Shakespeare to students, it is because he thinks Shakespeare has so much to say to them and to him, and because learning how to enter into a full exploration of the text of Shakespeare seems to him the best way of learning how to *listen* to Shakespeare. Learning how to hold a book, how to enunciate clearly, how to project, how to modulate tones, how to place characters, how to control stage fright—all these now become of importance in relation to the *life* of the literary text. The student's eye is not on development of an instrument, or of a personality, only, but on life as literature conveys it. Too great a satisfaction with self is not the best of preparations for the study of letters.

The teacher who has come to value advanced courses dealing with a limited number of writers has doubtless found that the extensive and intensive study of one man has increased the expressive range of interpreters with regard to that one man. Once they have been persuaded of the close correlation of mind and body, voice and spirit, most students will find that an increase in the intellectual range is the surest way to an increase in the whole emotional range. Meaning, for them, becomes not lexical meaning, not abstracted or extracted meaning, but whatever is included in *both* sides of that dichotomy we have been observing—intellect-emotion. And it is served not simply by "mechanical" means, not simply by "natural" means, but by both sides of *that* dichotomy. It employs not simply scholarship, not simply performance techniques —but both sides of *that* dichotomy. The teachers who pay lip service to performance but really care only about discussion of literary texts are not properly meeting their obligations as teachers of interpretation. The teachers who pay lip service to literature but really think of it only as something to perform are not meeting their obligations—and there are many such teachers.

Interpretation moves, as it has always moved—and as all the performing arts are always likely to move—between two dangerous shores. One may be wrecked on either. But all the seas between are navigable, and the voyage is wondrous.

∿

RESPONSE

Richard Haas
and David A. Williams

Professor Bacon has identified the dangerous shores of interpretation as they appeared to him in 1960: the bifurcations of the discipline's interests. He says "these bifurcations are simply underscoring the dilemma which exists, has always existed, and always will exist in the art of reading." We are not convinced that theorists realize that our discipline is an oral study of literature which need not divide text from delivery, logic from emotion, or reason from passion. But judging from our history, as Professor Bacon so wisely did, it seems we may be wrong—unless, of course, we learn from our past.

It is apparent in his essay that Bacon steers a course closer to the literary shore than the delivery shore. And although he accepts intuition as a navigational guide, he means an "informed intuition" that does not accept the flaccid assertion of "That's what the poem means to me." But the position established by Bacon appears to offer considerable latitude in theoretical approach to interpretation. Both shores are dangerous, he says, "but all the seas between are navigable." He is right. The seas between the shores are full of theories and performances. The theories and performances, however, will not appear the same to those viewing from a position close to the delivery shore as they appear to those viewing from the literary shore. These differences in perception suggest that interpretative evaluation might be based more on the evaluator's position in the "seas" than on the performance itself.

Another discussion point created by Bacon's essay is the matter of audience. The consideration of audience is not absent in the essay, but it is also not a functioning element of the dangerous shores metaphor. Possibly his statement "that interpretation provides the student with the fullest kind of reading" implies that the greatest value of interpretation is humanistic—the value gained by the interpreter in his "participation in the life of the text." Such participation employs the poem as "a point of return" and not as "a point of departure." The question could be asked: Is departing from the poem an act of embracing an audience and diminishing the humanistic value for the interpreter or simply a manifestation of an interpreter accepting his performance obligations?

A general challenge to the dangerous shores came to the editors from a few students. They pointed out that since 1960 a theoretical distinction has emerged which alters the interpreter's definition of literature and his definition of himself. This distinction, simply stated, establishes the interpreter as a creative artist, who, having recognized the meaning of literature, investigates the meaning of that literature in oral performance. As creative oral performer, he pursues and exploits in oral performance all that he finds around him to heighten and intensify the experience for an audience. He acts as any creative artist acts; he uses all that exists for a performance and stresses the literature with no more emphasis than any other feature of the performance. Apparently, they sail their ships closer to a delivery shore than Professor Bacon would recommend; but then, they would say the shore metaphor is not for them. "Language is speech," they would say, "and literature is an event of performed speech; so what I do is fulfill precisely what literature is. As a creative artist, I perform fully an unfulfilled speech performance." But then, don't recreative interpretative artists do that too?

The editors are not trying to challenge Professor Bacon. His essay is an acknowledged hallmark in the theory of interpretation. We have attempted rather to point out some dimensions of his essay which could evoke profitable discussion. As stated in the introduction, each essay should be read for its value *and* for the dimensions that provoke commentary.

∾

Today, looking out upon the straits that Troilus spoke of and Bacon demarcated, the theoretical positions bobbing around might appear to resemble flotsam and jetsam rather than an organized body of theory. Some of the theories even appear to bump angrily into each other. But then, it has always been so. And, we presume, the controversy makes for improved theory, though we wonder if our history cannot provide us with clearer navigational guides.

In 1895, S. S. Curry realized the weakness of remaining ignorant of the past and called for a study of elocutionary history in a paper delivered before the National Association of Elocutionists. He believed a history would reveal the enduring truths of the discipline and would coordinate the efforts of all elocutionists. Today, we have had many historical studies and the knowledge in these studies has been both disappointing and rewarding, but always informative. As Professor Bacon is reported to have said: "One is reassured to know he has ancestors."* And modern interpretation theory is sufficiently diverse to *require* a knowledge of the past.

Selected Readings

Beloof, Robert. "Oral Reader and the Future of Literary Studies," *The Speech Teacher* XVIII (January 1969), 9–12.

Bowen, Elbert R. "Promoting Dynamic Interpretative Reading," *The Speech Teacher* VII (March 1958), 118–120.

* Quoted by Alethea Mattingly in her paper, "Historical Studies in Interpretation," delivered at the Western Speech Communication Association, Fresno, 1971.

Campbell, Paul. "Communication Aesthetics," *Today's Speech* XIX (Summer 1971), 7–18.

———. "Performance: The Pursuit of Folly," *The Speech Teacher* XX (November 1971), 263–274.

Cunningham, Cornelius C. "Aims and Techniques of Oral Interpretation," *Western Speech* IV (May 1940), 1–5.

Geiger, Don. "Oral Interpretation and the Teaching of Literature," *The Speech Teacher* XI (September 1962), 202–207.

Hargis, Donald E. "Interpretation as Oral Communication," *The Central States Speech Journal* XI (Spring 1960), 168–173.

Irwin, Ray. "The Bases of Criticism in Oral Interpretation," *Today's Speech* XIV (February 1966), 5–7.

Marshman, John T. "Speaking the Speech," *The Central States Speech Journal* X (Winter 1959), 64–66.

S. S. CURRY

Importance of Studying
the History of Elocution
and Vocal Training

Whoever wishes to make safe progress in any department of science or art must "hold the past firmly by the hand." Man can consciously use the materials of his fellowmen gathered today or ages ago. He who does not do so is weak; at any rate, he cuts himself off from the greatest means of growth and support that can be found in the world.[1] The historical method must be used in all departments of knowledge.

Notwithstanding, however, the common acceptance of these principles there has long seemed to be a tendency among elocutionary students to ignore the history of their art. Many a teacher has seemed to desire the unconscious condition of the bird and to build his nest on some high limb as he thinks out of his own ideas without joining what little he can do to all that has been done before him.

Many boast that they have not studied with anyone and seem to glory in the fact that they do not know the methods which have

---

[1] "The scholar, . . . and we think student too whatever his field, can scarcely afford to be ignorant of what has gone before, for true it is that 'He who knows only his own generation will remain forever a child.'" Stated by Alethea Mattingly in her paper "Historical Studies in Interpretation" delivered at the Western Speech Communication Association Convention in 1971 [editors].

been arranged by others. The modern speaker often desires that no one shall ever know that he has taken a lesson in elocution! The delivery of the average speaker, as a rule, is such that he should have no anxiety on that score. His audience will never suspect that he has received assistance from a teacher able to read his needs and to apply such training as would develop his true personality and realize his possibilities.

No one who has struggled with the problems will fail to realize how difficult it is to write such a history. Vocal expression is the most subjective of arts. Every teacher of elocution who has ever amounted to anything has studied with other men; has received his traditions face to face with those who preceded him. Professor Monroe was taking lessons from others the last year of his life. The true teacher never refuses to be taught by others, never adopts some little system founded upon some temporary expedient that may have proved helpful to some individual; or bases his methods on his own natural endowment, his success in some contest.

But granting all this, every teacher and student needs to have the whole field illuminated; and the only light which will serve as a safe guide must come from the study of elocutionary history. In fact, the study of history is the most effective means of leading the teacher and the student to realize the very fact that delivery and all vocal art is personal and must be improved by a present mirroring of a soul to itself by another soul.

Allow me to present to you certain advantages which may be gained by the application of historic methods to various departments of vocal training, and vocal expression.

1. Such a historical study, were the materials accessible, would prevent mistakes. Ignorant people must live over again all the old exploded heresies simply because they do not look into history and find the light of experience which shows the natural result which follows certain conditions and causes.[2]

2. The historic method enables us to appreciate what is really new in the theories of the present time. If we know the past we

[2] See the discussion of this point in the Choral Reading essay elsewhere in this volume [editors].

can realize the advances that are being made, we can distinguish the true discovery of principles, from what is mere ingenuity or oddity or the result of mere vagaries, and what is really far behind the methods of other days.

3. One who is familiar with the struggles of the past will be able to feel the needs of his own time, and having come to understand and to feel the current of history, and having seen the mistakes of the past and realized the struggles of other days to advance his work, he will be able to grapple with the problem of his own age more effectively; he will be less subservient to any particular system, less liable to ride a hobby.[3] He will be able to look at his work from many points of view, he will be able to realize its need in general and to meet each individual case more adequately. Besides, he will be able to realize the true hindrances to his work; he will understand why it is not making greater advances, why it is not better appreciated. He can feel the remote causes of the difficulties which he has to face now, and above all he will be able to feel wherein the greatest dangers lie.

4. The historical method prevents egotism. The man who holds some little idea and, thinking that he has something that no one else in the world has ever known, imparts it to students as if it were the greatest secret in the universe, when he finds out that what he is trying to teach is more than three thousand years old and has been applied by thousands of teachers, such a light breaks into his narrow and egotistic soul that he is really able to see beyond his little sphere.

5. A study of the history of his art broadens the mind of a teacher or a student and enables him to realize its relation to other departments of knowledge and other forms of instruction. He realizes better the true nature of his own art, its limitations, its possibilities, its function, and its true power.

[3] "Today's interpreter can better steer his course, we believe, when, informed of the past, he perceives the present and envisions the future." Quoted from Mattingly's WSCA paper, 1971. See also Breen's statement quoted in the editor's discussion of Floyd's response to Parrish's "Interpreting Emotion in Poetry" [editors].

6. There would be an appreciation of the changes that have taken place in the style of speaking and of acting and of public reading, the causes of these, and the lessons entailed regarding the new methods for their development.

With a history of our field, artists could realize the relation of the art of vocal interpretation to other arts . . . and the world might be brought to see something of what we owe Thomas Sheridan and his plans for the reform of education one hundred fifty years ago.

❧

RESPONSE

Elbert R. Bowen

What? Do we really have to defend the history of our art?

It is no surprise that Curry, "the great eclectic," would make a pitch for it. His desire to learn and to use all valid methods of training is obvious to anyone who has read him. In his *Province of Expression,* he said, "comparison with results obtained in the past is one of the safest tests of truth."

Curry is a major figure in any historical survey of the development of modern concepts in oral interpretation. Among several astute men, Curry especially saw the follies of excessive and exclusive attention to techniques of performance. In their teaching, speaking, and writing, Curry and others led the way back to the essentiality of human response to literary meaning, a contention we take for granted today. *We* must study Curry, realizing all the while that had *he* not studied his predecessors of all persuasions, he probably would not have made his own contribution.

Let's look at this matter with reverse logic: to ignore our academic forebears (such as Plato, Aristotle, Cicero, Quintilian, Mason, Burgh, Sheridan, Walker, Cockin, Austin, Whately, Porter, Rush, Murdoch, the Bells, Delsarte—if you can find him—Curry, Corson, Clark, Winans, Woolbert, and so many others I so dangerously fail to list here) is to deny that they ever thought anything of value, either valid or not. Can anyone afford to take that chance?

On this occasion I should, I suppose, produce an inductive demonstration of the efficacy of historical study; but, in spite of a horrifying realization of the woeful, if not willful, ignorance of historical backgrounds in many teachers and most students in oral interpretation, I rather choose to ride off on a tangent. For being a student of all theories and methods, Curry is both admired and criticized. Let's face it: "eclecticism," in our day, is often a dirty word. We expect a theorist to drive a clear-cut philosophical route. Although Curry veered sharply off the elocutionary expressway shouting "impression precedes expression," he studied everyone in the field and adopted any idea or procedure he found usable. Furthermore, he studied the philosophers and the psychologists with a gusto that most of us should, but usually do not. As a result, the modern student regards Curry's writings as diffuse and ambiguous. "Eclecticism" tends to create "ambiguity," and "ambiguity" is too often accepted as "inconsistency," and everyone knows that inconsistency is no damn good.

Whether they intend to or not, the scholars appear to slap a besmearing implication of inconsistency onto Curry's ambiguity. In the impressive spread of his dozen or more books (nine on my shelves) it is too bad that Curry could not have, in *one* of them, boiled it all down to a crystal-clear explication of his final, pre-resting-place theory, just to please the yelping dogs. But he did not.

What I am really getting at is this: in these days of consistency and disambiguation,* the "literary wing" seems to regard those who are interested in both literature and oral communication as pledging inconsistent allegiances. I am prone to rewrite a bit of old fraternal cant out of my college days: "I'm mighty proud to be a Synthesist."

---

* Katherine T. Loesch, in her essay, "Literary Ambiguity and Oral Performance" *The Quarterly Journal of Speech,* October 1965, pp. 258, 259), borrows the term *disambiguate* from Katz and Fodor. "To disambiguate means to select a single interpretation from alternative possibilities."

✑

RESPONSE

Frances L. McCurdy

In 1895 Samuel Silas Curry urged the members of the National Association of Elocutionists to become familiar with the past in order to grapple more effectively with the problems of their own age. He called for a comprehensive history of interpretation. His plea is still to be answered. The essays *The History of Speech Education* edited by Karl Wallace, Mary Margaret Robb's *Oral Interpretation of Literature in American Colleges and Universities,* Eugene and Margaret Bahn's *A History of Oral Interpretation,* along with other monographs and unpublished dissertations, provide much valuable historical material; but the comprehensive histories, either of theories or practice, are still to be written.[1]

Too much of the energy of writers in the field of interpretation has been channeled into textbooks that offer no new viewpoint and add little to what others have previously said. The field would be better served by studies of theories and methods, past and present, than by a plethora of textbooks. Many questions remain to be answered. Marion Kleinau has called for research into "the interior world of the interpreter as he interacts with himself about the literary work (a sociopsychological act) and as he interacts with his audience (a social act)."[2] Others who have emphasized the performance of literature stimulate questions about means and ends.

[Footnotes are by editors.]

[1] Jere Veilleux in "Towards a Theory of Interpretation," *The Quarterly Journal of Speech* LV (April 1969), 105 begins his essay with the statement: "The history and theory of oral interpretation as a performing art has been a much-neglected research area."

[2] Paper presented as part of a committee report on research in interpretation at the SCA convention, December 1970. For work related to Kleinau's call for research regarding the interpreter's interaction with his audience, see David A. Williams's "The Effects of Positive and Negative Audience Response on the Oral Interpreter: A Multiple Indicator Approach," unpublished dissertation (University of Utah, 1971).

Focus on performance of literature is not synonymous with the eighteenth-century emphasis on *pronuntiatio*[3] as an end in itself but does point up the wisdom of Mr. Curry's reminder that "the real reformer is one who . . . knows what has been done before."[4]

Mr. Curry's comment is equally relevant in its reference to the need for a study of the past as a way of realizing the relation of interpretation to other departments of knowledge. The increasing interest of departments of English in the embodiment of literature and the research by psychologists, sociologists, and others in non-verbal elements of communication makes *it desirable that interpretation should determine its particular substance and contribution to instruction.* In the past two decades interpretation has been temporarily absorbed by a series of interests. Choral reading, explicative analysis, rhetorical analysis, linguistic study, and readers' theatre, one after another, have taken center stage. *Interpretation must determine where its focus is to be placed and precisely what its art consists of.*

Selected Readings

Anderson, Robert G. "James Rush—His Legacy to Interpretation," *The Southern Speech Journal* XXXIII (Fall 1967), 20–28.

Barclay, Martha Thomson. "Major American Emphases in Theories of Oral Interpretation from 1890 to 1950," unpublished dissertation, University of Minnesota, 1968.

Bassett, Lee Emerson. "Elocution Then, Oral Interpretation Now," *Western Speech* XIII (March 1949), 3–8.

[3] *Pronuntiatio,* one of the five canons of rhetoric, was the classical term for delivery.

[4] Professor McCurdy is stating a concern that too much nonhistorical research in interpretation has been directed to a performance orientation interested primarily in what to perform, how to perform, and the responses wanted from an audience. She does not object to an interest in performance, but realizes that it is not the complete act of oral interpretation.

Drake, Christine. "A Critique on 'The Curry Method,'" *The Southern Speech Journal* IX (March 1944), 112–117.

Faries, Elizabeth. "A Defense of Elocution," *The Southern Speech Journal* XXIX (Winter 1963), 133–140.

Fritz, Charles A. "From Sheridan to Rush: The Beginnings of English Elocution," *The Quarterly Journal of Speech* XVI (February 1930), 75–88.

Gray, Charles W. "What Was Elocution?" *The Quarterly Journal of Speech* XLVI (February 1961), 1–7.

Guthrie, Warren. "The Development of Rhetorical Theory in America, 1635–1850: The Elocution Movement—England," *Speech Monographs* XVIII (March 1951), 17–30.

Howell, Wilbur Samuel. "Sources of the Elocutionary Movement in England: 1700–1748," *The Quarterly Journal of Speech* XLV (February 1959), 1–18.

Mattingly, Alethea Smith. "Follow Nature: A Synthesis of Eighteenth-Century Views," *Speech Monographs* XXXI (March 1964), 80–84.

Matton, Donald J. "Jonathan Barber and the Elocutionary Movement," *Speech Teacher* XIV (January 1965), 38–43.

Parsons, Marion Robinson. "Diary of a Problem Child," *The Quarterly Journal of Speech* XXXII (October 1946), 357–367.

Robb, Margaret. "Looking Backward," *The Quarterly Journal of Speech* XXVIII (April 1942), 323–327.

Vandraegen, Daniel E. "Thomas Sheridan and the Natural School," *Speech Monographs* XX (March 1953), 58–64.

In her response to S. S. Curry's essay, Professor McCurdy said that "*interpretation must determine where its focus is to be placed and precisely what its art consists of*." The history of an art can reveal the enduring values of that art and, when analyzed in a modern setting, can provide an understanding of the art's focus and permanence. For instance, when H. L. Ewbank reviewed Ebenezer Porter's *The Rhetorical Reader* (1835), he was impressed by the contemporary attitude of its theory and said, "We need to find out how much of the 'modern' is really new.* In Curry's plea for a historical study, he said about the same thing. And another question should be raised: How much of that which was "good" in the "old" have we lost in our efforts to be modern? While it is easy to dismiss the elocutionists, it is obvious that what we say today about oral interpretation has been determined, in part, from what the elocutionists said then.

The following excerpts are brief theoretical and attitudinal statements by established elocutionists. These few excerpts are not intended to capsulize our elocutionary past. They are presented here as a stimulus for further study of the contributions made by elocutionists, a perspective into the alleged elocutionary "malpractice," and primarily as a basis for comparison with modern interpretation theory.

* *The Quarterly Journal of Speech Education* XIII (November 1927), 474–476.

Some Elocutionary Positions

THE RHETORICAL READER

Ebenezer Porter

1835

There are others [elocutionists], who would discard any systematic instruction on this subject, and yet allow that one important direction ought to be given and incessantly repeated, namely, BE NATURAL. But what is it to be natural? The pupil will understand, probably, that he is to read in the manner that is most easy to himself, or that gives him least trouble; that is, the manner to which he is *accustomed*. Bad as that manner may be, the direction has no tendency to mend it; because he supposes that any new manner would be unnatural to him. But you correct him again, and tell him to *be natural*. The direction is just, is simple, is easily repeated; but the infelicity is, that it has been repeated a thousand times, without any practical advantage [page 16].

PRACTICAL ELEMENTS OF ELOCUTION

Robert I. Fulton
and Thomas C. Trueblood

1893

Just as attention to critical processes in written discourse will retard for a time easy thought and composition, so will attention to the details of elocutionary drills temporarily impede naturalness, and the student becomes self-conscious. But when these principles become a part of his being he comes back to nature again refined by the process. The principles or science of an art though severe and a temporary hinderance, after a while become our own involuntary means of success, for having thoroughly learned them we become unconscious of them.

In the words of Prof. Genung, "*Art at its highest and nature at its truest are one.* The result appears ideally free from pain and effort; this, however, not because art is not present but because the art is so perfect as to have concealed its process." Chancellor W. H. Payne of Nashville University says: "*Science consists of knowing, art in doing; the principles which art involves science evolves.* The direct route to the perfecting of an art is through a clear comprehension of the principles that are involved in the art" [page 3].

[These two positions enforce the requirement of naturalness. Yet it seems the reason for the naturalness is to develop an easy handling of elocutionary technique which would appear natural to an audience. It remains for us to know the pedagogy which leads a student to develop a performing style appropriate to (natural to) the literature.]

PRACTICE BOOK

Leland Powers

1910

Fundamental Statement

Every expressive manifestation has its cause in the mind. If the cause is mental the manifestation is also a mind act. When the mental concept, becoming vital enough to demand expression, is carried out in definite thought pictures through the trained and obedient voice and body, under mental guidance, the result is *a mental concept made visible.*

It is a complete thought. The expressional process is as much a mind action as the concept itself; they are both a part of the same thing—the concept incomplete without the expression; the expression impossible without the concept [page 1].

[Has Powers established an elocutionary version of the "Dangerous Shores" or has he attempted a philosophical union of the "Dangerous Shores"?]

THE PROVINCE OF EXPRESSION

S. S. Curry

1891

In fact, whenever motions of the body or tones of the voice call attention to themselves, they distract the attention of the auditor from the thought, and in so destroy expression [page 29].

[If Curry means "expression" as the performance of understanding, has he established a middleman role for the oral interpreter?]

THE PROVINCE OF EXPRESSION

S. S. Curry

1891

It is the delicate suggestion that awakens the imagination and touches the fountain of feeling. Not only does the speaker's own feeling depend upon imagination; it is necessary to awaken the imagination of his auditors. A speaker cannot give his emotion to his fellow-man, but he can awaken their own [page 90].

A HANDBOOK OF ORAL READING

Lee Emerson Bassett

1917

Our first duty in reading aloud is to get a clear understanding of the meaning of what we read. Whether we read the literature that instructs, or tells a story, or describes a scene, or portrays a character, we must give the meaning the author intended to convey in every phrase and sentence. There can be little delight in "the vision of the sky" when the lines

> Slow fades the vision of the sky,
> The golden water pales,

are read with such emphasis on "water" and dropping of the voice on "pales" as to suggest to the listener that the foreground of the picture is composed of water *pails*. . . . Thoughtless utterance of words often results in such misstatement and misrepresentation of meaning. It never reveals the finer shades of thought nor contributes to words the significant variety of living speech.

Words are not the whole of speech, nor is the utterance of them all there is to reading. The meaning conveyed through them is determined by the way they are spoken [page 15].

[Compare the different ideas Curry and Bassett have regarding communication. How do these differences reveal theoretical attitudes regarding the interpreter-audience relationship? See the debate between David A. Williams and Eric Matthiesen on reader-audience paradox in oral interpretation in the following three issues of *Interchange: Student Thought in Speech Communication:* September 1971, September 1972, and December 1972.]

THE PROVINCE OF EXPRESSION

S. S. Curry

1891

A speaker may have an emotional responsiveness to thought, and both ideas and emotion co-ordinated under the control of will; and he may have a voice and body perfectly attuned, until all the channels of expression are responsive; but still he may fail to have adequate expression by mere misconception, misuse of the means, or through lack of skill in execution [page 253].

The statement that if a man has the thought and is stirred by the feeling he will be likely to say it right, is true, if the man were normal, if all the channels of expression were open and if the man were free from bad habits. But to give no attention to habit or right or wrong modes of execution, to have no regard for un-balanced emotional conditions or perverted channels of expression, is to abandon men to all sorts of wild impulses and to reduce all oratorical delivery to chaos [pages 333, 334].

[How do you presume Ebenezer Porter or Fulton and Trueblood would respond to Curry's remarks? For that matter, how would a more modern theorist respond? Consider how Bacon's statement ("Dangerous Shores") regarding "informed intuition" fits here. In these two statements, Curry is implying a number of attitudes important to the oral interpreter today: the kind of knowledge constituting "impression," the fullness of response to literature, the need for control of expressive technique, performance expectations, and the purpose(s) of interpretation.]

EVOLUTION OF EXPRESSION

Charles Wesley Emerson

1905

Analysis

The basis of intelligent vocal interpretation of literature is careful analysis. One cannot express shades of meaning that are not in the mind; until one clearly perceives the motives and relationships of the selection, he cannot reflect them to others. Too much cannot be said upon the importance of thorough thought and study of a selection previous to any effort toward expression. It is needless to explain that one cannot give what he does not possess; and it is equally self-evident that one gains by giving. . . .

Like every organism every true work of art has organic unity; it represents a unit of thought, the *Whole,* made up of essential

Parts. Each part is a part of the whole, because in its own way it reflects the whole. The perfect unity of an organism or of a work of art results from the service rendered by each part to every other part.

Here, then, is the logical order of analysis: first, the *Whole* or unit of thought; second, the *Parts;* third, the *Service, or use of the Parts;* fourth, the *Relationship of the Parts* which is the highest service and results in revelation [pages 16, 17].

∾

[Emerson's position in this brief statement could be found in a number of successful oral interpretation books today. Four of his remarks seem particularly worthwhile for discussion. First, Emerson used the words "reflect" and "give" for the manner of the interpreter's communication. In statements read earlier in this section, Curry and Bassett used different terms, thereby implying different attitudes toward communication and different relationships between the interpeter and his audience. Second, Emerson's statement that a thorough study of the literature should precede "any effort toward expression" implies a concern for arriving at a manner of delivery prematurely (see the essay on expression printed elsewhere in this volume). Third, the idea that the interpreter "gains by giving" brings back Bacon's statement regarding the humanistic value of interpretation. It also implies that new discoveries can be made by the interpreter during performance. What do you think are the nature of these discoveries during performance? And fourth, Emerson's method of analysis, appropriately "evolutionary" in nature and interestingly free from the dictum of the "author's intent," might be deemed simplistic by some modern theorists and satisfactory by others. Is Emerson's method of analysis sufficiently satisfactory for today's interpretation interests?]

PRACTICAL ELOCUTION

J. W. Shoemaker

1883

". . . to *comprehend,* to *appreciate,* and to *communicate* . . ." [page 17].

THE PROVINCE OF EXPRESSION

S. S. Curry

1891

Inward emotion causes an outward motion; inward condition, an outward position. Thus expression is, "the motion of emotion," the presentation of a vast complexity of physical actions which are directly caused by psychic activities [page 25].

HOW TO TEACH READING IN THE PUBLIC SCHOOLS

S. H. Clark

1898

Get the thought, hold the thought, give the thought [page 118].

❧

[The "formulas" for interpretation, stated above, all have a particular merit and generally reflect an accurate theoretical capsule of theories. Could "formulas" be created for the positions of today's theorists?]

In the preceding quotations, you undoubtedly found a number of theoretical perspectives which sound familiar as statements within one of today's theories or which are in agreement with your own understanding. Even if you discarded each of the quotations as irrelevant (which we doubt) you still utilized the past to help fashion or streamline your understanding of interpretation theory.

Another selection which reveals the relevance of the past is S. H. Clark's "The New Elocution." Competing against the dangerous shores of his day, the so-called "mechanical" and "impulsive" schools, Clark attempted to establish a common interest between them. He felt that much of the mechanical school was overly concerned with the vocal techniques of delivery and that the impulsive school was caught into an unreasonable dedication to the inner being or psyche and excluded textual consideration and artistic vocal expression.

Clark's paper should be set in its cultural perspective for a proper understanding. He delivered his paper before the National Association of Elocutionists in 1897. In his audience were elocutionists respected today for their modern views, people of the caliber of Chamberlain, Curry, Ayres, Trueblood, and Fulton. Clark may have included these people as followers of the "new elocution." Also in the audience were people who represented the maligned dimension of elocutionary study, people who presented papers on "The Elocution of Jesus," presented programs of bird whistles and tableaux, taught physical culture, "poses plastique," and "Antediluvian Art, old when Noah went into the Ark."* If the tone of some of Clark's comments seems a bit harsh, it must be remembered that he believed the conditions of the NAE warranted such frankness to revive its deluded membership.

The modernity of Clark's position has been recognized by many theorists today. Some students, speaking as though they were disciples of Clark, have speculated that their interpretative abilities could have been developed as well under Clark's "new elocution" supervision as under today's theory, literary criticism, rhetorical criticism, etc. The point is: Clark frequently makes great sense to the modern interpreter.

* Throughout the *Proceedings of the National Association of Elocutionists,* from 1892 to 1905, many descriptions can be found concerning the practices of the membership. The "Antediluvian Art" quotation is from the comments made by Henry Gaines Hawn during the Eighth Convention in 1899, pp. 156, 157.

S. H. CLARK

The New Elocution

What is the meaning of the motto of the new school, "Force out the expression through the thought"? It is this: "If the mental action is right the expression will be right." So much misunderstanding exists regarding this statement that it will be necessary to explain it in detail.

Whenever a learned person proves to be a poor speaker, we hear the criticism: "Why doesn't he read well? Surely he knows what he is talking about." This criticism shows very plainly that it has failed to grasp the meaning of the principle that mind governs expression. By "mental action" is meant the whole realm of the activities of the mind, such as reason, imagination, and emotion.

There are two terms that need definition: "Vocal technique" and "vocal expression." Vocal technique is the training of the voice for the purpose of developing a quality free from impurities, and of securing flexibility, range, volume, etc. Training in vocal expression is the development of the power to discern all shades of thought and feeling, and to manifest them through the voice. We are all acquainted with the various exercises for obtaining control of the voice and for developing its range, etc. These exercises are intended simply as vocal technique, and will produce results. But no claim can be made that they will materially affect the interpretative powers of the student. It is therefore urged, in favor of the method here presented, that it will achieve equally good results and at the same time develop the ability of the pupil as an interpreter.[1]

Another argument in favor of vocal expression training is that by it the pupil's technique is developed just as fast as his interpretative ability, and no faster. And why should it be faster? So long as a pupil can not interpret, of what avail is a certain formal technical ability?

In a word, we should say that training in vocal expression leads the student to a careful, critical, and sympathetic study of literature as literature, with the special object of developing his powers of appreciation. Then his conception of the author's thought and emotion is used as a means of developing the powers of expression. It is undeniably true that if a pupil can but catch the spirit of a line and can abandon himself to that spirit, no better way can be devised for improving the voice.[2] The pupil's voice can better be developed to express all shades of thought and feeling by getting him to appreciate them, than by working his voice up and down the scale, and by skips and slides, so often meaningless. Of course, merely understanding is not enough. The student must practice until he can *be* understanding, and *be* feeling at the moment of utterance.

We object to the mechanical school on the ground that it makes a great many pupils unnatural and affected. It is only be-

[Footnotes are by editors.]

[1] "Interpreter," used here to mean the student of elocution, is probably one of the earliest uses of the term for our discipline. Robb states that with the publication of Clark's *Interpretation of the Printed Page* (1915) and his "shift in emphasis from the technique of delivery to the subject matter itself . . . indicates that *Elocution* [had] become *Interpretation. . . .*" Mary Margaret Robb, *Oral Interpretation of Literature in American Colleges and Universities* (New York: H. W. Wilson, 1941), 176.

[2] For another use of the concept of "abandon," see Floyd's interpretation of Lewis's quotations in her response to Parrish's "Interpreting Emotions in Poetry" (pp. 170–171) and in the discussion following her response.

cause a few teachers have succeeded in spite of the method that it has endured so long as it has. Every effect produced by the old school, with the exception of a few accidents in impersonation, and certain accompaniments of intensest feeling, can be obtained by the new school in a rational way through a stimulation of the mental activities, and with far less danger to the pupil's individuality.

It seems to me, in view of what has been stated, that the superiority of the new method has been made clear. The average student is born with the technique of speaking. What he needs more than anything else is the ability to interpret (using that term in its broadest sense), and the power to make manifest to his audience the conception of his author. Our drills in expression aim to give him this power. Where they fail, it is owing to the mental or emotional restrictions of the pupil, and in such cases we are better off than the old school. For it tries to cover up inability by a very perceptible imitation, while we develop the pupil as far as his ability will permit, and are far more likely, by our method, to increase that ability than is the mechanical school.

Another feature of the pedagogy of the new elocution is that it strives after gradation. A study of psychology teaches us that certain steps must precede others. The new elocution starts with analysis of the text, training the student in the interpretation of simple passages, training him to appreciate and to express simpler forms of emotion. As his power of discrimination grows, he is led to subtler analyses; and as his appreciation of the profounder emotions develops, those emotions are studied and practiced. Perhaps the difference in the two methods can be made clear by a simple illustration. I know certain teachers who begin with developing the different qualities in the pupil's voice. Now, granting that the large, soulful quality of the voice may be called the orotund, is it not a violation of every principle of psychology to attempt to develop that quality unless the pupil can conceive the sublimer thoughts and emotions that will find expression in the orotund quality? Almost invariably the result of striving to get orotund quality into the voice without training the pupil to conceive and feel the emotion behind the quality, leads to loudness without soul. The orotund quality is more than mere loudness. It is soul largeness, and is often much less forceful than the normal quality. That is to say, a sublime piece of literature can be read with the fullest effect and yet not be heard beyond a radius of twenty feet. It is the peculiar suggestive quality of the orotund that we aim to develop through literary interpretation; and, therefore, using this one illustration as a sample of our whole method of graded work, the pupil must be led by easy stages from the simpler and more common forms of emotion up to the sublime, and through his endeavor to manifest these various shades of feeling a genuine orotund is developed. This is what is meant by grading the instruction.

I have been told a hundred times that we have no technique. Technique! The average elocution teacher to-day could not pass a primary examination in the technical work of the new elocution. Our technique requires a lifetime to master. Tell us we have no technique? We are all technique. We take all that is valuable in Rush, Delsarte, and the rest, and train our pupils in every possible form of expression revealed to us by these scientists; but our knowledge of psychology teaches us that we must seldom or never separate those forms from the state of mind that creates them.

The second distinguishing characteristic of the new school is its attitude toward literature. Let me say once more that it is not claimed that the past did not use good literature. In fact, it probably used a higher class of literature than the elocutionary world, as a whole, does to-day. The reason for this was that there was not the amount of poor literature in those days that we have now, and, consequently, the elocutionists dealt with a higher class of material. But we must remember that the average elocutionist had no real sympathy with good literature, and, consequently, sought out the cheaper and more catchy kind, until to-day the elocution world is flooded with cheap and meretricious productions that are turned out to supply the demand of so large a number of elocutionists. The new elocution will have nothing to do with poor literature. Its pathos must be genuine sentiment, its humor must be pure and clean. We hold every time a pupil recites or studies a cheap production, his artistic sense is thereby marred. Cheap literature reacts upon the mind and soul, destroying the keener sensibilities, and hence the art. Another reason why cheap literature is so prevalent on the elocutionary platform to-day is that it is easy for the reader to render, and for the audience to understand. It is palpable, tangible, and therefore meets with a certain amount of success with half-educated audiences. But the latter are no judges of literature, and know still less of the recitational art. If we are training our pupils simply to make fun and to give an audience thirty thrills in thirty minutes, let us keep at this style of literature. But the new elocution will have none of it. It holds that the particular function of elocution is not to amuse, not merely to entertain, in the popular sense of that term. Our art does entertain, but entertains the highest faculties.[3]

Since, then, our art is the handmaiden of literature, we must understand literature. And so the new elocution spends a great deal of its time in careful and critical analysis of English masterpieces. This analysis is truly educative, of both intellect and emotion. All the effects of literature and its technique are carefully studied with the object of inspiring a genuine love and enthusiasm for literature, and until that love and enthusiasm come, there can be no such thing as artistic vocal expression. There are no two sides to this question. I am willing to acknowledge that there is room for a difference of opinion as to details, but as far as the principle is concerned I glory in my dogmatism. The presentation of a piece of literary art in its true proportion is one of the most difficult tasks of the reader, and it is in this task that so many of the profession fail. Details are overdone, gesture is overworked, all kinds of useless externals are introduced, until there is so much detail that you can not see the forest for the trees. I ask you candidly, how many in the profession are there who can interpret for a cultured

[3] For more modern attitudes regarding the interpreter's selection of literature, see Geiger's discussion in *The Sound, Sense, and Performance of Literature* (Glenview, Ill.: Scott, Foresman 1963), 73; and Chloe Armstrong's essay, "The Literature: Choosing Material for Oral Interpretation," *Perspectives on Oral Interpretation,* ed. John W. Gray (Minneapolis: Burgess Publishing, 1968).

audience Shakespeare, Milton, Browning, Tennyson. No doubt there are quite a few, numerically speaking, but proportionately, I doubt if they form ten percentage of the whole profession. If it is argued that the fault is in the pupil, I reply that it is just here that the new elocution has introduced a new feature into the work. It insists, as a part of its training, upon the development of the pupil's powers of literary interpretation.[4]

The third and last of the striking characteristics of the new school is its art. Recognizing that if recitation is an art, it must have a close connection with the other arts, the student is led into a study of art in general and literary art in particular. We strive to understand all the arts as far as possible and to learn from them such lessons as will make artists of us.[5]

As a result of the art-training and the training in literature, the pupils of the new school have a higher ideal of literature, of art and of life. They recite *to* an audience, not *for* them. Their ambition is to serve, so to speak, as ministers of literature; to interpret the great ideals of the poet's mind; and they deem their highest praise not that which says, "What a beautiful voice he has," or "What graceful gestures!" but "What a beautiful poem that is."

Another result of the training of the new school is that it leads to independence. The student is continually thrown upon his

[4] See Breen's essay on Chamber Theatre elsewhere in this volume for another statement regarding the critical function of performance and the relationship of the performance to the audience. Note also Geiger's discussion of his definition of interpretative performance as "a critical illumination publicly offered in behalf of literature" in the preface to *The Sound, Sense, and Performance of Literature.*

[5] For other discussions of interpretation as an art, see S. H. Clark's "Recitation As Art" in Chamberlain and Clark's *Principles of Vocal Expression and Literary Interpretation* (Chicago: Scott, Foresman, 1899), 316–337; C. C. Cunningham's *Literature as a Fine Art* (New York: Thomas Nelson and Sons, 1941); and Alethea Mattingly's "The Art of Interpretation" in the second edition of *Interpretation: Writer, Reader, Audience* (Belmont, Cal.: Wadsworth Publishing, 1970), 3–12.

own resources. And so, after his days of instruction are over, he is largely independent of his teacher. Many, many readers to-day of some ability dare not attempt a recitation of any depth without the advice of a teacher.

One wing of the new elocution has held that after the pupil has the thought and feeling, he should go ahead and recite. It let out of sight the fact that recitation deals largely with the work of others. Therefore, if the selection contains any personation, there is the danger of obtruding our own personality. It is Shylock's thought, or Sir Galahad's thought, that must govern the expression, and if we are not careful we shall present our anger or our joy, rather than that of the character we are personating. The outcome of the method referred to has been that many of its disciples have no self-control. They do not guide their interpretation. One time they read well; at another, wretchedly. We must remember that in art there must be spontaneity and control combined.[6] I think, however, that we are getting to appreciate this more and more and we may hope for a reform in the near future.

The new elocution is not always understood because many teachers and a large part of the public have no conception of literature and of art in general. A pupil may have made remarkable improvement in literary interpretation, his powers of discrimination may have developed in a most appreciable degree, but because he happens to render a selection not requiring extravagant gestures and tremendous voice-power his improvement is not discerned. Alas! too many judge elocution by the amount of voice the pupil may have and the number of his gestures.

The new elocution is essentially educational. It spends most of its time developing the student's powers of discrimination in the realm both of intellect and of feeling. It deals only with literature that is good, and so stimulates the pupil to a higher conception of literary art by introducing him to the fundamental principles of art in general, and thus trains him to be artistic in his own realm.

[6] See Paul Campbell's "The Psychology of the Interpreter," *Oral Interpretation* (New York: Macmillan, 1966), 124–130.

It measures its success by the mental and imaginative growth of the student, combined, of course, with the artistic ability to express his conceptions.

Our first convention at New York fought a most bitter fight for the term "elocutionist." It held that since that word truly designated our profession we should not give it up because it had become synonymous with rant and affectation. That convention held that we should not resign the word but redeem it. Words mean what we make them mean, and so I say it remains for us to make the term "new elocution" stand for all that is best and highest in art.

Discussion

Miss Gertrude McMillan: It is very difficult to argue a subject with one from whom we have learned much.

I wish to emphasize at the beginning that I do not take issue with the speaker of this morning in regard to his *teaching*. My discussion concerns only the use of the term "new elocution."

Elocution is not an invention nor a discovery. It is as old as the human race, for it is part of man himself. The era of Pericles was the Golden Age of Oratory and the Drama, and elocution has yet to attain the perfection it reached centuries ago, in early Greece. The ideas and precepts of Demosthenes and his followers must be realized and improved upon by the readers and the teachers of the 19th century, before there is an intelligent demand for a "new elocution"; but to the term "new elocution" exception must be taken from the fact that it is misleading and incorrect. We have not earned the right to a title which signifies that the knowledge and experience of the past were practically worthless and antagonistic to the best teaching of to-day. Indeed, such a term belittles our profession, implying that hitherto it has *not* been the subject of scholarly research. While it may have been lacking in popularity in the past and was without a sufficient number of competent teachers, still that which is excellent has always been the same.

The speaker frequently used such expressions as these, "*our* method," "there is a school called the new elocution," etc., which would indicate that a certain number had banded themselves together to found a school representing their views, and that they all taught the same thing. But to the contrary, it is exceedingly difficult to ascertain just what is meant by the term "new" elocution, and who is the true representative of the widely varying systems bearing that name. One theory is the development of the individuality, and the abolition of rules. Another adheres most strictly to the science and technique.

What right have these apostles of the so called "new" elocution to claim certain great readers and teachers of the past as representatives of their methods? It is quite probable that they do not wish to be claimed for one thing! Why not say instead: The best in the new is only the old.

We have just been told that another characteristic of the *new* elocution is that "mental action precedes true expression." What responsible person ever believed the contrary? If mental action was lacking in Charlotte Cushman, Wendell Phillips, and Edwin Booth, what perfection might have been attained in their art, had they but known of this valuable truth promulgated (?) by the "new elocutionists!"

I will repeat that the object of my paper has been under no circumstances to criticize the methods of the speaker preceding me, but to show that so great is the similarity of thought between himself and other members of the profession, that the special term applied to his instruction is at present unjustifiable. The time will never come when we can array one school against the other, until there are *universally acknowledged* representatives of each. Mr. Clark, for instance, says that the old school was mechanical, and yet we fail to find who it was that stood for such a system. There is not a demand for a *new* elocution. We should glory in our art because it *is* old. Reading has not yet reached its greatest possibilities; but that is not all of which elocution consists. It is the broadest of all arts.

Mr. Clark: If anybody else but our fair speaker had said half the hard things about me that she did, I should have been angry;

but as she objects rather to the name than to the thing, I can accept her criticisms.

Her closing words are eminently appropriate. I agree with her that when we are educated up to the ideal held by the new elocution —pedagogically, spiritually, artistically—we can drop the qualifying term. That is exactly my contention. Let me repeat my claim: The new elocution combines in one method all that was best in the past and adds something new. It is not held that each of its details, so to speak, is new, but it can not be denied that as a whole, it is in method and result, the highest ideal of elocution we have thus far had. No doubt we shall in the future see another new school, which shall be superior to the present, *as a whole,* as the present is to the past.

The young lady says, in her bright optimism, that we have no poor elocution—for that is what her words imply. I beg to differ. The great majority of elocution has been and is very, very bad.

❧

RESPONSE

Richard Haas
and David A. Williams

In 1905, eight years after Clark's presentation of "The New Elocution," the NAE dropped "Elocutionists" from its title and the Association became known as the Association for the Advancement of the Speech Arts. The practice of elocution continued, of course, but the academic disregard of elocution had frightened off many speech educators from emphasizing delivery. In fact, the study of delivery was eventually relegated to a minor role as the field of interpretation changed course and tried the shoals of the other dangerous shore.

From the demise of elocution, interpretation grew—first as

a child to be heard and not seen, to the eclectically based discipline we know it to be today, which, for many, explores fully again the limits of the interpreter's performing skills. Ships, however, are able to change course more smoothly than theoretical positions. Oral interpretation carried the elocutionary stigma for years. One statement reveals rather surprisingly how little a change in name affects an understanding of what a "new" performing activity means. As late as 1924, W. M. Parrish wrote, "Speaking is a much broader activity than interpretation. The common element in them is, of course, elocution. But while elocution is *all* of interpretation it is only a small part of public speaking."[1] It is hard to believe Parrish made that statement, since the major thrust of interpretation, and even elocution in its later days, had stressed the importance of literary study.

An even greater problem emerged for interpretation, the acting-interpreting dilemma. The current misunderstanding of the two forms of expression can be traced back to the early part of this century when Woolbert and others declared that interpretation differed from acting in *amount of movement used in performance.*[2] Clearly, this view is not held today.[3] Although the degree of movement in performance is a possible difference between an acting performance and an interpretive performance, it is by no means the only or even the best way to draw a distinction—if a distinction must be drawn at all. The interests of the two performers, their purposes, their roles within the writer-reader-audience relationship are more often used to discuss the "distinction."

[1] Wayland Maxfield Parrish, "Public Speaking and Reading—A Plea for Separation," *The Quarterly Journal of Speech Education* X (June 1924), 280.

[2] See Robb's *Oral Interpretation of Literature in American Colleges and Universities* (revised edition) (New York: Johnson Reprint Co., 1968), 205.

[3] Lee Roloff, "The Roles of the Interpreter and the Actor," *The Speech Teacher* XXII (March 1973), 144–147.

Selected Readings

Barclay, Martha Thomson. "Major American Emphases in Theories of
    Oral Interpretation from 1890 to 1950," unpublished dissertation,
    University of Minnesota, 1968.
Bassett, Lee Emerson. "Elocution Then, Oral Interpretation Now,"
    Western Speech XIII (March 1949), 3–8.
Faries, Elizabeth. "A Defense of Elocution," *The Southern Speech
    Journal* XXIX (Winter 1963), 133–140.
Gray, Charles W. "What Was Elocution," *The Quarterly Journal of
    Speech* XLVI (February 1961), 1–7.
Mohrmann, G. P. "The Language of Nature and Elocutionary Theory,"
    The Quarterly Journal of Speech LII (April 1966), 116–124.
Parrish, W. M. "Elocution—A Definition and a Challenge," *The
    Quarterly Journal of Speech* XLIII (February 1957), 1–11.

DAVID A. WILLIAMS

Impersonation: The Great Debate

To even breathe the word "impersonation" in some circles of interpretation is tantamount to playing Russian roulette with six bullets
in the cylinder of the gun. Indeed, impersonation has been cheered
and leered, clarified and kicked, buried and born again. One would
have to be some kind of heretic to pick up the issue, let alone
advocate it, as a legitimate form of training for the oral interpreter.
However, no event, discussion, or dictum has changed or really
clarified the question of acting versus interpretation or impersonation versus interpretation. Whether it be in the classroom or convention, the same old questions are still being discussed. Too few
students are aware that "impersonation" versus "interpretation" was
debated back in 1915. The showdown came in the form of a great
debate between Maud May Babcock and Rollo Anson Tallcott.
Miss Babcock delivered a paper at the convention of the National
Association of Academic Teachers of Public Speaking, Chicago,
1915, which was later published in *The Quarterly Journal of Public
Speaking,* 1916. Professor Tallcott responded to the Babcock article
in the next issue of the same journal in an article titled, "The Place
For Personation." Miss Babcock countered in the October issue of
the same journal. Whether impersonation had a place within the art
of interpretation was debated and dropped for the moment. It was
not until 1940 when Gertrude Johnson published her anthology
Studies in the Art of Interpretation that impersonation once again

was discussed at some length. Miss Johnson included the Babcock-Tallcott debate in her section titled "Forms-Interpretation-Impersonation."

Although it would be ludicrous, not to mention dangerous, to establish a formula as to the limits of reader's theatre or of solo interpretation, the arguments and the issues raised by Miss Babcock and Mr. Tallcott are a logical starting point for the student of interpretation interested in this problem of interpretation versus acting or impersonation. Indeed, the debate presented by Miss Babcock and Mr. Tallcott represents a timely discussion which has endured. Today's student might be surprised to find that his "new" arguments for or against impersonation are not new. Once again we find the importance of studying the history of our art in order to gain a better perspective of where we are and where we are going. It is hoped that a synthesis of the major points presented by Babcock and Tallcott will preserve the issues for some and enlighten others who have not yet encountered the debate. Finally, a collection of thoughts on impersonation by other scholars will be offered in an attempt to show how many of the arguments have been preserved.

The most ironic feature of the Babcock-Tallcott debate was the inability to agree on definitions of terms. Babcock offers a definition of interpretation by suggesting it is a presentation of any form of literature without the aid of dress, furniture, stage settings, make-up, or any literal characterization in voice or action.[1] I doubt if we could or should live with this definition today, but Tallcott accepts it. He disagrees that interpretation by this definition should be the *only* legitimate form of presenting literature and suggests a more modern "midway" course. He prefers to describe four distinct forms of presentation. The first he describes as "interpretative reading"; the second, "impersonative reading," where only suggestive characterization is introduced; the third he calls "straight personation";

[1] Maud May Babcock, "Interpretative Presentation Versus Impersonative Presentation," *The Quarterly Journal of Public Speaking* II (January 1916), 18.

and the fourth, "acting."[2] Miss Babcock defines "impersonation" as an attempt to give exact, literal characterization in voice, action, and makeup, in realistic surroundings of dress, furniture, and stage settings."[3] Tallcott feels her definition best describes acting and not impersonation. He suggest there are times, depending on the literature, when the performer would want only to suggest, but also times when he would want to use literal voice and body characterization. The definitions never really become an issue: each scholar seemed to disregard the other's definition and went on presenting his respective case. Historically, impersonation has never been properly defined to satisfy all who would address themselves to the issue.

Miss Babcock next moves to the crux of her argument and her basic indictment of impersonation. She argues that any form of presentation that destroys the unity and harmony of a selection or distracts the listener from the purpose of the author should be discarded. She feels impersonation destroys the unity and harmony of a selection by directing the listener's attention to the "how" rather than to the "what" of the reading. The impersonator calls attention to himself and to the mechanics of his presentation each time he changes character or makeup or costume or setting. Any such change tends to cause the audience to lose interest in the unity and harmony of the selection.

Miss Babcock's point is well taken and applicable to a discussion of reader's theatre or solo performance today. If the audience becomes more aware of the "how" rather than the "what," the reader may be going beyond the realm of suggestion. Miss Babcock cannot see why readers would desire to exploit themselves as impersonators or imitators of "bells" and "beasts" with music and costume unless it is to surprise the audience "with the startling and extraordinary, the unusual and marvelous."[4]

[2] R. A. Tallcott, "The Place for Personation," *The Quarterly Journal of Public Speaking* II (April 1916), 116, 117.

[3] Babcock, p. 18.

[4] Babcock, p. 21.

Miss Babcock next poses a question: "Shall the audience be the instructor and tell us how best to proceed?"[5] Tallcott would give the audience what they want to see even if it is imitation and exhibition. Babcock feels it might be difficult for the entertainer to "sacrifice the delicious praise of the public, but the great artist always decides that the content is the only thing worthwhile."[6]

Tallcott responds to the question of the reader and his audience. He knows at least one person who uses bells, bugles, etc., because it "entertains and pleases in a clean and wholesome way some few of the good people in the world who do not care for cheap claptrap of the vaudeville, but who are perhaps not quite 'up to' the appreciation of pure interpretation. . . ."[7] He carries the point further by asking a question of his own: "Besides, who can say with authority that certain imitations do not convey the author's purpose so well?"[8] He feels Miss Babcock is begging the question when she says that imitation "beclouds and befogs the author's meaning."[9] If it does becloud there is no place for it, but Tallcott adds that Miss Babcock has not proved this. He also feels Miss Babcock has not come to grips with the issue of whether some literature is meant for impersonation.

Tallcott argues from a very modern point of view. The literature dictates how much impersonation one will use. He stresses that certain kinds of literature that give pictures of specific character types are best performed by impersonation. The issue for him is that literature demands a certain presentational form and one should not preclude the use of impersonation in the presentation of certain literary forms.

Moving from the audience issue, Miss Babcock next turns to the treatment of specific literary forms. She feels the lyric is a good example for interpretation and not impersonation, and warns that one should be careful in indirect discourse, especially descrip-

[5] Babcock, p. 21.
[6] Babcock, p. 21.
[7] Tallcott, pp. 119, 120.
[8] Tallcott, p. 120.
[9] Tallcott, p. 120.

tion, not to go too far. Her answer as to how far one can go has become a classified guide for the interpreter in the twentieth century.

So long as we remain the spectator, allowing the emotion to affect us as such, and do not become the participator, the illusion will be sustained. In other words, if the scene is held as if enacted, but we do not become an actor in the scene, we may allow our feelings and emotions full rein.[10]

Many textbooks in interpretation since Babcock reflect on this important issue. Miss Babcock objects to impersonation in direct discourse because often indirect discourse becomes bland and is "swallowed up." She maintains that equal attention should be given to both direct and indirect statement so that a balance is achieved.[11]

Tallcott agrees that lyric, lyric monologue, narrative, and descriptive readings can best be done by interpretative presentation. At the same time, he insists that a "play in which the characters, their peculiarities, mannerisms, and contrarelationship to each other are paramount may be most effectively presented by impersonation."[12] He adds that complete book readings where characterization is of primary importance should be impersonated. He cites examples of Dickens and some of Browning's dramatic monologues, and maintains the monologue and soliloquy may best be presented by what he terms "straight personation."[13] While properties, stage settings, costumes, and makeup are not needed, he does call for literal characterization of voice with pantomimic action. He feels that even with literal characterization, the audience is free to imagine all of the properties the person might be using.

The issue then becomes, at least for Tallcott, whether impersonation has a place at all as an art form. Specifically, he asks: (1) if there is a legitimate place in the lyceum for literal characterization and pantomime in the presentation of literature; (2) whether

[10] Babcock, p. 22.
[11] Babcock, p. 23.
[12] Tallcott, p. 117.
[13] Tallcott, p. 118.

this form of presentation destroys the unity and harmony so that it cannot convey the author's meaning as well; (3) and finally, whether it is more artistic not to personate? Using the analogy of a mathematics teacher, he explains that the teacher does not start his pupils with trigonometry, but begins with simple numbers and works up to the higher level. He insists that if we want audiences to appreciate literature, we should employ methods that the audiences can best appreciate. He then makes his point: "Today good interpreters are not in demand in the lyceum, because they want to force their audiences into calculus before they have had arithmetic."[14] Our interpreters need to give a little "rudimentary entertainment in the way of good personation along with their interpretative numbers. . . ."[15] If this were done, the lyceum would not become vaudeville, and good reading would in time come to be appreciated. As to whether interpretation is more artistic (a charge of Miss Babcock's), Tallcott explains that "it is more artistic to know when not to impersonate than not to personate at all."[16] He feels there is literature that will permit impersonation, and we can teach the student to discriminate when and where to use impersonation. He summarizes his position:

I believe that a reader, whether he be a college professor or a lyceum entertainer, should be able to adapt his program to the audience and to give both interpretation and personation. It will not disgrace him. On the other hand, by avoiding extremes, he will win to a higher and nobler appreciation of literature those who would stay away from his second performance—or, what is worse, go to vaudeville instead— if at first appearance he had given them nothing but pure interpretation.[17]

Explaining that she had received many letters from friends urging her to answer Mr. Tallcott, Miss Babcock responded to Tallcott in the October issue of *The Quarterly Journal of Public Speak-*

[14] Tallcott, p. 121.
[15] Tallcott, p. 121.
[16] Tallcott, p. 121.
[17] Tallcott, p. 121.

ing, 1916. She said she sees no reason for Mr. Tallcott to take issue
with her since his plea is for entertainment in the lyceum. She now
says she sees nothing wrong with impersonation for the "kiddies"
and "older people."[18] She does not object to the doing of such
stunts, but she does object to doing them under the "misnomer of
elocution, reading, interpretation, public speaking, and reciting."[19]
The public becomes confused as to what to expect unless the per-
sonators are advertised as just what they are. Earlier in the debate
she had stated, "Impersonation cannot, therefore, be considered as
helpful in interpretation, or even harmless, but must be set down
as absolutely baneful to platform presentation, and hence to be
discarded."[20] She now explains that impersonation is permissible in
the lyceum as long as it is called just that and not interpretation,
"that there is a place on the lyceum platform for literal characterization and pantomime, but 'not' in the presentation of literature. . . ."[21]

She next turns to the issue of audience. She explains that she
has yet to meet an uncultivated audience, one which could not
appreciate good literature, even in the western wilds. She adds:
"Audiences lead 'us' to comprehend the greatest, the highest, and the
best!"[22] Earlier she suggested it was unwise to let the audience decide which is better, interpretation or impersonation. She poses
the question: "Shall the audience be the instructor and tell us
how best to proceed?"[23]

In response to Tallcott's analogy of interpretation and arithmetic, she retorts, "demonstrated that even a 'child' may understand
calculus if 'presented right.' "[24] The best reading she has ever heard

[18] Maud May Babcock, "Impersonation Versus Interpretation,"
The Quarterly Journal of Public Speaking II (October 1916), 340.

[19] Babcock, "Impersonation Versus Interpretation," p. 340.

[20] Babcock, "Interpretative Presentation Versus Impersonative Presentation," p. 19.

[21] Babcock, "Impersonation Versus Interpretation," p. 340.

[22] Babcock, "Impersonation Versus Interpretation," p. 341.

[23] Babcock, "Interpretative Presentation Versus Impersonative Presentation," p. 21.

[24] Babcock, "Impersonation Versus Interpretation," pp. 341, 342.

was given by S. H. Clark and Alfred Ayres. They were great, she maintains, because they chose to suggest rather than to impersonate.

She concludes with an appeal for correct labeling of art forms.

May we not then discard these tickling phrases, 'stepping down to earth,' 'adapting the program to the audience,' 'educating people to appreciate literature,' and interpreters, entertainers, or impersonators conform to 'pure food' laws by correct labeling? If this is done we shall have taken a great step forward toward a consummation for which many of us have been laboring for years, that there can be no misunderstanding as to reading or entertaining.[25]

It is not the purpose of this paper to evaluate the Babcock-Tallcott debate to determine a winner. Most scholars of interpretation are very aware that with the publication of S. H. Clark's *Oral Interpretation of the Printed Page,* 1915, interpretation, not impersonation, became the accepted artistic form of presenting literature. This does not mean to imply that the advocates of impersonation remained silent. Phidelah Rice felt that impersonation is primarily "an act of the mind, of the dramatic imagination. . . ."[26] When the impersonation is well done, any aids used by the performer will be in complete correspondence with this mental concept. Although Professor Rice agrees that too much inpersonation may discredit the artist, she sees nothing inherently wrong with the form. Even Curry felt impersonation had its place. "The principle is not the mode of the art, but the art principles that are embodied; everything must be consistent and harmonious."[27] Miss Babcock would never admit that impersonation could be used without destroying the unity and the harmony of the literature.

Walter Bradley Tripp argues yet another consideration—the ability of the performer. If the student has little impersonative

[25] Babcock, "Impersonation Versus Interpretation," p. 343.

[26] Phidelah Rice, "The Art of Impersonation in Play Reading," *Studies In The Art of Interpretation,* ed. Gertrude E. Johnson (New York: D. Appleton-Century, 1940), 79.

[27] S. S. Curry, "Personation And Participation," *ibid.,* p. 122.

ability, he should reduce the percentage of impersonation. He feels that even a "mediocre interpretation is infinitely better than a 'bad' impersonation."[28] While the literature is a primary consideration, and perhaps the audience is a factor, Mr. Tripp comes to grips with the sticky criterion of talent. The reason many of us can accept one impersonation while rejecting another is based primarily on the ability of the performer as well as the literature. It is quite possible for two individuals to impersonate the same selection, yet a critic may accept one and reject the other. The real issue then becomes the ability of the performer, that is, perhaps, impersonation is more difficult than mere suggestion. There are only a handful of students with enough talent and ability who can do it well. On the other hand, if this be true, almost anyone might be able to suggest the ideas inherent in the literature.

Gertrude Johnson would not suggest that impersonation is a harder form or a higher form, but she does argue that "we are not ready to be suggestive if we haven't been literal."[29] She suggests that the "deadly lack of vital or actively motivated response in most reading indicates a need for every student to 'act things out,' in the hope that when such literal action and response is reduced to suggestive action for interpretative purposes, some muscular memory will set off vital empathic responses."[30] This idea has been retained by Charlotte Lee and others. Miss Johnson agrees with Parrish when he says it is "impossible to lay down laws to govern in all cases the proper degree of impersonation, and the appropriate quantity of emotion and gesticulation."[31] Miss Johnson does not discriminate between what types of literature should be imper-

[28] Walter Bradley Tripp, "Impersonation Versus Interpretation," *ibid.,* p. 134.

[29] Gertrude E. Johnson, "Impersonation, a Necessary Technique," *ibid.,* p. 128.

[30] Johnson, p. 125.

[31] W. M. Parrish, "Impersonation And The Art of Interpretation," *Studies In The Art of Interpretation,* ed. Gertrude E. Johnson (New York: D. Appleton-Century, 1940), 114.

sonated, but explains that all forms of literature may receive impersonative treatment and not lose value. However, in the case of the monologue, she insists on "complete impersonation."[32]

Both Babcock and Tallcott agree that the lyric is best given by interpretation. Martin Cobin, writing as late as 1959, disagrees, "In actuality, however, the lyric poem may call forth impersonation more readily than do other forms commonly thought of in this respect."[33] Smith and Linn agree, "Isn't it, then, a sound principle that a reader should orally present the chosen text in 'whatever manner will most completely communicate his comprehension of the text'?"[34] Ultimately one must ask how much impersonation should be used? No one has yet devised a system to indicate the amount of characterization, although some have tried.[35] Aggertt and Bowen suggest that it depends on three factors: the type of literature, the composition of the audience, and the aesthetic distance inherent in the reading situation.[36] While many in the field agree that these criteria are sensible, at least one scholar can not accept them. According to Miss Johnson, if one uses time, place, and audience to determine the extent of impersonation that could be used in a given situation, one "presupposes some rather extensive training before such decisions could be valid."[37]

One could go on endlessly juxtaposing different points of view, all of which contain a certain amount of validity, but sooner or later, after poring over the literature of interpretation versus impersonation, one comes to the conclusion that little has been resolved. In discussing acting, mono-acting, and interpretation of drama, Charlotte Lee comes to the conclusion that the "versatile

[32] Johnson, p. 128.

[33] Martin Cobin, *Theory and Technique of Interpretation* (Englewood Cliffs, N.J.: Prentice-Hall, 1959), 239.

[34] Joseph F. Smith and James R. Linn, *Skill In Reading Aloud* (New York: Harper and Brothers, 1960), 379.

[35] Tripp, p. 133.

[36] Otis J. Aggertt and Elbert R. Bowen, *Communicative Reading,* Second Ed. (New York: Macmillan, 1963), 8, 9.

[37] Johnson, p. 125.

artist will be able to handle all three."[38] The interpreter can use makeup, costume setting, lights, music, etc., but the task as expressed by W. M. Wayland Parrish remains the same: "to represent the truth of the poet's conception."[39] How exactly this is accomplished will always differ somewhat in degree and means. Seymour Chatman best summarizes the point: "Since he does not have and does not want a specific model, what the interpreter seeks is not so much exactness as plausibility or to use a forceful term from aesthetics, 'verisimilitude.' "[40]

Comment

At worst, any discussion of impersonation is "old hat," at best, purely academic; and after reading the *Dissenting Academy,* no educator wants to be stigmatized as being "academic." Whether the student of interpretation is academically avid about impersonation or casually curious, we believe the Babcock-Tallcott debate is the place to begin for twentieth-century comment. Surely, for a more complete and historical perspective one would have to go back much further in time. Indeed, a more penetrating analysis of the debate which would consider the background of the current theory at that time, and the personalities involved in the debate, would be a worthwhile project. Our comment, however, takes the form of certain conclusions based on the debate and subsequent theory of impersonation as an art form.

Our first conclusion concerning the debate over impersonation versus interpretation is that it is purely academic. As in most art forms, rules are ridiculous. Conventions change because of "whims"

[38] Charlotte I. Lee, *Oral Interpretation,* Third Ed. (Boston: Houghton Mifflin, 1965), 363.

[39] Parrish, p. 113.

[40] Robert Beloof, Chester Clayton Long, Seymour Chatman, Thomas O. Sloan, and Mark Klyn, *The Oral Study of Literature* (New York: Random House, 1966), 106–107.

not "whys." Too many variables are involved despite the voluminous collection of words on the subject. The social scientist, if we allow him in the discussion, would laugh at anyone who would try to measure and define the limits of characterization. What is too much for some turns out to be not enough for others. The same seems to be true of the magic word "suggestion." The same questions raised by the Babcock-Tallcott debate are still being discussed.

Ultimately, it is up to the reader to decide how much impersonation, if we could agree on this term, and how much suggestion is needed in order to "blow life" into a given piece of literature; we don't want it any other way. The student should be completely free to experiment within the dictates of the literature. When a student is dealing with a character, there is a tendency to impersonate. Today, that is accepted as interpretation. It becomes a matter of *degree* of impersonation. The degree of impersonation depends on the strength of the character or the density of the persona. A poem with an obvious persona may require a high degree of impersonation; and yet, since the persona does not completely fill the poem or exhaust the poem's effects, a performance of that poem, with considerable impersonation, does not eliminate considerations of suggestion. Suggestion is a dimension of impersonation and impersonation is a dimension of suggestion. In a practice session the student should begin with a full impersonation and then "cut it down" by seeing what he can suggest without losing the strength of the character or persona. The interpreter works for economy of movement in order to suggest the character while always keeping the literature in primary focus. Combining Babcock's idea of keeping the unity and harmony of the literature with Tallcott's desire for impersonation for certain forms of literature, one finds that today we have an acceptable hybrid of "tasteful impersonation." The reader must take his cue from the literature in determining how much he can impersonate. The literature is his best "coach."

Our second conclusion is based on a feeling, an inference regarding the instructor of interpretation. The background, tastes, scholarship, and interest of the instructor will usually dictate the pedagogical policy taught in the interpretation classroom. Who taught your teachers? Who taught Miss Babcock? The student need not look too closely at the writings of Alfred Ayres to see where Miss Babcock was getting her arsenal of ideas. We are not condemning this practice, but we are inferring that the student may be reticent to try a new style of interpretation because he knows his paternal pedagogue will disapprove. All of which brings up the question of whether the student is performing for his instructor or for his audience, or assuming the responsibilities of the literature. Some theorists believe the reader must do all three. This presupposes that the audience and the instructor have the same tastes, which too many times is not the case. We believe that because the student's primary responsibility is with the literature, he should not prematurely worry about his audience or instructor. Broad minds are needed if we are to hear "correct readings."[41] "Let's see if it will work" should be our credo, not "No, you can't do that."

The audience is involved in our third conclusion. Have we really sought to determine whether the audience prefers impersonation? Should we cater to the wishes of the audience providing we can ascertain what it really wants? A recent dissertation which traces the current practices and theories of interpretation found that the audience was the most neglected aspect of interpretation.[42] If any one single issue emanates from the great debate, it is the audience factor. Current theories on the subject run from Hunsinger's high regard for the communicative process between the reader and his audience to Bacon's belief that the interpreter may worry too much about his audience. Some feel that the communion must be between the reader and the poem, others stress the communion with the audience. What is the reader's responsibility? Should he bring great literature to his audience in hopes of "educating" them or should he read what he knows they will like? Scholars in the area have supported both ideas. Indeed, it is likely that we can do both.

[41] For further discussion of "correct readings," see Don Geiger's essay on the locus of a poem found elsewhere in this volume.

[42] Martha Thompson Barclay, "Major American Emphasis in Theories of Oral Interpretation from 1890 to 1950," *Speech Monographs* XXXVI (August 1969), 311.

Our fourth conclusion is based on an inference about what is taking place at readers' theatre festivals. Some of the same questions that were raised over the impersonation issue are once again raising their ugly little heads. What about costume, sets, props, music, etc.? Once again professional pedants are raising a supercilious eyebrow and screaming "impersonation." Once again the question of "how far one can go" is raised. It all reminds us of the Babcock-Tallcott debate, and we fear the discussion will resolve about as much. After listening to some critics at such events, we wonder if they will ever be capable of "enjoying" literature again. Many are too quick to point out that the reader slid into acting or impersonation. We can remember a festival at the University of Arizona where Dr. Janet Bolton presented her very fine production, "Four Women West." No scripts were used, the performers were dressed in period costumes, and small properties were used with suggestive lighting and music. We are certain some in the audience could not enjoy this very fine and memorable performance because they were bothered that the performers were impersonating. We think Dr. Bolton, Tom Turpin, the script writer, and the students of the University of Southern California were justified in their presentational form of this script. It worked—it worked beautifully—but it worked only because the script, direction, and performers were right. A change in any one of the three ingredients could have changed the outcome. Although it is difficult to explain, one must "see" a production before one can make any such value judgment such as too much or too little impersonation. This leads to our final conclusion.

We would like to declare a moratorium on the use of the word "impersonation" in interpretation circles. We all have been guilty of reacting to the connotation, the stigma, of the word without objectively trying to determine whether it might be used for some literature and by certain performers. We are convinced that the tremendous popularity of interpretation is due in part to the fact that different methods and styles of reading have been allowed to prevail. The lack of rules has been healthy. The nature of literature, the nature of performance, the nature of individuals require a flexibility—a fluidity—lest we become stagnant. Let us revisit the impersonation debate on paper, not in practice.

Selected Readings

Allen, Annie H. "The Impersonation of Plays," *The Quarterly Journal of Speech* XX (February 1934), 57–72.

Cunningham, Cornelius C. "Trying to Pos the Impossible," *Western Speech* XII (April 1948), 11–13.

Lowery, Sara. "Impersonation As a Style of Interpretation," *The Southern Speech Journal* XIII (November 1947), 65–69.

The older scholar might wince at the naiveté of such a question as presented in my title, but I wonder if the younger student, one who missed the heyday of choral reading, could answer the question. This essay is dedicated to the younger student with a hope that its contents will either illuminate, reaffirm, aggravate, or add a dimension of discussion for the student who missed the first funeral of choral reading.

I am also writing this essay out of speculation. Choral speaking is back, but if we are not careful, if we do not learn from the past, we could bury the art for the second time. I see and hear the new advocates of group reading making the same mistakes that ruined the art in the late thirties and early forties. The literature is being used and misused.

DAVID A. WILLIAMS

Whatever Happened to Choral Reading?

Thirteen years ago Professor Agnes Curran Hamm asked the same question that I pose above. She asked: "Why the professional cold shoulder?" At the close of her 1960 article in *The Quarterly Journal of Speech,* she appealed to her readers to respond to her question. Since she posed this question, only two have responded—Professor Clive Sansom, Tasmania, Australia, and I. Perhaps no one else cares. At the close of this essay I hope to show that we should have cared and that we should care today.

Professor Sansom worked with Marjorie Gullan in England for many years. Miss Gullan was singularly responsible for the tremendous success of choral reading in this country in the 1930s. Mr. Sansom discussed some of the "malpractices" of choral reading found by Miss Gullan in her last visit to the United States. Miss Gullan found: (1) unsuitable material was used; (2) music and sound effects overpowered the literature; (3) lines were broken "irrespective" of the poem's form or meaning; and (4) "harmonizing" occurred to the extent that the audience was more concerned with the sound than the sense.[1]

Because Miss Gullan was a visiting professor at the University of Southern California, the popularity of choral speaking began in the West and spread to the East. It is difficult to pinpoint the first choric production in the States, but surely Mabel Smith Reynolds's production of Rosetti's "Sister Helen" in January 1926 would qualify as one of the earliest.[2] Many who attended the November Western Speech Convention, 1931, were impressed by Miss Elizabeth Jenks's students from San Jose in their presentation of choral speaking. Professor Dorothy Kaucher, who saw the production, explained that "one is probably safe in saying that the future of 'choral speech' in this part of the country is assured."[3] The success, however, seemed to be short-lived, and the statement did not prove to be "safe." Choral reading began its decline in the next decade.

To many the art was only a passing fad. Many instructors launched into productions merely as a change of pace from what they were teaching in order to come up with something novel for the students. Too many who tried their hand at choral reading simply were not informed or equipped in the art. Rose Walsh

[1] Agnes Curran Hamm, "Why the Professional Cold Shoulder?" *The Quarterly Journal of Speech* XLVI (February 1960), 80, 81.

[2] G. F. Reynolds, "Concerted Reading," *The Quarterly Journal of Speech* XVIII (November 1932), 659–661.

[3] Dorothy Kaucher, "The Verse Speaking Choir," *The Quarterly Journal of Speech* XVII (February 1931), 72.

prophesied the decline as early as 1935: "There are always too many ready to snatch a new thing and plunge into operation before they are properly prepared, and it would seem that the revival of choral speaking is threatened with that danger."[4] She continued using stronger language suggesting that choral speaking might well go the route of elocution and be "degraded with hit or miss attempts, stopping at insipid sensational 'recitations.' "[5]

Although there were some fine performances, true to the literature and which made good use of the medium, too many were just plain bad performances which disenchanted many who were previously interested in learning about the art. Rather than being discreet in the selection of the material, all kinds of literature were attempted. Mona Swann, in her book *An Approach to Choral Speech,* warned of this problem. The material suited to choral reading is limited and when these limits are "transgressed, the Speech-Choir loses its value as an artistic instrument. . . ."[6] The pure lyric and other subjective kinds of literature are ill-suited for choric treatment. Evidence indicates that too much experimentation using ill-suited literature, as well as other gimmicks, brought the medium into disrepute.

R. H. Robbins cites the principle which must be employed before one can decide on using a choric approach: "Our criterion must be 'Why choric; why not solo?' If this is done, there need be no fears for the permanence of choral speaking as a distinct art form."[7] This advice unfortunately went unheeded by too many.

In 1939 Agnes Curran Hamm presented a word of caution to those who would try choral reading, in her article "Choral Speaking—A Word of Warning." If any teacher, especially one unfamiliar with the rationale and techniques of the medium, attempts

[4] Rose Walsh, "Whither The Verse Speaking Choir," *The Quarterly Journal of Speech* XXI (November 1935), 462.

[5] Walsh, p. 466.

[6] Mona Swann, *An Approach to Choral Speech* (Boston: Walter H. Baker, 1937), 11.

[7] R. H. Robbins, "A Further Justification of Choral Reading," *The Quarterly Journal of Speech* XXIV (October 1938), 442.

to use choral reading in the classroom, "it will not be long before Choral Speaking falls into disrepute."[8]

Charlotte Lee best summarizes the inherent problem which is applicable to choric speaking, impersonation, or reader's theatre: "There cannot be too much emphasis placed on the fact that choric speaking is not an art form per se but a branch of the larger art of oral interpretation. It is a 'means' toward an end; not an end in itself."[9]

One cannot read a book dedicated to the treatment of choral reading without becoming acutely aware of its potential. Indeed, any given text on the subject laboriously defends the art beyond all expectation. In fact, most texts begin with a stronger defense as far as educational and practical elements are concerned than for the art of oral interpretation. Depending on one's point of view, the prefacing comments almost become paranoid in the defense of the art.

A number of theses have been concerned with choral reading, but none have been concerned exclusively with its rise and fall and current status. No doubt one could find other reasons than those presented here that lead to the decline of interest in the art. However, I thought the reader, as well as the researcher, might better be served by turning to responses of scholars who have worked in the medium and allowing them to present their candid opinions as to what happened to choral speaking. In a letter soliciting a response from each of the following individuals, I implied that although I did not think choral reading was read, I did believe that identification of the remains might be difficult. My assertion led to the following responses:

Agnes Curran Hamm

When a proven speech technique is a pleasure to teach and a pleasure to learn, why is it ignored by the speech profession as a

[8] Agnes Curran Hamm, "Choral Speaking—A Word of Warning," *The Quarterly Journal of Speech* XXV (April 1939), 22.

[9] Charlotte I. Lee, "Choric Speaking," *Making Words Come Alive,* ed. Cornelius Carman Cunningham (Dubuque, Iowa: William C. Brown, 1951), 186.

whole? When this same technique (choral reading) is one of the most effective methods of speech training, why is it not widely used? And when this technique can make oral interpretation an exciting, even thrilling experience for many students, why are most teachers limiting themselves to the one-to-one method?

These questions have been asked for years by the few teachers who have been using, enjoying, and getting results from choral reading, but the questions remain unanswered.

One wonders if choral reading has been given a real chance in the big universities or even in the high schools. In high school, when choral reading is taught, it is just a unit in a general speech course, and this is also true in some universities. As a six-week unit, it doesn't amount to much; at the end of this time the group is just beginning to grow. The students have fun together; they learn a few poems, get some speech training, and so the time is well spent. But the art does not develop—it is aborted.

Choral reading develops slowly and this is good—weeds make haste. But is its growth too slow for our push-button world—our jet age? It takes many hours and weeks of practice for a group to think, feel, and speak as an artistic unit. It means *work*—work on the part of the teacher as well as the students. Good students like to work—what of the teachers? Perhaps the training of teachers is at fault. If one looks at the history of this art, one realizes that training has been sporadic and inadequate.

As part of this history, I must be forgiven for including myself. Ugh! To be part of a "history" makes me sound as old as I really am. But here goes: Early in 1929 the president of a small girls' college in St. Louis, Maryville College, heard Marjorie Gullan's work in London and immediately decided she had to have it in her college. She sent me over to London on a year's scholarship to study with Marjorie Gullan, while a graduate of Miss Gullan's school came over to begin choral reading at Maryville College in September of 1929.

After the year with Miss Gullan—full-time day school plus additional classes in the evening (phonetics at the University of London), I taught at Maryville for four years. Then I married and moved to Milwaukee where I taught at Mount Mary College for thirty years.

During all these years I had many speech choirs—some were truly exciting; others were less good. I arranged "Hiawatha" as a choral drama to be used as a dramatic vehicle for the speech choir, and the Expression Company of Magnolia, Massachusetts published it. We presented this first in St. Louis and then in Milwaukee. In Milwaukee, one member of our audience, a professor at Marquette University, was so impressed that he said the show ought to be presented professionally and commercially. Naturally, it wasn't. But the professor did not forget the show. In 1950 he was a member of the board of the Delphisches Institute in Germany that was to present "The Delphiade," an international drama festival in Freiburg, Germany in 1952. When he was asked who should represent the U.S.A. in "The Delphiade," he recommended Mount Mary College in a presentation of "Hiawatha." We accepted the invitation! Two weeks after the Freiburg performance of "The Delphiade," with nine nations participating, the performance was repeated in Verona, Italy in their famous old amphitheater. Thirty-six students were in the speech choir that carried the narrative and took part in the choreography throughout the show. They found it a creative and thrilling experience.

So there have been exciting times in my choral reading career, as well as the day-to-day joy of using this effective technique. I only regret that more teachers don't share my pleasure, and I can't help repeating my question of February 1960: "Why the professional cold shoulder for choral reading?"

Margaret Robb

I don't think choral reading is dead. The emphasis on public performance as a choir is no longer present, partly because it became too much of an exhibition and not enough of an interpretation of the literature (too much attention to costume, perhaps). It was a fad which may have been superseded by Reader's Theatre, which again is a group presentation and may use some choral reading from time to time as the material dictates.

When the material calls for more than one voice to carry the emotion, we naturally use choral reading. Not only the Greek plays but others such as "Murder in the Cathedral" require a chorus to intensify the emotions of the play. Folk ballads and psalms suggest to us a number of readers reading together. When the rhythm of lines must be intensified, a group interprets—even the musical may make use of this kind of reading ("The Music Man" uses several examples of this kind of group presentation).

I believe choral reading is a very good technique for teaching children, especially those who may have some handicaps. The teacher reads the poem and invites participation during the next reading. Suggestions will come from them about solo parts. They love incremental readings of choruses, etc. Maybe a child who is very timid and couldn't stand before the class and recite a poem will have a lovely time reading/speaking the poem with others and might even volunteer to read a solo line later on.

Even with the young, I think some distinction should be made about material. A sonnet is a very personal poem and is not improved by group reading. In fact, it may be ruined. Children write poetry which is personal and not in need of a group voice. They understand this and are quite sensitive to the person of the poem. Who is speaking? What kind of voice?

You see, my idea for a book would be: How can and when should choral reading be used, not why it is no longer being offered as a class.

Sara Lowrey

It is my opinion that interest in choral reading may have declined due to many factors—as an art form, it seldom stands alone effectively. It served a purpose in Greek Drama to interpret the feeling of the populace. It served a similar purpose in plays by T. S. Eliot. It seems to serve purposes in religious drama from the Hebrew literature of the Bible to modern rituals. I think it can be used effectively in teaching from the elementary school through college. Literary appreciation can be enhanced through classroom experiences in choral reading.

As an art form it seems often to appear artificial. As Amy Lowell said, "Art becomes artificial when form takes precedence over spirit."

I have witnessed charming programs in the Greenville Public Schools after my inservice courses with teachers. Before our choral reading classes, teachers seemed afraid of poetry, not knowing how to let students experience rhythms and other dramatic values in poetry. They learned how to let the children express their own creativity through acting out poetry, integrating the choral experiences with individual poets and parts.

I have always felt that choral reading served a better purpose as a means than as a performance per se.

Eugene Bahn

It seems to be a part of human nature to be attracted to the new and the unusual. Therefore, when choral speaking first became popular, through the admirable work of Marjorie Gullan and her disciples in America, the response was tremendously enthusiastic. Many teachers and departments of speech organized work in this "new" form of expression. Choral speaking basked on the crest of this wave for a relatively long time and still rests on it even though the wave is not as large, or as sonorous, as it once was.

This subsidence is not unique. Throughout the history of speech education there have been movements which have arisen, from century to century and even from decade to decade. Some have survived and others have had a short life.

Choral speaking, however, is not dead. Indeed, it holds a significant place in the speech and educational world, and if it is not on the peak of the highest wave, it is still in view and is in the company of other highly respectable movements.

When choral speaking first appeared in the twentieth century, it was relatively new to the modern world. As we look back, it may have had other significant contributions to make to speech which were not discernible at that time. It may well have reduced tendencies toward elocution in its submergence of the individual into the group, and it certainly gave precedence to what is heard as opposed to what is seen. This made exaggerated bodily action less important, which was a very significant achievement. At the opposite end of the pole, it gave freedom of expression to the increasing number of those who felt that the only answer to elocution was to omit all gesture and emotional response whatsoever. In this light it might possibly be said that choral speaking helped support the approach to oral interpretation which was subsequently accepted in this century as "natural."

If choral speaking is not practiced as much as it was, as some will contend, it will be of interest to look for the reasons. One of these may be found in the nature of contemporary literature, for certainly the literature itself has something to do with the interpretative approach.

One authority held that poetry for choral speaking should have strong and compelling rhythm, vivid and striking diction, and variation and contrast in mood or thought—all moving to a climax.[10] Further, poems with a general viewpoint (rather than very personal material), straightforward, and not too difficult or too introspective were preferred.[11] An authority no less than Marjorie Gullan observed that "contemporary American and English verse is almost all that which is called 'free,' which means that it is often not to be distinguished from prose of a rather jerky order."[12] Moreover, she maintained that this poetry is mainly "a direct statement" and ignores imagery. "Modernist" poetry, Miss Gullan affirmed, is not interested in developing a definite theme. While this is a valid observation of some contemporary literature, it is not true of all of it, for certainly there is much imagery, considerable rhyme and much rhythm in modern verse. There is, however, a tension in it which does not appear to be in earlier traditional poetry. Moreover, it often needs to be heard several times to be understood. Much modern poetry is complex, it often appeals to the intellect and it

[10] Marjorie E. Burdsell, "Choral Speech in the English Class," Marguerite E. DeWitt, *Practical Methods in Choral Speaking,* (Boston: Expression Co., 1936), 182.

[11] *Ibid.,* p. 181.

[12] Marjorie Gullan, "Spoken Verse," *ibid.,* p. 211.

is personal and subjective. So perhaps the nature of our poetry has, as far as adults are concerned, something to do with the popularity of choral speaking.

Children's literature, on the other hand, still carries along with its verse a strong traditional thread in that its rhythm is definite and unmistakably clear. It is here that the two elements meet of the child's instinctive love of rhythm and a literature that nurtures that rhythm.

Choral speaking is an excellent means of developing a sense of rhythm and its concomitants, tempo and pausing; therefore, that literature which has rather definite rhythms is frequently used first in choral speaking. Such qualities are found readily in well-known traditional literature, and particularly in traditional children's literature, which, in any case, the child should hear. Choral speaking has been, and will continue to be, of inestimable value in bringing poetry and children together.

However, it is necessary at this point to draw a distinction between the public presentation and the classroom usage of choral speaking. While there are probably not nearly so many public choral speaking programs as there were, there is considerable use of choral speaking in the classroom. One well-known person in this field, Carrie Rasmussen, believed that choral speaking in the elementary grades should be focused on classroom activity and not on public performance.[13] When it is used in the classroom, rather than for public performance, it will usually not be given the publicity involved in public presentations, such as is today more apt to be attendant on a Reader's Theatre or Chamber Theatre production. Moreover, choral speaking is, in some instances, included in courses with the title of "Reader's Theatre," "Group Reading," or some other general term. Thus the public will not be aware of the extent to which choral speaking is used.

Choral speaking has certain speech and educational values that have warranted, and do warrant, its use from the standpoint of literature and the growth of the individual. As Agnes C. Hamm says, choral speaking is an excellent medium for improving both

[13] Marjorie E. Burdsell, *ibid.,* p. 186.

tone and diction, especially in terms of a group. In addition it helps
the shy as well as the forward student.[14] These facts will not be
overlooked by the perceptive educator, and such educators will give
choral speaking the support it merits in the educational system.

Conclusion

Among all of the communicative breakthroughs in the twentieth century and the push for scientific research, choral reading
seems anachronistic. In my judgment no one has really refuted its
benefits, both practical and aesthetic. There seems to be a small
group of partisans who work in utter obscurity to the obsequious-
ness of the masses. Without appearing to be a heretic or a devil's
advocate for the status quo, I think the speech profession has overlooked a dynamic interest which may have cost us a number of
students, for those who count numbers, not to mention a "bread
and butter" course for elementary teachers.

My observations are naturally based on many inferences: (1)
there is a demand for choral speaking in the elementary grades and
perhaps the secondary schools (how much of a demand has never
been calculated); (2) there are a few qualified people currently
teaching choral reading; (3) only a very few English and speech
departments teach choral reading. If you can accept these observations, they seem to indicate a need to "get it together." Pedagogically, we have lost a very viable part of our curriculum. If the
English departments are willing to cooperate, and there is evidence
they will, and if we in speech are creative enough and energetic
enough to build a solid course in group performance for the elementary teacher, we may find our lost child, choral reading.

Furthermore, conversations with people who directed choral
reading productions in the thirties indicate that today's Reader's
Theatre productions are not so different from choral reading of the

[14] Agnes Curran Hamm, *Choral Speaking Technique* (Milwaukee:
The Tower Press, 1946), 6, 7.

thirties as might be imagined. In fact, many choral reading productions emphasized solo readings with only occasional choral renditions, and only then when the script required choric effects. Additionally, the productions did not employ costumes or sets and the performances were not positioned in a singing chorale arrangement, but rather were "blocked" to establish a pleasing stage picture and to accommodate whatever movement was required. It seems, then, that Reader's Theatre is much more an outgrowth of choral reading than we have heretofore accepted. Even John Masefield's descriptions of the productions at the verse-speaking choir contests he conducted in Scotland sound like descriptions of a Reader's Theatre presentation. Granted, Reader's Theatre productions today seem mature and sophisticated compared to what we know of choral speaking, but it should be recognized that choral reading of yesteryear died for reasons we might accept more willingly today.

Hopefully, we will learn from the past as S. S. Curry hoped, and choral reading will once again take its place as a viable art form for certain kinds of literature. Because interpretation is concerned with the text, the concern should always be whether the choral approach is right for the literature. At the 1972 SCA Convention in San Francisco, 1972, Professor Jean George Congdon built "A Case for the Choral Interpretation of Drama in Reader's Theatre." She offered sage advice: "Choral orchestration seeks to 'explore' rather than 'exploit' the text; to 'clarify' rather than distort meaning."

Selected Readings

Griffin, Christine. "Choral Reading—A New Use," *Today's Speech* VII (September 1963), 14, 30.

Hopkins, Bess Cooper. "English Teachers Need the Speech Choir," *The Southern Speech Journal* XIX (March 1954), 214–223.

Kaucher, Dorothy. "The Verse Speaking Choir," *The Quarterly Journal of Speech* XVII (February 1931), 64–73.

Meader, Emma Grant. "Choral Speaking and Its Values," *The Quarterly Journal of Speech* XXII (April 1936), 235–245.

Paul, Vera A. "Choral Speaking as a Phase of Oral Interpretation,"
    The Southern Speech Journal XIII (November 1947), 62–64.
Robbins, R. H. "A Further Justification of Choral Speaking," *The
    Quarterly Journal of Speech* XXIV (October 1938), 437–442.
Walsh, Rose. "Whither the Verse—Speaking Choir," *The Quarterly
    Journal of Speech* XXI (November 1935), 461–466.

During the first twenty-five years of the twentieth century, interpretation continued its trend toward the literary shore. But for many it was still primarily elocution[1] and a skill rather than an art.[2] In 1922, Ralph Dennis, Dean of the School of Speech at Northwestern University, spoke out for eclecticism and the humanistic values of interpretation. Fifty years later, his essay was called a "classic in its own right."[3]

Although his style is dated, Dennis's ideas are not out of date or even out of step with the current wave of humanism. Dennis was not interested in theories; he was interested in people. He helped put the interpreter back into the discussion of the interpretative process. He warned of fetish and the passing fads of schools and systems. He spoke of a "plus" which is difficult to define. To endorse his "plus" is to reject much of interpretative process as we know it today; but to deny his "plus" is to deny what most interpreters have seen and heard in certain special readings. Wallace A. Bacon will comment on the exuberance of Dean Dennis by putting the "plus" in the perspective of current theory.

[1] W. M. Parrish, "Public Speaking and Reading—A Plea for Separation," *The Quarterly Journal of Speech Education* X (June 1924), 280.

[2] W. M. Parrish, "Interpretative Reading," *The Quarterly Journal of Speech Education* XIII (April 1927), 160–168.

[3] Martha Thompson Barclay, "Genesis of Modern Oral Interpretation: 1915–1930," *The Speech Teacher* XXI (January 1972), 40.

One Imperative Plus

My theme is this: In addition to all the teachings of all the schools of expression, in addition to the values of the "think the thought," "feel the emotion," the Delsarte, the rush, of any old or any new group, call it what you please, there is an imperative plus a *something needed* if the interpreter of literature is to be a really great interpreter. And secondly, it is my opinion that any attempt to regulate platform reading by rules which define, limit, condemn, or regulate—rules often growing out of personal limitations—serves but to narrow our work, to introduce controversy, to destroy more than to build. Imagine a line running across this page, six inches in length. Let it represent the skill and power of a reader. Rules and regulations may be laid down which guide the individual for about one-half inch of the way. The rest must be left to the personal powers, instincts, capacities, and tastes of the reader. To do more than this is to kill his art.

Now back to the main theme! I belong to the eclectic school in interpretation. I see values in almost every system which has been devised, values of major or minor importance. This may be a strength or a weakness, I do not know. I understand Mark Sabre when he says, "I've got the most infernal habit of seeing things from about twenty points of view instead of one . . . I've no convictions; that's the trouble. . . . I can always see the other side of the case. . . . You can't possibly be successful if you haven't got convictions. . . . What I call baldheaded convictions. You know, you can't possibly pull out this big, booming sort of stuff they call success if you're going to see anybody's point of view but your own. You must have convictions . . . only one conviction . . . that you are right and that every one who thinks differently is wrong to blazes." Anyway, I agree with the "think the thoughters," the tone system, the "feel emotion" crowd, etc. They are right, as far as they go. No one of them holds all the truth. From all of their picking and choosing, we get valuable material, good enough for a system for today, but steadily needing additions and subtractions if it is to meet tomorrow's needs. For we die at the top when we think we have found the last word. The youngsters will show us that we are wrong, will discard some of our pet schemes for something better, something which more meets the needs of the new generation. Fundamentals of a sort will always exist but they should never be made fetishes by those who would continue to grow.

What is the aim of interpretation? To re-create life as it has been put into printed words. To find and re-create the beautiful, the good, the worthwhile, the universal, the truth as it has been put into books.

What is needed if one is to do this well? An education, brains, an emotional nature which is quickly responsive, a voice and body tuned to quick responsiveness. But grant these, grant training under one or all of the various "systems," grant platform experience and skill, and there is still needed the imperative plus before the real interpreter of life and literature is made.

What is this plus? I am not sure that I can put it into words. It is too easy to become high-flown, long-haired, ecstatically aesthetic. But with my feet on the ground, talking to practical folk, let me try it. A moment ago I used three words, "interpreter of life." Let's start there. To interpret life one must know life—through many beautiful, happy, sad, painful, toilsome, lighthearted, heavyhearted, journeys into the land of experience; journeys made in the flesh, mayhap; mayhap in the spirit, in the imagination. But you must have been there. Out of this course comes a philosophy (simple and crude it may be—but it is), a vision of man and mankind. You may get this without reading a book, though that is a doubtful method. You may get it through books alone, again a doubtful method with lopsided results. You may get it through both sources, books and life—the best way, I think.

Winchester says that literature is a record of the emotional life of man. Shelley said of the drama, as he might have said of all great literature, that its highest purpose "is the teaching of the human heart, through its sympathies and antipathies, knowledge of itself—in proportion to the possession of which knowledge every human being is wise, just, tender, tolerant and kind."

Kerfoot, in his *How to Read,* quoted in Miss Johnson's good book, says, "We have nothing to read with except our own experiences—the seeing and hearing and tasting and smelling and touching that we have done; the fearing and hating and hoping and loving that has happened to us; the intellectual and spiritual reactions that have resulted; and the assumptions, understandings, prides, prejudices, hypocrisies, fervors, foolishnesses, finenesses, and faiths that have thereby been precipitated in us like crystals in a chemist's tube."

But turn to *The Nigger of the Narcissus,* last edition, and read Conrad's statement of faith and you have what appeals to me as the best possible statement of what I am attempting to say. He says, "The artist appeals to that part of our being which is not dependent on wisdom; to that in us which is a gift and not an acquisition—and, therefore, more permanently enduring. He speaks to our capacity for delight and wonder, to the sense of mystery surrounding our lives: to our sense of pity, and beauty, and pain: to the latent feeling of fellowship with all creation and to the subtle but invincible conviction of solidarity that knit together the loneliness of innumerable hearts to solidarity in dreams, in joy, in sorrow, in aspirations, in illusions, in hope, in fear, which binds men to each other, which binds together all humanity—the dead to the living and the living to the unborn."

I may intellectually know meanings, but if I am to interpret, I must know meanings emotionally, must connect them with life, all

human life. Not long since, I heard a college student read Kingsley's
THREE FISHERS. She understood the words, but when she read,

> For men must work and women must weep,
> And there's little to earn, and many to keep,
>   Though the harbor bar be moaning.

it was apparent that never in her life of real or imaginary experience had she seen the poverty of China, watched the women of
Japan coaling a passenger boat, seen the peasant women of Europe,
known the meaning of The Man with the Hoe, or even in our own
Chicago stood on Halsted, or Milwaukee, or Blue Island of an
evening and watched with sympathetic and understanding eyes the
human stream as it wound home from work. She knew so little
and she didn't know so much. Similarly I might illustrate with
every poem of merit, with every bit of prose that depicts life:

> Oh Lord, give *understanding*—of life, of the great human
> spectacle the earth over, of the human heart.

Such is one imperative plus! Can we teach it? Yes. We can
plant the seeds, which may later grow. They must be planted. No-
where, in no other class in university, college, or secondary school,
is there such an opportunity given to a teacher to plant seeds that
make for vision, for sympathy, for warm personal contacts, as to
the teacher of interpretation and public speaking. Further, if he be
a teacher worth his salt, he *must* teach these things, largely by indirection.

And with this our task, we quarrel and quibble over termi-
nology, definitions, methods, systems. We say that all reading must
be thus and so. We define (and rightly, for we must be intelligent)
impersonation, personation, characterization, acting. And some of
us, moved unconsciously (I hope it is unconsciously) by our limitations, our tastes, score mercilessly those who use A instead of B,
or C instead of D, etc. Papers are read here to prove that he who
uses the technique of acting in his reading from the printed page

is outlaw; that he who characterizes is outlaw, that he who uses costume is outlaw, or makeup, or this or that. Fill in the words for yourself. I have heard artistic work in all these manifestations. So have you, if you are not narrow minded.

How can we measure platform art, or stage art? By this—does it appeal, does it get over—*to the judicious few as well as to the many?* That's a high standard, a practical standard. Can you meet it? Who does: Guilbert, Sales, Williams, Janis, Wilson? What's the next standard? That it appeal to the many without offending the few. And last—because so limited in its appeal—that it appeal to the few and bore to death the many. If we accept such measurements, what care we about personation or impersonation, characterization, or acting, except as they be good or bad mediums for the individual under discussion? Your real artist can get over to the few, to the many, separately, or to both in the same audience.

She wore a costume, therefore she was inartistic-nonsense. She impersonated, it was therefore terrible-nonsense. She almost acted the thing and it was therefore bad-nonsense. Did it live, was it true, did it get over to the audience, pleasing the judicious or at least not offending? There's the standard. We may say to the pupil, "You should not characterize so broadly." But if we say it, we must criticize not because characterization per se is bad, but because it is not the right medium for that particular reader. Exactly the reverse may be true of the next student to enter your room. You may say to the student, "Ah, that is acting, what you should do is personate." But we must not say it because we have a fixed dislike for acting per se, but because in that instance the student failed to make the truth live by acting and could and does make it live by personation. We should be pragmatists, with certain definite results we are trying to hit.

And now back to our original theme, the imperative plus. If a reader has the plus, not one bit care I whether he characterizes, acts, personates, or what method he uses. He shows me life through his personal slant, his concept, his vision. If he is sincere, true, honest, does not offend; if he moves me, makes me think, I am for him.

What is the cultivated man? What is culture? There are many

definitions. This one, "The cultivated man is the one who has the most contacts"—with music, art, literature, poetry, PEOPLE. And I don't dare omit the people. We who live in or on college campuses, who have lost the ability to understand the common folk, who interpret art as we think other people *ought* to like it, who have been educated out of a taste for the simple things of life, who can't see God in the servant, the clerk, the postman, the day laborer, as well as in our educated equals, our social equals, our money equals—if there be those of us like that, we have lost the imperative plus and have put down a minus sign in its stead.

Let's not quibble over terms, over methods. Let's get a better, bigger understanding of what this life is all about, let's find a meaning in it, let's learn how to re-translate, into living words and actions that will be understood by all the thoughts, the life values, the life interpretations which writing men have put into books.

∼

RESPONSE

Wallace A. Bacon

Dean Dennis's essay was published in 1922. The world is no longer what it was then. It may be that the big things don't change (eating, sleeping, living, dying), but the little things change constantly—and as someone has said, it is the little things that make all the difference.

It is possible to sympathize generally with many of Dean Dennis's views. It is true that "rules" are often death-dealing; no one ever handed down golden tablets on which were engraved the "principles" of interpretation. It is true that most of the old schools of instruction had virtues, and that an eclectic approach and a pragmatic attitude have more than passing merit. It is equally true that there is no substitute for a well-stocked imagination and an awareness of life. A parsimonious spirit is not the best equipment for an interpreter, who should learn to move outward from himself, not to hoard his virtues but to spend them freely.

Nevertheless, I find myself uneasy with Dean Dennis's heady optimism. While it is clear at times that he is actually aware of, and touched by, opposite or different views, he can say:

What is the aim of interpretation? To re-create life as it has been put into printed words. To find and re-create the beautiful, the good, the worthwhile, the universal, the truth as it has been put into books.

But the interpreter has negative capabilities: he can re-create the ugly, the bad, the worthless, the particular, the lie—as these have been put into books, too. And it isn't just a matter of re-creating, nor just a matter of life "as it has been put into printed words." The interpreter is creator as well as re-creater; the total experience which he in part creates and in part re-creates may be far from life as he knows it. Literature really isn't the "transfer" of life into words. Aristotle long ago disposed of that issue, surely.

A love of literature does not necessarily make one happier; not even, necessarily, healthier. It *ought* to make one more sensitive, more aware. It ought to help inform that sense of "otherness" to which the whole human experience surely should (but often does not) lead us. I think Dean Dennis claims far too much for the class in interpretation and public speaking, though it is true that such classes indeed often do provide for "warm personal contacts" within small groups. I know that his own classes *did* have the capacity to inspire students with his kind of optimism. I have heard his students say that. But I have also known them to speak skeptically of what seemed to some of them too-large generalizations. Is there perhaps something indiscriminate in the view of the imperative plus?

The difficulty with saying so is that it makes one feel, even while he says it, that he is being picayune. But truth also deals with the little things—the things that we have suggested make all the difference. While I might like to see life steadily and see it whole, I doubt that I or anyone else will ever manage to accomplish that. The best we can do is to keep the blinders off, to keep our eyes healthy, and to keep looking. We do die at the top when we think we have found the last word. We die, then, from top to toe; *rigor vitae* is *rigor mortis*.

One can be petty and intolerant, or one can try to permit *all* and end up holding nothing: tolerance is somewhere in between. One can define things to death; or one can try to get along without definition at all, but he will not succeed: the mind by nature seeks to organize. While Dean Dennis quotes Mark Sabre approvingly as saying "I've no convictions; that's the trouble," no one who ever knew Dean Dennis would think him lacking in convictions. He had them, and they were strong. What does it mean, then, for a teacher of interpretation to say, as he does, that beyond that "half-inch" where rules and regulations may guide the interpreter, "the rest must be left to the personal powers, instincts, capacities and tastes of the reader"?

I like, I must say, the enthusiasm for the spirit of the student; I like the sense of the student's *counting*. But the teacher who, beyond that half-inch of "rules," leaves all else up to the student is surely not earning his keep. Nor is it all a matter of encouraging him to be "wise, just, tender, tolerant and kind," to be "sincere, true, honest." This optimism, essentially sentimental, leaves out too much. There are times when a human being must be tough rather than tender, when he must compromise, when he must even feel one thing and say another. The disinterestedness of the pelican, the innocence of the lamb are not enough to fit one for the world; the courage of the lion is not, by itself, enough; the cunning of the fox is not alone sufficient. The kingdom of man, like the animal kingdom, has qualities of many kinds; one needs to know how to live with them, though this does not mean simply *adopting* all these qualities in oneself. One of the things to be said for the training required of the interpreter (though not alone for him) is that it teaches him to understand, vicariously, and to embody much that he could otherwise come to feel only in ways that would do him damage. He must have some sense of what it is to be mean, to be cruel, to be vicious—otherwise he could not enact literature that has these qualities. Does Dean Dennis really allow for literature that "offends"? Does the interpreter never do anything, say anything, that is an affront to taste? One may say "No," and so seem to answer the question by definition. I must say for myself that I have seen interpreters do things which I found, as a matter of personal taste, offensive to *me,* but which I could not say were, simply *in toto,* or *in vacuo,* offensive. There is literature that offends me, but that I cannot say is not literature. Surely *I* require educating, too, and it doesn't make me very comfortable simply to say, of an interpreter, "If he is sincere, true, honest—does not offend, if he moves me, makes me think, I am for him." I have been moved by interpreters when I was aware of the triviality of my being moved. And what does "makes me think" really mean? A bad performance of a bad text can make me think.

I could rewrite Dean Dennis so that we would seem to be saying pretty much the same things. But we really aren't saying the same things because we see literature (and probably life) in different terms. Doubtless the thing we both *would* agree on is that there is no *one* "way" to see either. He is more exuberant, at least in this essay; by contrast, I will seem parsimonious, though I do not think that I really am. Perhaps the world I live in has made me more aware of trouble, of uncertainty, of darkness; but it has not, for all that, made me less sure of its value. I am for it, as Dean Dennis is for it. I, too, am interested in the interpreter who makes use of a variety of methods, who creates and re-creates a sense of life—though I think that it is not just "his personal slant, his concept, his vision" that moves me, but his ability to match those with the "personal slant," the "concept," the "vision" of the work itself in all its tensiveness and in its full perspective—in a word, in all its *presence.* I think that literature really does not make "the truth" live. I think it presents; it creates presence. The interpreter in turn embodies, enacts. The truth of literature (to paraphrase Wellek and Warren) is that it seems true. Or (to paraphrase Aristotle) it may simply seem *probable,* and it often will not matter whether in fact it be *possible.* The interpreter is not a preacher, not a philosopher, not a purveyor of truth; he is a performer, he performs texts. While surely the "rules and regulations" are best kept few and far between, and while surely there is always something of the unteachable in the art of one who performs, the things he must be taught and can be taught are legion.

Selected Readings

Babcock, Maud May. "Teaching Interpretation," *The Quarterly Journal of Public Speaking* I (July 1915), 173–176.

Geiger, Don. "Oral Interpretation in the Liberal Arts Context," *The Quarterly Journal of Speech* XL (April 1954), 137–144.

Marshman, John T. "Art Approach to Reading Aloud," *The Quarterly Journal of Speech* XXXVIII (February 1951), 35–40.

Rarig, Frank. "Ralph Dennis," *The Quarterly Journal of Speech* XXIX (April 1943), 234–240.

Like Professor Dennis, John T. Marshman believes in the "plus" of interpretation. Marshman calls interpretation a paradox; perhaps many today would agree with him. Because oral interpretation is an art, it has always been difficult to define its artistic realm. Indeed, some have argued that as an art interpretation transcends definition; it is a "mystery."* Scholars continue to describe the process of what goes on between the writer, reader, and audience. Differences exist in opinion. We feel that diverse opinion is good for an art. It is only by investigation, discussion, and reciprocal modification of theories that an art can flourish. As you read Marshman's essay, try to discover if the paradox is still true today. Professor Janet Bolton will then put the paradox into perspective with her contemporary comment.

J. T. MARSHMAN

The Paradox of Oral Interpretation

It is an old and faithful saying, "Art that conceals art is the best art." Oral interpretation is an art in which there is a great and a peculiar danger of the artist's dishonoring this aged paradoxical aphorism. As oral interpreters we are prone to accentuate the voice

* J. T. Marshman, "The Mystery of Oral Interpretation," *The Quarterly Journal of Speech* XXIV (December 1938), 601.

and body technique as the "be-all and end-all" of interpretation until the technique stands out in such bold relief that no one listening can see, hear, or feel anything beyond. Ruskin declared such manifestation to be a "fatal fault" in any art. It springs largely from self-admiration and a love of exhibition. The highest art in oral interpretation, as in any other art, impresses itself without being remarked.

Perhaps we could say that the physical techniques, such as inflections of voice, qualities of voice, stresses of voice; and action, such as gesture and posture, are the anatomy of oral interpretation, while psychical techniques, such as processes of imagination, reasoning, memory, emotion, are the organism of oral interpretation. It might be that we could make our conception clearer by saying that the physical techniques are the individuality of oral interpretation, while the psychical techniques are the personality of oral interpretation. Do we express our personality through our individuality? It would seem that they are warp and woof of each other, even as anatomy and organism are inextricably intertwined.

It is practically impossible to avoid ambiguities and vagueness in an attempt to explain the acting and the reacting, and the resulting relationship of inner mental processes and the outward physical processes in oral reading. Such an exposition can not be very definite for one in dealing constantly with the processes of the functioning of the vocal and actional behavior in relation to the mental machinery, such as emotion, imagination; and, to say nothing of the processes akin, it is impossible to be very accurate in an analysis and classification of emotion and imagination. If we attempt to put a mental microscope on an emotion, it is not there, and if we watch for the emotion's return, if it comes at all, it comes back in a different compound.

We shall have to be content with the mental telescope in our examination processes, processes that seem so near to us and yet are so far away. If the artist is to analyze and classify, he must use the telescopic mind. Art must realize qualities instead of, as science with its microscope, conceive detailed relations. Art is concerned with the ends of living. Literature worthy of the name deals with ends and not with means. If we are to realize these ends and qualities as oral readers, we need telescopic minds. No two of us in our telescopic examinations will see the same ends in all their relationships. And this is as it should be since we are dealing with an art.

We do not mean to say that just any one can peer through his mental telescope into the firmament of literature and discern there worlds and suns and moons and stars. We shall need to know how to use the telescope, and we shall need to know what to look for, and we shall need to know where to look, and we shall need to know when to look. A mastery of such knowledge will perfect our subjective technique as oral interpreters, the technique that discovers truth and penetrates reality of great literature. It is a long and risky road that we must tread in coming to be unconsciously aware of the soul of literature.

What we are trying to say is that "one must be well charged with a great work of literature through long, sympathetic brooding before any attempt be made at defining, formulating, precipitating which 'refuse the soul its way.'" I think that it was Hiram Corson who said, "We must long inhale the choral atmosphere of a work of genius before we attempt any intellectual formulation of it; which formulation must necessarily be comparatively limited, because genius, as genius, is transcendental, and therefore outside of the domain of mere intellect. And even when we do formulate and precipitate through the intellect, it is done for the purpose of coming back to a greater perspective and solution of the whole." Not analysis then for the sake of analysis, but analysis for the sake of a greater synthesis.

All this is evidence to show that when men give themselves unreservedly to a high task, there is a "plus" which implements their power. It is this "plus" that we as readers must have. It is this same "plus" that gives us simplicity which may well be described as the truthfulness of nature. Charles Dudley Warner called simplicity the immortal element in literature. To think thoughts after writers truly and to feel their emotions genuinely and to read so that men see and feel, this is the highest art in reading, because it is coming back to nature; it is the childlike spirit of simplicity. "Nature at its best and art at its highest are one."

Let us come to a conclusion of the whole matter. The background and the discipline of an oral interpreter as an artist involves the discernment of the truth, of the world within and the world without; the penetration of the reality of these two worlds, and then the revelation of the spiritual elements in symbols of voice and action. This means that the oral interpreter not only must have a cultural background, but he must also have a mastery of the formal technique of communication. In other words, he must have the power of appreciation; and appreciation is a re-creation, a vitalizing anew, of the artist's soul and handicraft; and an incarnation of what the artist saw, thought and felt, taking unto one's self, and yet a taking that does not rob. Added to this he must learn to see, to think, and to feel in terms of a communicative technique that will overcome audience inertia, and that will find an emphatic response in those who listen.

If we are to overcome audience inertia and find an emphatic response, it will be necessary for every student and teacher of oral interpretation to develop a synchronized mental and physical technique without making hard and fast rules, for standardizing an art tends to mar the art.

Art is realized philosophy and science, for the principles which art involves, science and philosophy evolve.

In true oral interpretation, not only mental and physical techniques are one, but reader and listener are one. The printed words of literature become flesh, and the flesh becomes the spoken words of literature.

❧

RESPONSE

Janet Bolton

Texts and articles in the last thirty years indicate an escalating effort to identify oral interpretation as a study and to vindicate its place in the academic curriculum. Preeminence of the literary text is now almost universal: "expression" is subordinated to "oral study" and "appreciation." The dimensions and distinctions of an oral approach to literature have been difficult to explain, however, and to buttress often vague demarcations, theories have been appropriated from seemingly more established disciplines in English and speech communication. These transplants emphasize relationships to rhetorical analysis, to literary criticism and to communication theory; they may also suggest a superimposed identity—that oral interpretation itself is a chimera. Even those writers who continue to insist that oral interpretation is an artistic phenomenon subject to examination only within its own set of dynamics, evade reference to the long since excommunicated public performer.

To evaluate John Tryon Marshman's concept of oral interpretation in a contemporary perspective of demonstrable hypotheses and objective data would be to dismiss an older but completely viable construct. The reader must return to an era seemingly longer gone than thirty years. In personal outlook and by training, Marshman was a prototype of the dedicated teachers of the early twentieth century and of their views: Charles Wesley Emerson's expression as thought amplified; Hiram Corson's pairing of the voice and spiritual education; Robert McLean Cumnock's eclectic development of individual abilities; Ralph Dennis's "One Imperative Plus"; above all, S. S. Curry's philosophy of the speech arts as activation of all human powers. Marshman's career is one of the last testimonials: advanced degrees in literature and oratory, distinguished teaching in debate, oratory and oral reading, ordained minister, Chautauqua lecturer for ten years, president of the Speech Association of America in 1938. In a lecture on the history of speech education he recalled the schools of speech, oratory, and expression which were later incorporated into the colleges and universities:

In those early days I feel that the emphasis was largely on the instrumental value of speech education. In other words, these special schools in speech stressed the vocational utility of speech education. Their appeal to men and women was that speech, public address, was a practical subject, training them for specific vocations, such as law, ministry, politics, lecturing, and acting; also, in those days there was great interest in lyceum work. . . . From persons interested in some vocation these special schools recruited their ranks.[1]

I would interject here that the appeal of these schools and the public platforms was more than vocational. The lyceum platforms and Chautauqua tents, the orators, lecturers, entertainers, and artists were manifestations of a turn-of-the-century ideal—a rural and small town American dream that education and self-development were obligations of every human being. Marshman's generation established the speech arts as commitments involved in being rational, being moral, acquiring taste, being a member of society, being a man dedicated to self-realization. From this ideology, the element of subjectivity could never be eliminated. In this context, the key to oral interpretation as "mystery," as "paradox," makes definition beside the point.

The confident premise of "The Paradox of Oral Interpretation" is that oral interpretation is to be regarded as art—beyond explanation. The art of oral interpretation is what an artist interpreter does. It is a mystic process in which ambiguities and vagueness are inherent. Emotion, imagination, concept, voice, and action are in flux, so intricately related, so evanescent, that "it is impossible to be very accurate in an analysis and classification. . . ."[2] Marshman wrote: "Every great oral reader is more or less a mystic. He finds his style and technique (technique, subjective and objective, is style) as a mystic finds God in his own soul. The true reader finds his technique slowly drawn up from within out of a well of inner emotions and thought."[3] By its very nature, the mystic experience is neither apparent to the senses nor obvious to the intelligence; it is akin to spirituality, vision, and even rapture.

The miraculous paradox is mutuality of the psychic and the physical processes.

[1] Later published as "Trends in Speech Education in the Last Half Century," *The Speech Teacher* 4 (March 1955), 81.

[2] "The Paradox of Oral Interpretation," p. 32.

[3] *Ibid.,* p. 33.

The outward, or voice and body manifestations, may well be called the revelation process; the inward or mental and emotional procedure, may well be called the realization process. In the internal activity there is a subjective or psychical technique; in the external expression, there is an objective or physical technique. The two techniques are reciprocal in action; the one is not independent of the other. A mastery of subjective technique helps to the mastery of objective technique, and the mastery of the objective technique helps to the mastery of the subjective technique.[4]

This integration cannot be formulated; it is no less than unity of mind and body. The only means of describing the enigmatic coalition of "realization" and "revelation" is through metaphor, and Marshman summoned a host of these: anatomy and organism, warp and woof, camera and projector, painter and pigment, weaver and garment. He called for a "mental telescope" for the examination of art, instead of the scientist's microscope which merely reveals detailed relationships.[5] Scientific methods cannot be trusted: "There are realms where science does not contribute much; it has little to offer in understanding to the humanities; it contributes little to the imagination; in fact, too close application to it may be a hindrance. . . ."[6] The exploration of art cannot be charted, but with good guidance (i.e., a good teacher) the "firmament," the "broad ocean," the "continents of truth and beauty"[7] of literature may be apprehended. Apprehension results from contemplation, from being "well-charged" with the literary text before the intellect begins the work of analysis.[8] And when the intellect is finally loosed upon the text, it is to provide a higher synthesis. "We must long inhale the choral atmosphere of a work of genius before we attempt any intellectual formulation of it; which formulation must necessarily

[4] *Ibid.,* p. 31.
[5] *Ibid.,* p. 32.
[6] "Trends," p. 83.
[7] "Paradox," p. 32.
[8] *Ibid.,* p. 32.

be comparatively limited, because genius, as genius, is transcendental, and therefore outside of the domain of mere intellect."[9]

All of this leads not to concept but to celebration of the mystic office of the interpreter. A kind of transcendental syllogism seems operative. "Art is concerned with the ends of living rather than with the means of living. Literature worthy of the name deals with ends and not with means."[10] Therefore the task of the interpreter is no less than the exploration of human values—an ordination. And indeed Marshman stressed his ethical commitment: simplicity, humility, immolation of self in the literature, complete absence of display. "Fatal faults in art are hypocrisy, indolence and affectation."[11] The interpreter communicates ideal examples of moral choice and action in literature; he must recognize and embody these. His psychic techniques are developed to make him a "focus that accumulates the rays of the meaning and mood of the literature . . ." His physical techniques are means of radiating "these rays that others may understand and emotionally comprehend with him."[12]

In this oracular context, it is not suprising that audience response should be given little specific consideration. The audience is, of course, the recipient of the message, but the particularity of the audience is of no more importance than that of a congregation of worshippers. Witnessing the engagement between a great literary text and a worthy interpretative artist is an experience of grace, and an audience cannot but be moved and illumined.

The role of the teacher is not that of instructor, director or model. He is a guide, a Virgil companion on a Dantesque search. The teacher's knowledge cannot be imparted directly; he serves as

[9] *Ibid.,* p. 32. It may be noted that Marshman attributed this to Hiram Corson, but he was casually uncertain. The phrase, not the source, evidently seemed important.

[10] *Ibid.,* p. 32.

[11] "The Mystery of Oral Interpretation," *The Quarterly Journal of Speech* 24 (December 1938), 597.

[12] "Paradox," p. 36.

inspiring impulse, to cause the student to discover for himself the "language of the soul, the feeling of the heart."[13]

In summation, an art of interpretative reading is an integration of all the expressive means of the human organism—words, modulations of tone and action, ideation, knowledge, process of thinking, attitudes of mind and feeling, capacity for excitement and self-control. Its paradox is the human being himself, who, in Curry's influential words, cannot like a machine be manipulated from without, but . . . "is modulated from within."[14]

We do not leave the paradox behind when we examine present day views—only an older verbiage. The thrust today is inquiry rather than celebration, operational definition instead of metaphor. At this writing, two recent sensitive commentaries reaffirm unsolved problems. From Thomas Sloan's relation to Richard Palmer's work on hermeneutics to oral interpretation come echoes:

Paradoxically, language is temporal and fixed, interior and exterior. Its moment of existence is its moment of utterance, compounded as that moment is of past conventions and future expectations. It resonates from the interior of a speaker and creates a 'presence' . . . in space. Yet language can be fixed, as in memorized or written texts; and utterance is always in part a coming-to-explicitness, or explicitness itself, of the speaker's perception of the world he inhabits.[15]

Gary Cronkhite's paradigm of oral interpretation is "the study of the interface between a written symbol system and an oral-physical symbol system."[16] Three cognitive systems are involved: those of transmitter or author, interpreter or reader, and receiver or listener. Each of these is a *perceptual* interface.[17]

---

[13] *Ibid.,* p. 34.

[14] S. S. Curry, *Foundations of Expression* (Boston: Expression, 1920), 10.

[15] Thomas O. Sloan, " 'Hermeneutics' the Interpreter's House Revisited," *The Quarterly Journal of Speech* 57 (February 1971), 104.

[16] Gary Cronkhite, "The Place of Aesthetics and Perception in a Paradigm of Interpretation," *Western Speech* 34 (Fall 1970), 283.

[17] *Ibid.,* p. 284.

Neither contradicts Marshman's older view. Both emphasize the complexity of oral interpretation as the complexity of human perception and understanding. They do, however, posit means to explore this complexity. A paradox is a stated incongruity, frankly opposed to common sense or objective data, self-defeating as definition. A paradigm is a paradox resolved. If Marshman would not admit the ultimate possibility of a paradigm of interpretation, he would surely applaud the search.

Selected Readings

Marshman, John T. "The Mystery of Oral Interpretation," *The Quarterly Journal of Speech* XXIV (December 1938), 596–603.

Williams, David A. "Paradox Revisited," *Interchange: Student Thought in Speech Communication* II (December 1972), 8–10.

————. "The Reader Audience Paradox," *Interchange: Student Thought in Speech Communication* I (September 1971), 1–4.

Veilleux, Jere. "The Interpreter: His Role, Language, and Audience," *The Speech Teacher* XVI (March 1967), 124–133.

Dean Dennis has spoken of the "plus" in oral interpretation and Professor Marshman discussed the "paradox"; now Professor Parrish discusses another elusive term, "naturalness." The dilemma created by the confusion between the "natural" and "mechanical" schools of elocution continue to plague our understanding of what it means to be "natural" in oral interpretation.

Students are not always clear about their relationship with their literature and evidence frustration by saying the literature sounds "unnatural." At other times one will hear that the reader sounded "unnatural" in performance. There also seems to be a tendency for many interpreters to select literature that "sounds like me." Prematurely, they decide they cannot perform a work because it doesn't "sound right" for them.

Professor Parrish deals with the concept of "naturalness" and helps to develop the theory for today's interpreter. He first puts the issue in perspective by reviewing the history of the concept and then goes on to explain his theory. He establishes the basic point that the injunction "to be natural" has little to do with reading a poem because a poem is not a natural means of expression. This edited version of his article ends with the completion of his second point. His third point becomes the natural expression of emotion which he elaborates in the next essay, "Interpreting Emotions in Poetry."

Of interest to the reader will be Edmund A. Cortez's comment on Parrish's "naturalness" concept in *The Quarterly Journal of Speech* (December 1951). Cortez asked for a clarification of which emotion the reader should feel, the poet's or the interpreter's. He felt that the reader might be in a quandary because he does not know the poet's intention. Parrish answers Cortez in the same issue.

W. M. PARRISH

The Concept of "Naturalness"

It is commonly accepted, and has been since Aristotle, that naturalness in speech is a virtue. Whether in public address, in oral
reading, or in acting, the one who speaks naturally is assumed to
speak well. The implications of this assumption are seldom examined critically, and just as we assume, unmindful of quagmires,
floods, drouth, and tornados, that all the physical phenomena of
nature are good and beautiful, so the "natural manner" in speaking
is accepted and taught, though it might, as Professor Winans has
pointed out, "be stretched to cover stammering, mumbling, cleft
palates, thievery, and murder."[1]

It is also commonly taught that during the past two centuries
the "natural method" has been opposed by another method called
the "mechanical," and that the two are antithetical, and teachers are
classified as belonging to one school or the other. But if we examine
the works of even the most mechanical of the mechanists we find
that they too accept nature as their norm and guide. Let us look
at three who are sometimes regarded as the exemplars of the mechanical method: James Burgh, John Walker, and James Rush.

Burgh's, *The Art Of Speaking* (1762) is a collection of reading materials principally for young people, with a preliminary

[1] James A. Winans "Whately on Elocution," *The Quarterly Journal
of Speech* XXXI (February 1945), 5.

essay on delivery. This would now be classified as a work on "general speech," for Burgh is concerned with "a competent address and readiness" not only in parliament, at the bar, and in the pulpit, but also "at meetings of merchants, in committees for managing public affairs, in large societies, and on such like occasions." (It seems that conference speaking was not a development of the last twenty-five years.) Burgh never suggests that there is any other standard in speaking than that supplied by nature, and as was customary in the late eighteenth century, he regarded nature as an omnipresent, coercive force. Children, he says, should be taught to read with the "natural inflection of the voice" which they use in speaking. "Nature," he says, "has given to every emotion of the mind its proper outward expression," and he introduces his description of some seventy or eighty different "passions, humours, sentiments, and intentions" with the statement, "I hope it will be allowed by the reader that it is nearly in the following manner that *nature* expresses them." It seems to me that the candid modern reader will have to allow that his descriptions do not misrepresent nature. Even in his powerful and eloquent denunciation of cold and apathetic preaching he does not advocate anything that savors of affectation or artificiality. The underlying assumption throughout his essay is that "from nature is to be deduced the whole art of speaking properly."

John Walker's reference to nature for his principles and precepts is less apparent, but it is not entirely lacking. His numerous and complicated rules of expression are based upon grammatical structure, which surely does not make them unnatural, for any so-called natural expression of a thought, so far as it involves pause, emphasis, and the like, *must* depend upon the grammar of the language in which it is spoken. In treating inflections, he says he will point out those "which every ear, however unpracticed, will *naturally* adopt in pronouncing them."[2] And again he says that slides or inflections of voice "spontaneously annex themselves to cer-

---

[2] John Walker, *Elements of Elocution,* Second Ed. (Boston: D. Mallory, 1810), 72.

tain forms of speech,"[3] and that "the line is drawn by nature between *accent* and *no accent*.[4] He follows Burgh in his treatment of the passions, follows him to the extent of borrowing, almost verbatim, but with proper credit, about sixty of his descriptions of the passions. The passions, he says, depend upon quality of sound, and these qualities one acquires by feeling the passions. Like many of his contemporary elocutionists, he quotes Quintilian to the effect that one can arouse such feeling by imagining the circumstances which occasioned it. But he adds that we should also study the "effects and appearances of the passions,"[5] that we may be able to exhibit them when not impassioned. Here, then, are clear indications that for Walker nature furnished the norm for good speaking.

In a later work, however, *The Academic Speaker* (1789), designed to instruct schoolboys, Walker does stray far from nature and sets up a standard so artificial as to be utterly ludicrous. He would have the boy speaker extend his right arm at the beginning of his first sentence, let it fall at the end of the sentence, shift his weight and extend his left arm for the second sentence, and so alternate till the end of the piece. But, believe it or not, Walker defends this mechanical nonsense in the name of nature. "There are, indeed," he says, "some masters who are against teaching boys any action at all, and are for leaving them in this point entirely to nature. . . . Improved and beautiful nature is the object of the painter's pencil, the poet's pen, and the rhetorician's action, and not that sordid and common nature which is perfectly rude and uncultivated."[6]

[3] John Walker, *A Rhetorical Grammar,* First American Ed. (Boston: Cummings and Hilliard, 1814), 77.

[4] *Ibid.,* p. 141.

[5] *Elements of Elocution,* p. 308.

[6] These silly directions were incorporated into the American editions of William Scott's *Lessons in Elocution* and unfortunately had very wide circulation in America. I know of printings at Leicester, Concord, Montpelier, Philadelphia, and Greenfield. It seems that in speech *bad* teachings are always tenacious. Scott's *Lessons* was published in Edinburgh in 1779, ten years before Walker's *Speaker.* The "Elements

James Rush's detailed anatomization of speech, his newly created technical vocabulary, combined perhaps with his forbidding style and his idiosyncratic spelling and punctuation, have led many readers of his work to agree with Miss Robb that "this so-called scientific approach could not tolerate the natural method which shunned rules and took its cues from nature."[7] But if ever a man mistook his cues from nature it was James Rush in his *Philosophy of the Human Voice*. He does indeed indulge in sarcastic diatribes against Bishop Whately and the "natural manner" defined as mere "*animal* instinct," but he believes that his system, calling for "the regeneration of the mind . . . to a new life of accumulated knowledge, has necessarily a tendency, in *its* scientific instinct, toward the *natural manner* of a more comprehensive, refined, and effective Elocution."[8] Good speech as he conceives it should represent nature as the artist represents her—at her best, with her impurities refined away. The precepts for ideal speech must be "derived from the study of nature it is true, but applied to represent her chosen, corrected, and combined individualities; and thereby . . . to generalize and exalt even that Nature, in form if not in purpose above herself."[9] In this, of course, he is following strictly the Aristotelian aesthetic, though I have not observed that he anywhere refers to Aristotle's *Poetics*. It is from nature in this sense that he attempts to derive all his conclusions. He announces in his introduction that he will disregard any criticism of his work "that is not the result of a scrutinizing comparison of its descriptions, with phenomena of Nature herself."[10] And in his section "Of the Means of Instruc-

---

of Gesture," containing this passage lifted bodily from Walker, and a large helping of Burgh's descriptions of the passions, was apparently prefixed only to American editions, some of which were published as late as 1821. Miss Robb's *Oral Interpretation of Literature In American Colleges and Universities* does not clearly recognize these passages as direct borrowings from Walker and Burgh.

[7] Robb, *Oral Interpretation of Literature,* p. 86.

[8] Sixth Ed., p. 489.

[9] *Ibid.,* p. 55.

[10] *Ibid.,* p. 44.

tion in Elocution" he says, "I have endeavored to set before the reader, a copy of the all-perfect Design of Nature, in the construction of Speech."[11] And again, "the system here proposed has its Origin and its Confirmation in Nature."[12] It is obvious that Rush's intention was to set forth a thoroughly natural system of elocution.

It should be apparent from what has been said so far that the terms *natural* and *mechanical* need careful definition, and perhaps also that our assignment of various writers to one school or the other need reexamination.

When we say that "natural" speaking is good, do we mean that it is spontaneous, or habitual, or conventional?

Does our reference to "natural method" mean method of speaking or method of teaching?

Do we make a distinction between "naturalness" as the *norm* of good speech, and "naturalness" in our method of achieving this norm?

Does "naturalness" mean the same thing when applied to extemporaneous speaking, to reading factual matter, reading poetry, and to acting a part in a play?

Does the "natural" expression of an author's emotion mean that one must *feel* the emotion and express it as if it were one's own?

Is the "natural" representation of an emotion or a character (such as Hamlet) to be achieved by giving vent to one's instinctive behavior, by studying one's own emotional behavior, or by studying the behavior of others?

When we assign a writer to the "natural" or the "mechanical" school, do we notice first whether he is merely describing how the voice may operate, or prescribing how it *must* operate?

Is it always true that "natural" expression is good, and "mechanical" expression bad?

These questions need answers. The concept of "naturalness" has received little critical examination, except for Professor Winans's study of Whately referred to above, and a study by Richard Murphy,

[11] *Ibid.*, p. 484.
[12] *Ibid.*, p. 534.

"Natural and Mechanical" in *The Emerson Quarterly,* in 1937.[13]
The word *natural* has so many meanings that it will be useful to
us only when we make clear in the sense in which it is employed.

First, it seems to me, we must distinguish between the spontaneous or habitual utterance which feels natural to the speaker,
and utterance that *seems* natural to the audience. If a student is
frightened, inhibited, or affected, we quite properly encourage spontaneous utterance as a corrective to these unnormal interferences
with "natural" speech. We wish to free him from any hindrances
to what is for him the normal functioning of his agents of expression. What we mean is, be at ease, be sincere, be your normal
self. Such advice may serve well enough for one who is delivering
extemporaneously his own thoughts, though even in such cases we
must make reservations, for, as Professor Winans has so well
pointed out, it seems natural for some people to be unnatural.[14]
Even when expression *feels* right to the speaker, it may not be
adequate as communication, may not deliver to the hearers what he
wishes and intends to deliver, and may not seem natural to them.

When, however, our student is reading the thoughts of another, interpreting a poem, or acting a part in a play, the injunction
to be natural has little more value or applicability than it has for
riding a bicycle or shifting gears. It is not natural for one to
speak in rhyme or blank verse, or to think, feel, or behave as
Hamlet or Macbeth. And the highly imaginative language of poetry
is in no sense for the average person a normal medium of expression. These are not, like eating, sleeping, and talking, instinctive
activities such as all normal human beings engage in. It is natural, of
course, as is sometimes argued, for children to act, and perhaps also

---

[13] Other criticisms of Whately may be found in James Rush's
Philosophy of the Human Voice, Sixth Ed., 1867; George Vandenhoff's
Art of Elocution, 1855; J. C. Zachost's *Analytic Elocution,* 1861; Hiram
Corson's *The Voice and Spiritual Education,* 1892; S. S. Curry's *The
Province of Expression,* 1891; and in my *Reading Aloud* (New York:
Ronald, 1932).

[14] James Albert Winans, *Public Speaking,* Revised Ed. (New
York: Century, 1917), 28–30.

for adults—and puppies and kittens—but it is *not* natural for them to act parts in plays that others have designed for them. The early elocutionists—Mason, Burgh, Sheridan, Rice, Enfield, and Walker—taught that the pattern of *reading* should be based upon the reader's practice in energetic conversation,[15] a method which Rush disparaged as mere "self-imitation." And some of them taught poetry should be read exactly as if it were prose. But most of them were aware that it is not *natural* or easy for one to read as if he were speaking, or, as Whately put it many years later, "It is by no means natural for any one to *read* as if he were *not* reading, but speaking."[16] And Walker and Sheridan at least were aware that poetry poses additional problems for the reader.

There are involved here two applications of "naturalness" which may lead to different, and even contradictory, results. When we instruct a student to read naturally we can only mean that he is to speak and behave as he ordinarily does, that he is to be himself. But when we praise a reader's performance for its naturalness we probably mean something quite different, since we may not know what his ordinary, or customary speaking is like. We mean rather that it *seems* natural—seems appropriate to the material or the character he is representing. The interpreter, especially if he aspires to be a "creative artist," must not then merely yield to his own raw instinct, but must design a pattern of expression that will conform to the audience's conception of what is natural for the given content and situation, and then express the meaning of his selection through this predesigned pattern. Such expression may not *feel* natural to the reader, may not conform to his instinctive or accustomed manner of speech, for in this sense "naturalness" is not necessarily good. Natural speech is good speech when it *seems* natural to a properly qualified audience or, what is the same thing, to a properly qualified teacher.

[15] William Cockin is an exception. He argued, in his *Art of Delivering Written Language,* 1775, that nature prescribes one manner for speaking and a different one for reading.

[16] Richard Whately, *Elements of Rhetoric,* New Revised Ed. (New York: Sheldon, 1869), Part IV, Vol. I, p. 9.

The limits of this paper do not permit a definition of these qualifications here.

Second, we must distinguish between a natural performance as just defined, and a natural method of achieving such a performance. Just as a reader may by following a spontaneous natural method achieve an unnatural result, so he may by an unnatural, or even mechanical method achieve a performance that will seem natural. Whether in self-instruction, or instruction by a teacher, the difference between a natural and a mechanical method is not easy to define. Burgh has been decried as a mechanist because he described the normal expression of the passions, and Walker because he formulated rules of expression, and Rush because of his detailed analysis of vocal action. Does a description of normal expression or a formulation of rules for it, make one a mechanist? If so, who of us shall escape the charge of being mechanical? We look upon Whately and Winans as dyed-in-the-wool naturalists, but Whately points out which words are to be emphasized in a passage of the *Liturgy,* and his text is peppered with words in italics, which, I take it, is an indication to the reader that those words are emphatic. And Winans prescribes the rule that, "The speaker should look at his hearers squarely," and he instructs the student in preparation to "indicate" echoes, new ideas, contrasts, phrase limits, etc.—details that are sure to remain in his mind while he is performing. It is not a simple matter to distinguish between a natural and a mechanical method of teaching. And I cannot agree with Professor Guthrie that there was, or is, a "sharp conflict" between them, anymore than I can agree with him that only one school held "that the best delivery was to be gained from 'nature'."[17]

Perhaps it is not as important to distinguish between the two methods as many of us have supposed. It would be easy to say that the end result is all that counts, and that it does not matter whether we achieve naturalness by a natural or a mechanical method. But we do not want our pupils to be mere puppets, manipulating their arms and voices for purposes that they do not understand. They

[17] See Warren Guthrie, "The Elocutionary Movement—England," *Speech Monographs* XVIII (March 1951), 30.

should themselves appreciate what they read, as well as arouse appreciation in their hearers. Our obligations as teachers should have priority over our obligations as coaches. And so it seems to me that we should prefer a method that helps to concentrate the reader's attention on meaning over one that does not. If this is so, then any device or scheme that helps to keep the meaning in the reader's focus of attention should be unexceptionable even if it is mechanical. I cannot share Professor Winans's contempt for the practice, recommended by Sheridan, of sometimes marking on the manuscript an emphatic word or a pause. Such a notation made by the student during his preparation may be very helpful in *reminding* him, amid the distractions of the platform, of a meaning he would otherwise miss. Following mechanically someone else's notation is, of course, a quite different matter. I would observe also that the average student when he does understand what he reads, and has his mind on it as he reads, will generally communicate the meaning adequately. The result is that we actually give, and need to give, very little time to teaching elocution. Perhaps ninety percent of our effort goes to teaching the meaning of literature, call it grammar, rhetoric, linguistic structure, literary criticism, or what you will. Primarily we are teachers, not of elocution, but of interpretation.

≈

RESPONSE

Alethea S. Mattingly

Through the years many writers have discussed the relationships between art and nature, and, as George Steiner observes, the two terms "trace a maddening pattern across the weave of criticism."[1] In some periods of time the concept of naturalness exercises

[1] George Steiner, *The Death of Tragedy* (New York: Knopf, 1961), 34.

a more coercive force than in others. Whenever the words *nature, natural,* and *naturalness* appear, however, one needs to understand in what sense they are being used. Asking for clear definitions, Parrish recognizes the ambiguities of such terms. *Nature* has, indeed, been a "word-of-all-work."

To Aristotle, and equally to men of the Augustan age, nature was seen as an ultimate standard, as the essential meaning and final aim of life, and the end of art was conceived to be a revelation to man of the ideal perfection of nature. To medieval man nature was "an agent obedient to the dictates of a divine Will"; for the Renaissance man nature implied all of its classical meanings of balance, moderation, regularity, simplicity, symmetry, typicalness, and uniformity, all of them subservient to order or rationality. But the question soon arose: Does ART imitate NATURE, or does ART improve NATURE? By the time of the eighteenth-century English elocutionists, referred to by Parrish, the problem had become one of reconciling "adherence to Nature with adherence to the rules of Art, and both with the requirements of reason and good sense."[2] Two schools of oral reading developed, both advocating adherence to nature but differing somewhat as to how nature assists art. The so-called mechanical school saw nature as a rational concept, the natural school viewed it as an emotional one. The teachings of the two schools are best understood in relation to the two concepts[3] which continued to cross, recross, and overlap. In speech education repetitions and echoes of the two schools were heard in this country throughout the nineteenth and into the twentieth century.

[2] Basil Willey, *The Eighteenth Century Background* (New York: Columbia University Press and London: Windus, 1941), 18. Cf. Arthur O. Lovejoy, " 'Nature' as an Aesthetic Norm," in his *Essays in the History of Ideas* (Baltimore: Johns Hopkins Press, 1948), 70–77.

[3] See Alethea Smith Mattingly, "Follow Nature: A Synthesis of Eighteenth Century Views," *Speech Monographs* XXXI (March 1964), 80–84; *The Mechanical School of Oral Reading in England, 1761–1821,* unpublished doctoral dissertation, Northwestern University, 1954. Also see Daniel E. Vandraegen, *The Natural School of Oral Reading in England, 1748–1828,* unpublished doctoral dissertation, Northwestern University, 1949.

One critic, R. G. Collingwood, discerns two senses in the modern usage of *nature:* one sense meaning the sum total or aggregate of natural things, the other sense denoting not a collection but a principle or source, "something which makes its possessor behave as it does," the source of behavior being "something within itself." Collingwood believes that the word *nature* presently does not commit one to nature as either single or multiple, and he calls behavior *unnatural* when it is caused by constraint of some kind. "If a man walks fast because he is strong and energetic and determined, we say fast walking is natural to him," but if a dog on a leash pulls his master along, the man's fast walk is unnatural, arising from constraint or compulsion.[4] Similarly, can we say that a speaker's or interpreter's delivery is unnatural when it evidences constraint in voice or body and seems unrelated to an inner source prompting spontaneous expression?

Actually, current textbooks and teachers of interpretation do not appear to find the word *natural* very useful, if one can be judged by a scrutiny of the indexes in leading textbooks in the field. When the word is used today, the meaning implied is that the interpreter is at ease with himself and his audience. "Ease" evidences itself in a balance between activity and tension. It is felt or seen in the body and heard in the voice.

Without using the more frequently recurring words *perception, empathy,* and *aesthetic experience,* Parrish, in speaking of naturalness, touches upon matters continuing to concern and often perplex the interpreter. The questions he raises about emotion relate directly to . . . concepts of art, poesy, and the enactment of a literary text. General agreement exists that the interpreter seeks a relationship to the text that affords him the aesthetic experience of the literature. Indirectly, Parrish asks about the essence of that experience.

The interpreter's view of literary art or of the poem itself—poem in the largest sense of that word—will largely determine the answers to Parrish's queries about emotion. What does a poet

[4] R. G. Collingwood, *The Idea of Nature* (Oxford: Clarendon Press, 1945), 43, 44.

create? What *is* a poem? Poets themselves sometimes answer the question in a poetic fashion: consider Archibald MacLeish's "Ars Poetica" or Marianne Moore's "Poetry." Frost calls a poem "a performance in words," and Dylan Thomas labels it "a formally watertight compartment of words." Critics speak of the poem as "fictive utterance,"[5] as both expression and artifact, and as a construct of language embodying experience. Philosophers and aestheticians discuss *illusion* in relation to art and to literary art in particular, Susanne Langer stating that "the *illusion of life* is the primary illusion of all poetic art." She reminds the reader that illusion is not delusion. Rather, illusion in literature is "the appearance of 'experiences,' the semblance of events lived and felt . . . [organized] so they constitute a purely and completely experienced reality, a piece of *virtual life*."[6] *Life,* she notes, can be used in a biological sense or in the sense of *what happens;* in the latter sense a poem has life. Moreover, the poem has a life of its own, presenting a "world" of illusory events, a "world created as an artistic image . . . to look at, not to live in. . . ."[7] Like other objects of art, the poem is a created form symbolic of human feeling.

Accepting such a view of the poem, the interpreter will say with Langer that the poet presents not feeling but ideas of feeling, not emotion but ideas of emotion, not life but imagined living, or what Henry James called "felt life." The challenge to the writer is to "command" the reader's experience, to give the poem an air of "reality" and at the same time keep it a "fictive utterance." The challenge to the interpreter is analogous. Both writer and reader create virtual images or semblances. Illusion, Arthur Koestler tells us, "is the simultaneous presence and interaction in the mind of two universes, one real, one imaginary," and the aesthetic experi-

<hr>

[5] A view developed by Don Geiger, *The Dramatic Impulse in Modern Poetics* (Baton Rouge: Louisiana State University Press, 1967).

[6] Susanne Langer, *Feeling and Form* (New York: Scribner, 1953), 212.

[7] Langer, p. 228. See Langer, *Mind: An Essay on Human Feeling* (Baltimore: Johns Hopkins Press, 1967), Chaps. 4–7.

ence requires our living on two planes at once, depending, as it does, "on that delicate balance arising from the presence of *both* matrices in the mind; on perceiving the hero as Laurence Olivier and Prince Hamlet of Denmark at the same time; on the lightning oscillations of attention from one to the other, like sparks between charged electrodes."[8] The experience has both an intellectual and an emotive aspect. Emotions can serve self-interest or they can be self-transcending. In the aesthetic experience they are the latter, or, in other words, perception of the poem involves aesthetic or psychical distance.[9]

In the light of what Langer, Koestler, and others say, let us proffer some answers to questions about emotion raised by Parrish and Cortez. First of all, as performing or expressive agent for the poem, the interpreter seeks to express what he perceives in it. Emotion may be an element in the totality of the poem—art can express feelings other than emotion—but the emotion is neither the poet's nor should it be the interpreter's own, actual emotion. Indeed, if the interpreter makes it his own, he is guilty of the "affective fallacy" described by W. K. Wimsatt and Monroe C. Beardsley in *The Verbal Icon* (1954). By empathy, a highly complex function which space forbids exploring here, the interpreter perceives the "voice" and finds the feelings within the poem. His mind hears, his voice obeys; his mind feels, his body obeys. He makes audible and visible the "world" of the poem. Craftsmanship will be involved, but it serves the poem, not the interpreter's self. Like the dancer or the actor, the interpreter conceives emotions and enacts them, he does not "vent" his own. Many persons find it difficult to differentiate between imagined feelings and their symbols and an emotion felt in response to actual events. "Indeed,

[8] Arthur Koestler, *The Act of Creation* (London: Hutchinson, 1964), 306.

[9] See Edward Bullough, " 'Psychical Distance' as a Factor in Art and an Aesthetic Principle," *The British Journal of Psychology* V (June 1912), 87–118; and Beverly Whitaker, "Edward Bullough on 'Psychical Distance,' " *The Quarterly Journal of Speech* LIV (December 1968), 373–382.

the very notion of feelings and emotions not really felt, but only imagined, is strange to most people."[10] Yet, Sartre argues that "all human action takes place before the gaze of objectifying consciousness" and that man is a consciousness of "*acting* emotions, roles, and states."[11] Imagination and distancing or objectifying, in that case, are mental functions familiar to everyone, and Edie believes that "The eidetic structures of ordinary and aesthetic imagination are one."[12]

The import of emotion in literature and in actual life, however, can differ. We do not find in the poem exact replicas of our own day-by-day emotions, but we conceive the depth and extent of the virtual images of passions felt by an Antigone, an Othello, or a Willy Loman. At least, we do so when the poet has found an "objective correlative," and as interpreters we seek our own "objective correlative" in the act of embodying the experience in the poem.

At that point the interpreter may find himself returning to a question which has long confronted man: Is there a universal pattern, instinctive or learned, expressive of a given emotion? Ray L. Birdwhistell's research indicates that no one pattern for anger, fear, or the like can be found. Cultural differences exist, as he explains in *Kinesics and Context* (1970), and within a particular culture one can detect subcultural patterns. Moreover, kinesics or "body language" relates to the spoken language; bodily expression is conditioned in part by the syntax of the utterance, just as we know vocal intonation is. Nevertheless, within a national or ethnic group certain conventions of expression indicate meanings. Perhaps departures from cultural patterns and conventions seem *unnatural*.

In summary, my response to Parrish's article has been to say that concepts of art and poesy are central in a theory of interpretation. The primary concern for the interpreter is not so much to be or seem *natural*—whatever that term means—as to become *aware* of the poem as an aesthetic object embodying "virtual life."

---

[10] Langer, *Feeling and Form,* p. 181.

[11] James M. Edie, "The Problem of Enactment," *The Journal of Aesthetics and Art Criticism* XXIX (Spring 1971), 312.

[12] Edie, 304.

Such life is imagined thought and feeling. Imagination is the *sine qua non* for the interpreter as for the poet. Through its power the interpreter can create a performance revelatory of the poem, making seem real what is not actual, and showing as present what is absent. How best to acquire the ability to do so or to teach it may never be fully understood.

Selected Readings

Burklund, Carl E. "Hyacinths and Biscuits," *The Quarterly Journal of Speech* XXXI (December 1946), 469–474.

Cortez, Edmund A. "Concerning 'Naturalness,'" *The Quarterly Journal of Speech* XXXVIII (April 1952), 208, 209.

Freeman, William. "Whately and Stanislavski: Complementary Paradigms of Naturalness," *The Quarterly Journal of Speech* LVI (February 1970), 61–66.

Henderson, Ellen C. "Some Prinicples of Oral Reading," *The Quarterly Journal of Speech* XX (April 1934), 287–299.

Lowery, Sara. "Gesture Through Empathy," *The Southern Speech Journal* XI (January 1946), 59–62.

Parrish, W. M. "More About 'Naturalness,'" *The Quarterly Journal of Speech* XXXVIII (April 1952), 209.

Emotion is the stuff of literature, but it is not the "stuffing" of literature. It is not there as the dressing in a turkey. Emotion is created by the poem. Since the oral interpreter is concerned with literature, his question as to how one engages the poem to ignite the emotions for both the interpreter and the listener becomes very important. Is there such a thing as too little emotion, too much emotion, or the wrong kind of emotion? It is the poet's job to get us to feel the emotion by stressing the object. In performance, the interpreter must focus on both the object and the emotion, while at the same time attempt to keep his own emotion under control. The audience can add another complication in this process when it decodes the emotional tone of the poem. Professor Parrish deals with these sticky problems in his essay, "Interpreting Emotions in Poetry." Professor Floyd comments on Parrish's ideas and goes on to clarify the interpreter's relationship with the poem in our age, an age that might be reluctant to embrace the complexity of interpreting fully the emotions in poetry.

W. M. PARRISH

Interpreting Emotion in Poetry

In this paper I wish to develop a suggestion made in my recent essay, "The Concept of Naturalness." I am concerned with the nature of emotional expression in poetry and the oral interpreter's relation to it.

It has long been assumed that poetry is involved with emotion. From Aristotle's catharsis of pity and fear to T. S. Eliot's doctrine of the objective correlative, both poets and critics have held that poetry is distinguished from other writing chiefly by its emotional appeal.

Well known is Wordsworth's statement that poetry originates from emotion recollected in tranquility and becomes a "spontaneous overflow of powerful feeling." Milton characterized poetry as sensuous and passionate. Bliss Perry said that it "begins in excitement, in some body-and-mind experience." Masefield said that enchantment is the main function of poetry, and that it has always to come from the excitement of the poet.

Various recent writers in describing the effect of poetry have said that it causes goose flesh, or shivers down the spine, or a sensation in the pit of the stomach, or that it is a taking off of the top of the head. The modern critics, for all their attempts to redefine poetry, are still generally agreed that it is primarily concerned with emotion. Yvor Winters calls a poem a statement "in which special pains are taken with the expression of feeling." Kenneth Burke says that literature as art "is designed for the express purpose of arousing emotion." Elder Olson supposes that the end of poetry is "certain pleasures, produced through their play upon our emotions." T. S. Eliot defines his objective correlative as a formula for setting off a particular emotion. And if we take rather his statement that "poetry is not a turning loose of emotion, but an escape from emotion," we still have the assumption that it is concerned with emotion. And Herbert S. Langfeld, the psychologist of aesthetics, says, "All art expresses emotion. That is the function of art; that in the last analysis is the meaning of art, to give pleasure."

In all this consideration of emotion there has been little attention paid to a definition of emotion, or to an examination of just what is communicated from poet to reader, and how. What does it mean to "express" an emotion? We tend to accept naively the notion that a poet, moved by emotion, puts his emotion on paper; that an interpreter reading the poem is moved by the same emotion; and that by reading the poem aloud he communicates it to his hearers, who thus experience the same emotion that moved the poet to write. A little reflection will show that this "bucket brigade" theory of the transference of emotion is too simple and too inexact an explanation of what really happens.

Let us note first that the emotions, as commonly understood, and as commonly defined by psychologists, are sharp, upsetting physiological and psychological disturbances—psychosomatic, if you like that word. Now it is the experience of the race that such disturbances cannot be expressed in language. As we say, we are speechless with rage, too frightened to talk, dumb with fear, too sad for words. Language is not an effective medium either for expressing emotion or for perceiving the emotions of others. If we try to express them, our words are confused, disordered, and broken; and poetry is utterance that is highly disciplined, orderly, carefully designed. *Thought* may be formulated and expressed in language, but emotion finds expression rather in tears, or action, or gesture. Neither a poet nor anyone else can successfully put his emotions on paper.

What, then, does get onto paper? We should note that besides pure emotions (rage, fear, shame, love, hate, grief, etc.), we have certain related symptoms or experiences which psychologists call affective states or processes. But the psychologists seem uncertain as to when a state or an experience is affective, or how it is related to emotion. For instance, is the pain you feel from a sore tooth an emotion? Is the pleasant warmth you feel as you lie in the sun an emotion? Or that comfortable fullness around the middle after a hearty meal? Or that kindly attitude toward little children? Or the excitement of expectation before a football game? Are we to classify as emotional our sensations of pain and pleasure, our appetites and their satisfaction, our desires, interests, sentiments, moods, motives, aversions, comforts? Or such things as liveliness, vivacity, artistic enjoyment, inspiration? There seems to be no sure answer. I do not find that psychologists differentiate clearly even between feeling and emotion. All of these types of experience may have an emotional tinge, an "affective tone." And it is some of these that a poet generally gets into his poem, rather than a pure emotion. Perhaps as often as anything else it is his *attitude* toward things that he expresses. I certainly am not competent to distinguish between these various forms of emotion. The best I can do is lump them all together under the terms *feeling* and *emotion.*

Second, we should note that it is possible to be moved by another person's emotion without feeling the same emotion that moves him. Our emotional response is not necessarily a sharing of his emotion. For instance, if your child has an earache, you may suffer for him, but you don't suffer from an earache, even an imaginary one. You can feel sympathy and sorrow and pity before you know the cause of his misery. If you come upon a friend who is grieving over the loss of his mother whom you have never known, you may sympathetically grieve with him, but you don't feel what he feels—a sharp sense of personal loss. Your pity and sorrow for these sufferers is not what they feel at all. And if that child is not yours, his expression of pain may move you only to irritation and annoyance. Under certain circumstances your friend's grief may cause you to feel anger, or pleasure, or fear. We say that emotion is contagious, but it is not always so by any means. A child's tantrum does not ordinarily excite in the observer a sympathetic tantrum. It may rouse rather a feeling of grief, or contempt, or humor, or even fear. And surely our responses to the emotions expressed in poetry may vary in similar ways.

Third, it seems indisputable to me that many poems are not expressions of the poet's feelings, and they may not have anything to do with emotion or feeling. Poets often write about things other than their feelings. A poem may be purely descriptive or rational, an expression not of what the poet feels but of what he thinks, or has observed. It may be a representation of some scene, or event, or mood, or experience, designed to reveal its significance or essential meaning. It may be motivated not by an emotion but by an idea, or merely by a pleasing pattern of words. Stephen Spender's description of the making of a poem contains no mention of his feelings, except his feeling of relief when the poem is finished. He begins with an idea, and he develops it and works it into a poem by acute concentration, by "sweat and toil." Apparently no feeling is involved in the process.

A poem may be a product of the poet's imagining, dealing with things he has never experienced, as is Coleridge's *Rime of the Ancient Mariner*. Poets are not always writing about their own feelings. In many of our best poems the poet does not appear at all, and though he *may* have been prompted by some emotion, he makes no mention of it. His own feelings are not the subject of his poem. This is true, for instance, of Shelley's *Ozymandias* and Markham's *The Man with the Hoe*. And if he does express an emotion, it may not be his own. Many so-called lyric poems are really dramatic. That is, though the poet speaks in the first person, he expresses not his own thoughts and feelings, but those he imagines other people have. "It is not necessary," says Eliseo Vivas, "to assume that the actual emotion that is worked up by the poet into the poem is the actual occasion of the creative act." And T. S. Eliot says, "Emotions which he has never experienced will serve his turn as well as those familiar to him," and, "The emotion of art is impersonal."

Fourth, we should note that when a poem *is* occasioned by some emotion of the poet, that emotion will be greatly altered in the attempt to express it. We find our emotions changing their form or evaporating when we try to put them on paper. If Keats really felt the heartache and numbness he mentions in his *Ode to a Nightingale,* he must have had his feelings considerably modified as he tried to put them into words that would fit the complicated stanza form he chose for the poem. Louis Untermeyer says, "The poet must separate himself from his emotion in order that he may express it, must view it objectively, must depersonalize it."

Fifth, it seems to me that these considerations indicate that a reader's response to emotional representation in poetry will depend upon whether the emotion is personal or general, and upon the poet's method of representing it. Surely it makes a difference whether the emotion is a personal one caused by a specific immediate experience, or whether it is a communal feeling such as all normal readers will share. Wordsworth, in his sonnet *To Sleep,* expresses the yearning restlessness of a specific attack of insomnia. But he does not give his readers insomnia. He is not expressing an emotion that we are expected to share. Our feeling is rather sympathy for his suffering. Robert Burns's love for his various Nells, Peggys, Jeans, Megs, and Marys was doubtless real, but it was personal—not a love that we can share with him. We don't know the girls. Rather we find a sympathetic pleasure in *contemplating* his loves. We may, of course, try to identify ourselves with him and feel what he felt, but not necessarily, and it seems to me we can't quite succeed in this.

Wordsworth's sonnet, *The World Is Too Much With Us,* makes a different demand upon us. It expresses a sentiment that the general reader may be expected to share. And some of the lyrics in Tennyson's *In Memoriam* are public prayers in which all readers are expected to join. And some of Shakespeare's sonnets express a communal, not a personal, emotion.*

Quite different in their method of appeal, but similar in result, are those poems which, without reference to the author or his emotions, merely present a picture, an incident, a story, an object, in such a way that the reader will be moved in some desired way. Such a poem is Shelley's *Ozymandias.* It is purely descriptive in method, containing no reference to the author's feeling. Of the same nature are Robinson's *Mr. Flood's Party,* and Chesterton's *Lepanto,* and all narrative poetry. In these the reader will probably feel about what the poet felt.

A still different method of appeal is made in that poetry which is dramatic, in which the poet represents some other person as voicing his thoughts and emotions. These are not the poet's emotions at all, and often they are such as neither poet nor reader will wish to experience. Such emotions may arouse quite different emotions in the reader. For instance, the distress and frustration of the poor gentleman in Browning's *Up At a Villa—Down in the City* will move the reader to a kind of tolerant amusement. And the cheap,

* See Thomas O. Sloan's statement "that the oral interpreter does not merely 'perform' a poem but makes a conscious effort to get others to join him in the dance" in "Restoration of Rhetoric to Literary Study," *Speech Teacher* XVI (March 1967), 93.

savage malignity of the monk in *Soliloquy of the Spanish Cloister* moves us to contempt and disgust, but tinged with amusement, too. Macbeth's murderous rage moves us to horror and fear.

Is it not apparent, then, that a reader is not always expected merely to echo an emotion felt by the poet?

Of course, our concern is with a more difficult and complicated problem than I have so far considered. We are not primarily concerned with a simple author-reader relationship. We are concerned with oral interpretation, and the intrusion of an interpreter between author and receiver is a factor which greatly complicates the problem of emotional transference. It is a problem that is not considered at all by literary critics, and one which I think we interpreters have not sufficiently considered.

Before we look into it a little let me summarize what I have been trying to point out. First, poets do not always write in a state of emotional agitation, are not always motivated by emotion, do not always express emotion, are not concerned exclusively with emotion, and sometimes are not concerned with it at all. Second, the sharp inner disturbances of pure emotion cannot be expressed in language and put upon paper. What gets onto paper is likely to be merely a suggestion of some affective state, whatever that may mean, some mood, attitude, feeling, disposition, or sentiment. Third, the observing of an emotional manifestation does not often cause the observer to experience the same emotion. Fourth, any feeling the poet had to begin with will be modified and refined in the process of trying to put it into language and fit it into a verse pattern. Fifth, a reader's response to a representation of emotion in poetry will depend upon the kind of emotion and the method by which it is represented. In reading some poems he will feel what the poet felt. In others he will merely feel sympathy for the poet. And in still others he may feel a quite different emotion from the one represented.

I recognize, of course, that a great deal of poetry gives pleasure and arouses feeling because of its form, its rhythm, rhyme, assonance, word music, etc., and does this regardless of whether it deals with emotion. I am not considering this factor here.

What, then, is the task of the oral interpreter with relation to the expression of emotion? First, we must distinguish between speaking about emotion, or even expressing emotion, and speaking emotionally. Even the dryest and dullest of matter, an algebra lesson for instance, can be presented with liveliness and animation. And one can express emotion without speaking emotionally. One can arouse deep feeling in others without himself feeling any emotion, just as cold print, or a cartoon, can arouse deep feeling. One can express emotion without feeling it. I find it difficult to do, but it can be done. I have been moved by a reader who himself remained unmoved by the feelings he was expressing, who, in presenting a pathetic incident was himself actuated chiefly by delight at his success in arousing the feelings of his audience. I feel sure that many actors do not feel the emotions which they express, and which they arouse in their audience. Certainly few actors are moved by their own humor, though the hearers may roll in the aisles. So then it seems plain that one may express feeling without arousing it in others, and he may both express and arouse feeling without experiencing it himself.

Now a good interpreter, of course, has control over his feelings. What should he do with them? I urge my students constantly to try to feel the emotions they are trying to express. I criticize them often for not reflecting the mood of the passage they are reading. I urge them also to read even cold didactic prose with animation and vivacity, that is, to read with feeling even when there is no feeling to express. In such a case the feeling is their own, not the author's. Whether this is wise teaching in all cases I do not know. I wish I did. I think we ought to recognize that in a given interpretation the same feeling need not be felt by poet, reader, and hearer. I think that at times both the poet and the interpreter may be cold and yet the hearer will be moved. I think that at times the poet's feeling may be communicated to the hearer by a cold interpreter. And with some poems you may have a very successful interpretation when no one of the three is really moved—with didactic or philosophical poems. All three parties might respond with appropriate and significant mental and imaginative activity, and yet not be moved by any feeling. Perhaps Milton's sonnet on his blindness could be so interpreted; or Hamlet's soliloquy.

But one thing of which I feel certain is that poet, interpreter, and listener often need not, and should not, feel the *same* emotion. If the poem does express emotion, and if the emotion is communal —one that all normal people may be expected to feel—then the chain of feeling may pass unbroken from poet to interpreter to hearer. Such a poem is Wordsworth's sonnet, *The World Is Too Much With Us.* Such also are some purely descriptive poems where the poet's feeling is not mentioned, as in *Ozymandias,* and *The Man With the Hoe.* In such poems, however, it seems to me that the interpreter *might,* without being moved himself, merely present the incidents and images and allow them to have their proper effect.

But what about such personal private expressions as Keats's *When I Have Fears,* or Mrs. Browning's *How Do I Love Thee?* If, as I have said, the silent reader is supposed to be an observer, not a sharer, of such emotions, what should be the attitude of the interpreter? It seems to me that he either may, or may not, assume the feeling of the poet. He may, if he wishes, put himself on the side of the hearer, and, while speaking the words of the poet, may identify himself with the audience and play the role of a sympathetic observer. Even if he decides to impersonate the poet he will hardly be able to experience the emotion that presumably moved the poet. Like an actor, he can assume an emotion without feeling it, just as we all may assume anger without really being angry, or pretend to be cheerful when we are not.

And in definitely dramatic poetry, that in which the reader is not expected to be moved with the same emotion as the character who is represented as speaking, what is the interpreter's role? Should he reflect the emotion of the characters, or that of the audience? Or should he be emotionally neutral? It seems to me that he may do any one of the three. In reading Browning's *Soliloquy of the Spanish Cloister* for instance, it seems to me that an interpreter may reflect the passion of the speaker and at the same time show his contempt and amusement at such a petty display of malignant hatred, and that he may, or may not, have his own feelings deeply affected. Or, in reading Drayton's sonnet, "Since there's no help, come, let us kiss and part," an interpreter may express sympathetically Drayton's emotion—relief, or pretend relief, over his renunciation of love—and at the same time express his amusement, which is presumably what the hearer should feel.

All this, I know, is very confusing and contradictory, and I think the reason is that the facts of poetic experience and communication are confusing and contradictory. We have always tended to make the interpretation of emotion too simple, and have thereby violated the facts. Since the workings of emotion are so various and so difficult to understand, and still more difficult to control, and since emotion, if it is always present, is only one of *various* elements in poetry, it seems to me that we would do better to concentrate our attention on those other elements which are more constant, more definite, and more readily studied: the formal elements of rhythm and word music, the ideational content, and most important of all, the images and symbols. If our interpreters can grasp these and communicate them to their hearers, emotion in both reader and audience can be trusted to take care of itself.

As Elder Olson says, "Emotion in art results . . . because we actively contemplate" a thing. "Our emotions are determined by the object of imitation." And D. G. James says that emotion is only "part of a total experience central to which is imaginative prehension," and "The central fact about poetry is that in and through it an imaginative object is conveyed." The primary concern of the interpreter, then, should be, not to feel emotion, or to arouse emotion in his hearers, but to present vividly the objects, incidents, images, and word-forms that are the stuff of which poetry is made.

I think we will do better to think less about feeling, expressing, and arousing emotion, and more about a clear "imaginative prehension" of what the poem says. We might well return to the idea of Horace that the function of poetry is not to affect our feelings, but to "profit and delight." Or, go farther back to Aristotle's notion that poetry, like the other arts, is imitation of nature, and that it succeeds when the poet, by his penetrating insight into the nature of things—persons, events, objects, scenes, moods, and truths—reveals to us their ideal forms.

ᴕᴔ
RESPONSE

Virginia Floyd

> I am simply calling attention to the fact that fine art
> is the only teacher except torture.
>
> —G. B. SHAW

Mr. Parrish's article, an elaboration of his ideas posed in an earlier essay entitled "The Concept of Naturalness," is richly diffuse. He raises many complex questions, related in one or another way to considerations of emotion, of the language of poetry, of the poet, and of course, the oral interpreter. To deal adequately with all of his questions and observations is not possible in my essay. In a general way, however, I find these considerations very exciting, *au courant.* For a great many reasons I am convinced that in the last third of the twentieth century questions about art are more exciting than ever. They invite healthy differences of opinions— the very yeast of art. They encourage precise definitions of the key terms that any one employs as he comes upon the necessity to define his principal concepts, albeit one writer's clarification of concepts as he perceives them may be another's notion of splitting hairs.

Because of what I have just said, I add posthaste that my *aperçu* in this essay is what I believe *now,* at this time. My dateline is today. Why? Because my views may change. We are dealing with large subjects when we reflect on "Interpreting Emotion in Poetry." Although I have been thinking through these concepts for a good many years, I know that I have not arrived at final answers. My definitions and notions may all be challenged. They should change or at least accommodate themselves to new knowledge and developments. Certainly I hope to gain insights. The incredible increase in the acceleration of the rate of change itself is difficult to assess when you are in the middle of it. You "feel" it happening all about you. And, as the late Abraham Maslow observed (1970): "Something big is happening. It's happening to everything that concerns human beings. Everything the human being generates is involved, and certainly education is involved. A new *Weltanschauung* is in the process of being developed, a new *Zeitgeist,* a new set of values and a new way of finding them, and certainly a new image of man."[1] You read numbers and ratios, such as the estimate that by 1975 the world population will be about three billion. With more people and more brains there may simply be more of the same kinds of thoughts we hold today. On the other hand, we could anticipate in the years ahead a substantial increase in the number of original and rare kinds of responses and thoughts. You realize that the present-day "Children of Change" are, according to biological time (not federal census ten-year-segmented-time), no longer children—and they have never experienced anything but the technological world we are living in where time has collapsed and the horizon has disappeared, but the institutions are still run generally by a generation out of tune with the new environment.[2] The child whose baby-sitter was TV has come of age knowing how to experience events instantaneously, knowing the largely nonverbal movement, and thoroughly acquainted with the metaphoric put-on of commercials and pop art.[3] Even as I write I take into account that "The Children" have indicated to a large extent that the *word* is dead as they move into a world of electronic experience. Film? Tape? Laser? The inputs of my generation are not those of many of my students. Hence, I expect my present beliefs will be altered.

I do, moreover, find excitement in our discourse about the interpreter's art—one of *performance of literature* (I now think oral or silent)—because we have increasingly found it fruitful to turn to other fields and branches of inquiry: to aesthetics, a comparatively recent addition to the philosophical family where I judge

[1] Abraham H. Maslow, "Peak Experiences in Education and Art," *The Humanist* XXX (September–October 1970), 29. The article was received before Dr. Maslow's death and appeared posthumously.

[2] Don Fabun, *The Children of Change* (Beverly Hills, Cal.: Glencoe, 1970), 7. This publication was prepared for Kaiser Aluminum and Chemical Corporation.

[3] Fabun, p. 26.

there is a considerable interest burgeoning in the aesthetics of artistic performance; to physiology; to biology; to psychology and to the psycho-pathologists who have been aiding us so greatly in understanding the concept of the body image; to applied anthropology for sound concepts of space, the literal, not "virtual," space of our bodies peripherally and directionally, and of the shape of movements in space; to the other arts, e.g., the dance; and to the field of English, of course (and I have named only a few of the branches). But we draw upon them only to help us with what I wish to focus on—the experience in performance of the poem itself. I am using "poem" in the older sense of it, not merely as verse but as the created product of the storytellers who act as the keepers of a culture.

What I take to be the paramount questions in Parrish's article are these: "What does it mean to 'express' an emotion?" and "What, then, is the task of the oral interpreter with relation to the expression of emotion?" He appears to answer his own questions. For one thing, he rules out the "bucket brigade" theory of transference of emotion as being an over simplification and an inexact explanation. For another, he notes that "language is not an effective medium either for expressing emotion or for perceiving the emotions of others."[4] Furthermore, he notes: "One can express emotion without feeling it." And he concludes his article with the observation that "the primary concern of the interpreter, then, should be, not to feel emotion, or to arouse emotion in his hearers, but to present vividly the objects, incidents, images, and word-forms that are the stuff of which poetry is made."

I am reluctant to do what I must, namely to "explain" my view of the theory of interpreting poetry because the result ultimately is impoverishment of the art. Explaining for me is a kind of language game in which I, an explainer, must use metawords, sometimes with verbal redundancy as the end result and myself as

---

[4] The context is his discussion of the experience of the race when sharply upsetting physiological and psychological disturbances leave one "speechless" or "dumb," etc.

a salesman giving a "hard sell" on what I believe is "meaningful," and seeking endorsements by others. Parrish, baffled about imprecise distinctions between feeling, emotion, and effective tone which he believes a poet "generally gets into his poem," lumps them all together under feeling and emotion. Mrs. Langer has pointed out that everybody talks sometimes about "expression of feeling," using feeling and emotion synonymously and including things that can be designated by names. I find rewarding her view of "feeling" as simply "anything that can be felt"—anything that registers in our awareness.[5] As she further points out, the advantage in such a use of the term is that it can take one back into natural history, there to connect with biology and biochemistry, and it can take one the other way; thus all activities of the mind can be derived from feeling. In a very early stage feeling can be divided into "sensibility"[6] and "emotivity."[7] Man, a symbol-making creature, does his thinking-conceiving through symbols, which are representations of an idea. I believe man's only symbolic means of logically expressing (or "projecting," as Susanne Langer speaks of this metaphorically) his awareness of an emotive or a direct body *feeling* resides in the arts, not in ordinary discourse. That is, in a poem one might find feelings of emotivity expressed, but, of course, one would recognize that they are not the emotions of anyone's real life. I presently think they would be perceptions of emotivity. "What you do when you make a work of art is to create, not a straight symbol . . . but an expressive form."[8] I hold, then, that a poem is a single expressive *form* (and by "single" I refer to a property of oneness or unity) possessing the capability for a liveness of its own. In that expressive form we intuit a quality that appears to be a characteristic of the work. The quality may be emotive.

[5] Susanne K. Langer, "The Expression of Feeling in Dance," *Impulse,* ed. Marian Van Tuyl (San Francisco, 1968), 15, 16. This volume is entitled "Dance—a projection for the future."

[6] Mrs. Langer means the peripheral feelings of the organism.

[7] Langer's term instead of "emotion" because it allows for many things below the limen of emotion but is still of the same cloth.

[8] Langer, p. 18.

The question of a poem's function has a long history in the Western world, and there have been many possible functions ascribed to it. This question is not one that I, as an interpreter, raise. It strikes me as a utilitarian question not raised by a poet or any other creative artist. The epigraph of this essay might seem, at first, to belie my position. However, I do not think so. Our negotiation as interpreters, with the symbolic presentation of human feeling in an expressive form we call a literary work of art, is an enabling negotiation; through it we simply learn about our inner lives, our experiences. A poem does not make anything happen, ". . . it survives/ A way of happening, a mouth."[9] That it "survives" in language leads to certain other complexities. To examine them would take me too far afield. It differs from real life, yet it shares with human life a pattern of tensions and releases of those tensions. Seeming paradoxes cloud distinctions here, but what I now think is that a poem is not actually a living thing like a plant. It is organic; yet it is simply appearance, reflecting the life of feeling, and a poet "gets" it from human life or from nature, but cannot name it or label it. I would presently argue that it comes to the creative artist as an image—and the apparatus of imaging and intuiting is complicated in the extreme. For the poet, and for scientists too of a certain caliber, the real joy is in the metaphor of perception. In *On Growth and Form* the distinguished morphologist D'Arcy Thompson makes certain observations about trees that may clarify my point here. He writes: "But the tapering pine-tree is but a special case of a wider problem. The oak does not grow so tall as the pine-tree, but it carries a heavier load, and its boll, broad-based upon its spreading roots, shows a different contour. Smeaton took it for the pattern of his lighthouse, and Eiffel built his great tree of steel, a thousand feet high, to a similar but a stricter plan."[10] Discussing the morphology of the organism,

[9] Lines from stanza two of the poem "In Memory of W. B. Yeats" from *Collected Shorter Poems 1927–1957* by W. H. Auden (New York: Random House, 1967). Reprinted by permission of the publisher.

[10] D'Arcy W. Thompson, *On Growth and Form* (New York: Macmillan, 1942), 29.

Thompson offers observations about the time element implicit in the idea of growth. The "space-time relation," as he calls it, cannot be neglected in a consideration of form.[11] Heeding this relation has import for the biologist and something to do with the way a certain eye (an artist's) is able *to see* and *to present* (using Parrish's word) a quality. The quality then seems to express a feeling. And this has a very great deal to do with the way an interpreter is able to perceive and to present the poem. To recapitulate, there is in art what Langer has called "metaphorical symbolism."[12] I believe that the relationship of an interpreter to expression of poetry is also metaphorical.

I have a final response to Parrish's essay and his concern about "the intrusion of an interpreter between author and receiver." It has to do with the interpreter's response to the single expressive form whose quality he intuits. A danger lies in the reader who retains the nonliterary attitude toward the poem and "does things" with it. I am here indebted to observations by C. S. Lewis on "How the Few and the Many Use Pictures and Music."[13] There are those readers who perceive and then "use" a work of art. Such a person offers to the work the same treatment he does to the teddy bear or an ikon (meaning here any two- or three-dimensional object intended as an aid to devotion). Both the bear and the ikon may be in themselves works of art, but their purposes are not to have attention fixed upon themselves so much as to stimulate certain activities in the child or worshipper. A teddy bear exists in order that the child may give it imaginary life and play with it. The better the playing the less the actual appearance of the bear matters. "We must not let loose," warns Lewis, "our own subjectivity upon the pictures and make them its vehicles. The real objection to that way of enjoying pictures is that you never get beyond yourself. The picture, so used, can call out of you only what is already there." He further notes that "the first demand any work of

[11] Thompson, p. 194.

[12] Langer, p. 20.

[13] Chap. III in *An Experiment in Criticism* (Cambridge: University Press, 1961).

any art makes upon us is surrender. Look. Listen. Receive. Get yourself out of the way."[14]

For the interpreter's reception of a poem is not passivity. It is, rather, an imaginative and a transcendent activity; ineffable, yes, but when we experience the poem, we sense an outward movement, the root meaning of "emotion." We have crossed over, gone beyond self. Ours is an age of miniaturized gadgetry and the "mini" fashion: the mini-look, the mini-dress, the mini-course, the mini-tour. The interpreter may be unfashionable, for he seeks no mini-experience but a fully embodied one wherein he surrenders, looks, listens, receives, and gets himself out of the way of the poem.

∿

RESPONSE

Richard Haas
and David A. Williams

The preceding two essays clash on a number of points central to the interpreter's art. Professor Floyd notes accurately that emotion or feeling resides within the poem. The poem's operation of itself, the interworkings of its "objects, incidents, images, and word forms that are the stuff of which poetry is made," creates its own emotion, it own liveness, an interworking of poetic elements that "registers in our awareness."

With that point made, she dismisses the interpreter's consideration of ever moving "another person's emotion without feeling the same emotion that moves him" by objecting to Parrish's contention that the interpreter *intrudes* between the author and the listener. The possibility of moving another's emotion without feeling that emotion yourself implies a particular relationship

[14] Lewis, pp. 16, 17, *et passim.*

with the audience to which she does not directly object, but rather offers the humanistic value awaiting the interpreter in the act of directly and deeply *surrendering* to the operation of the poem's own life and emotion. In this act of surrender, she feels the interpreter will be able to realize that "literature itself," as Professor Bacon says, "aspires, speaks, and the interpreter becomes language in its full and most significant sense. He is not a horn through which the poet calls, not a vacuum transmitting speech, but the embodiment of speech."[1]

When "the interpreter becomes language" and is "the embodiment of speech," Professor Floyd's observation that "the relationship of an interpreter to expression of poetry is . . . metaphorical" means that the performance of the text *is* the text. The humanistic value in this approach is appreciated by many interpretation and literary scholars.[2] It provides a way by which the interpreter fully realizes a humanistic growth by seeing, thinking, and feeling with a life other than his own.[3]

One of your editors tells the story of his first lesson in the act of surrendering to the poem's operation of itself and to the life found within it. In the last days of his undergraduate years, he was discussing poetry with friends when one handed him a poem he hadn't read. He gave it a brief reading and announced, "I don't like it." His friend replied, "That doesn't matter, Haas. Does the poem like you?" Haas admits he was sitting back expecting the poem to do something *to* him. Poems won't. You must go to them. "Look. Listen. Receive. Get yourself out of the way." As any good communication advice will state, "Try to see it from the other guy's point of view; what does *he* mean." To the interpreter, this advice means surrender to the poem so as to "gain the kind

[1] Wallace A. Bacon, *The Art of Interpretation* (New York: Holt, Rinehart and Winston, 1966), xvii.

[2] Allen Tate, *On the Limits of Poetry* (New York: The Swallow Press and William Morrow, 1948), 123, 279.

[3] C. S. Lewis, *An Experiment in Criticism* (Cambridge: University Press, 1965), 140, 141.

of realization of the work which occurs only when one can make some intimate and personal connection with it."[4]

Looking back now to Parrish's essay, his observations are not wrong, but different from Floyd's view of the interpretation of poetry.

Language is not an effective medium either for expressing emotion or for perceiving the emotions of others.

Parrish is right. Language is better suited for informational purposes. But because of this ineffectiveness, it makes poetry's ability to create feeling even more exciting and wondrous. W. H. Auden didn't think poetry was a way or a means to get something said as much as an activity by which the poet and the reader enjoyed hanging around words to hear them talking to one another.

. . . it is possible to be moved by another person's emotion without feeling the same emotion that moves him.

Parrish's examples make good sense. The interpreter's surrender to the emotional life of the poem, however, establishes greater similarity of felt emotions between the poem and the interpreter than that emotion achieved by sitting back and expecting the poem to talk to you. In performance, the difference is even greater. The interpreter who has surrendered to the poem performs the aspirations and manners of speech as he hears the poem create its own life-speech. This performing approach is clearly different from "using" the poem to create emotions not truly felt by the interpreter or truly shared with the poem. This is not to say that artistic performances cannot be created by "using" the poem; but such performances will not be of the type Floyd discusses. Nevertheless, Parrish is right. A skilled performing technician *can* so move his audience to emotional responses he does not feel. But why should he wish to?

[4] Mark S. Klyn, "The Terms of Feeling," *Western Speech* XXVIII (Summer 1964), 164.

. . . many poems are not expressions of the poet's feelings . . . [and even if that were so] poets are not always writing about their own feelings.

Since the date of Parrish's article, the intentional fallacy (viewing the poem as a message of the poet's communicative intent) has peaked and now is waning, even to the point of being called the intentional fallacy fallacy. Indeed, the poem can be viewed as the poet's message, as the utterance of the poem's "speaker" (persona), and as a poem without a designated "speaker," but one which, through its own "embodiment of speech," establishes its own speaking voice.

. . . the emotion will be greatly altered in an attempt to express it.

The word "greatly" is the major point of concern here. Any interpreter is aware of how a poem will mean something more or less, or maybe just different from day to day. This is one of the strengths of good poetry; it is always more than any one reading can gain. In performing-situations, most theorists applaud the personal touch an interpreter gives a poem. Parrish's next point should be brought into this discussion:

I think we ought to recognize that in a given interpretation the same feeling need not be felt by poet, reader, and hearer.

The poet strives for an expression of an emotion. His poem stands as the expression of that emotion and no attempt to explain that emotion will be the same as the poem. Also, the poet is not deceived to think that the poem is an exact pattern and expression of the emotion he felt. The interpreter, in his surrender to the poem, attempts to encounter that feeling as closely as possible; but then he has the additional task of expressing the poem as he feels and understands it. Therein lies another alteration of the emotion. If we add an audience, with its different personalities and perceptual sets, we add yet another step in which the emotion can and will be altered. Just how great the alteration is can be determined by the artistry of all involved. Exact precision in translation of emotion is impossible; but the striving for the ideal is rewarding and is the backbone of art.

Parrish suggests some different performing methods for the oral interpreter:

- to assume the feeling of the poet
- to put himself on the side of the hearer
- to impersonate the poet

And, specifically in dramatic poetry, Parrish offers additional suggestions:

- to reflect emotion of character
- to reflect emotion of audience
- to be emotionally neutral[5]

These suggested methods of performance fall into schools of thought regarding interpretation. As Robert Breen has said, "The successful oral reader is not conditioned by schools of oral reading but rather by the demands of the poem he is reading. It is a wise reader who will suit his interpretation to the style of the poem."[6]

Professor Floyd so fully discussed the aesthetic backgrounds of her position that she clearly established the diligence of the active encounter an interpreter must take to his study and art. We fully support her concern that the humanistic values in interpretation, through a diligent literary study, might be lost to those in a modern world who take a mini-approach to interpretation and who might mistake a mini-experience for the maxi-experience that awaits them.

[5] See Cornelius Carman Cunningham, "The Sepia School of Interpretative Reading," *The Quarterly Journal of Speech* XXVIII (February 1942), 37–41.

[6] Robert Breen, "Some Difficulties in Reading Modern Poetry Publicly," *Western Speech* XIX (October 1955), 245–249.

Selected Readings

Brennan, Joseph Gerard. "The Role of Emotion in Aesthetic Experience," *The Quarterly Journal of Speech* XL (December 1954), 422–428.

Geiger, Don. "Emotion in Poetry: The Oral Interpreter's Special Responsibility," *The Southern Speech Journal* XXI (Fall 1955), 31–38.

Klyn, Mark S. "The Terms of Feeling," *Western Speech* XXVIII (Summer 1964), 159–166.

In 1952, Tyson V. Anderson advocated the "conversational norm" in oral interpretation.[1] He was not precise in his description of the term, but suggested that a violation of the norm would be doing things that the reader would never do in spontaneous speech. Both the "mechanists" and the "naturalists" advocated natural epression. Does "natural" mean "conversational?"

All of us have heard students conversationalize poetry in an attempt to make it sound clearer. Would it be wrong? Robert Breen suggested that "the reader may characteristically use a conversational mode for his readings and thereby do disservice to the lyrical quality of the verse.[2] Most theorists would agree with Professor Breen. However, it might seem reasonable to read a modern poem conversationally because it appears conversational. But the poem might be deceivingly conversational and far more formal and structured than immediately realized.

In order to determine whether the conversational norm is still an issue today, we reprint William B. McCoard's article, "How Conversational Is the 'Conversational Norm'?" and two additional theorists, Elbert R. Bowen and Janet Bolton, discuss the point.

[1] Tyson V. Anderson, "Shall We Tell Them How to Say It?" *Western Speech* (January 1952), 25–28.

[2] Robert Breen, "Some Difficulties in Reading Modern Poetry Publicly," *Western Speech* XIX (October 1955), 249.

WILLIAM B. McCOARD

How Conversational is the "Conversational Norm"?

It would have been a good deal of help if Mr. Tyson V. Anderson in "Shall We Tell Them How To Say It?" had defined more clearly what he meant by his advocated "conversational norm." He points out that the "think-the-thought" method is not effective as a teaching method, since the fundamentals are omitted. By implication he suggests that one would get the fundamentals if one used the "conversational norm" as the approach.

Perhaps it ought to be pointed out he does not advocate that a selection should be interpreted using the nomal, everyday, run-of-the-mill conversational manner as the criterion. Obviously this would be too casual for the interpretation of literature that was written only because it was of more than ordinary importance. Writers do not write of those things of ordinary conversation—unless there is special reason for doing so, and then the ordinary is no longer ordinary. Art deals with experiences of heightened emotion even when it deals in bread and butter. So, Mr. Anderson must be referring to the use of a norm of conversation that is normal for the intensity of the art experience. If this is true, how is this knowledge likely to result in any great advance over the think-the-thoughters in development of the fundamentals?

Where Mr. Curry emphasized impression, Mr. Anderson is emphasizing expression. It is clear that neither can get along without the other—and that the use of the "conversational norm" is helpful as long as one recognizes that the reading situation is not "natural" but must seem to be so. In the last issue of *The Quarterly Journal of Speech,* Mr. Parrish pointed out that "naturalness in interpretation is to be approved, not when it feels natural to the reader, but when it seems natural to the hearer." This, of course, is what Mr. Anderson also says since the conversational norm for each interpretation is checked by the class reaction. Otherwise we should have the strange situation of each person continuing his speech faults and inadequacies merely because they seem "normal" to him.

✎

RESPONSE

Elbert R. Bowen

Previously I wrote a hasty first draft of this response, taking the position that the whole issue of the conversational norm, being as old as the hills, is not worth discussing further. I even quoted John Mason, 1748, who recommended conversation as a model for naturalness.[1] I thought all of us agreed that conversation has a quality that should be utilized in some degree in all our efforts to speak or read in public. Today, especially, when we so distrust any evidence of phoniness in a speaker, the conversational mode would seem to be the norm for all communicative speech. I therefore hesitantly proposed to change the subject, contending that if we wished some *real* controversy, we might better debate the "*communicative* norm." However, after taking time to reread some critical essays, I have discovered two things which should have occurred to me beforehand: one, that the question of the

[1] John Mason, *An Essay on Elocution, or, Pronunciation* (London, 1748), 30.

conversational norm is still with us; and, two, that the communicative norm is practically its Siamese twin.

Let us begin with a premise: "Virtually everyone in the field of oral interpretation believes in the *communicative* norm." True, there are among our colleagues a very few who so exclusively equate oral interpretation with literary criticism that they rule out communication as any sort of goal for the art. One of them expressed it to me: "I don't care whether a student communicates anything to the class. All I want is to see that *he* has the literature." Fortunately, such polarists are rare. Most who regard oral interpretation as primarily a critical endeavor still acknowledge that communication is a happy by-product.

Let us continue, with another premise: "Virtually everyone in the field of oral interpretation believes in the *conversational* norm." I would venture that even those who prefer elevated performances for some literature would justify some degree of conversational naturalness to assure communication.

From whence, then, comes any opposition to these two premises? Well, chiefly from those poets and critics who abhor the notion that a poem can be communicated orally. Notwithstanding Kemp Malone's words of praise for the oral reading of literature —dealt with elsewhere in this volume—I suspect that the majority of poetry scholar-teachers think much more like Samuel R. Levin, who writes: "Many textual ambiguities cannot be preserved in oral performances, simply because the stress-pitch-juncture system of English demands a resolution. . . . One can argue that ambiguity is built into poetry, and that resolution of this ambiguity represents not a service to a poem, but a disservice."[2]

Heavens! If poetry has ambiguities that oral reading inevitably resolves, and if oral reading does a disservice to the poem by resolving them, then the oral reading of poems containing ambiguity is *wrong!* Levin has chosen to assert that an "oral per-

[2] Samuel R. Levin, "Suprasegmentals and the Performance of Poetry," *The Quarterly Journal of Speech* XLVIII (December 1962), 366–367.

formance does not optimally represent the poem," and he suggests
the invalidity of the assumption that "oral performance of poetry
is superior to visual performance." My friends, if Professor Levin
is correct, we are goners!

A very few individuals in our midst are studying linguistics
and trying to answer Levin's type of attack. Most prominent is
Katherine T. Loesch, who contends that the oral interpreter, rather
than being forced by the language to disambiguate (to resolve
ambiguity), always has at his disposal a "non-disambiguating intonation."[3] Professor Loesch feels that the oral interpreter can and
should read in such a manner as to expose the listener to the
richness of ambiguous meanings. Says she: "Disambiguation in the
interests of communication can be self-defeating; the object to be
communicated may be maimed, crippled or partially destroyed in
the process. . . ."[4]

Thus, though Levin and Loesch are agreed as to the importance
of poetic ambiguity, Loesch maintains that the oral interpreter can
preserve ambiguity in his reading whereas Levin feels he cannot.

Seymour Chatman, also both a linguist and a friend to interpretation, disagrees with both Levin and Loesch: "Granted that
the critic may have the leisure to fondle ambiguities, I wonder
whether the oral interpreter can afford to." Professor Chatman
sums up his position quite specifically, with plenty of italics for
reasons the reader can discover for himself in the original: *"The
exigencies of public performance and public knowledge of poetry
being what they are,* where, at a given location in a text, alternative
intonations capable of disambiguating the syntax are available, the
oral performer *would be well advised* to disambiguate *if he means
to communicate at all."*[5]

To those of us who have long had faith in oral interpretation

[3] Katherine T. Loesch, "Literary Ambiguity and Oral Performance," *The Quarterly Journal of Speech* LI (October 1965), 260.

[4] Katherine T. Loesch, "A Reply to Mr. Chatman," *The Quarterly
Journal of Speech* LII (October 1966), 288.

[5] Seymour Chatman, "On 'Intonational Fallacy,'" *The Quarterly
Journal of Speech* LII (October 1966), 284.

as a performing art in behalf of literary messages, Chatman's argument is probably the most heartening. On the other hand, the Levin and Loesch positions raise serious questions for considerable thought by all of us.

Now, back to "conversation." The aforementioned linguists do a good deal of debating over the nature and function of what they call "normal" intonations in preserving or resolving ambiguities. Whatever normal intonations are, they apparently are not conversational!

Finally, I refer you to the critic Yvor Winters, who has written in the following vein: "A poem . . . is a formal statement; and the reading of a poem is thus a formal occasion. A poem is not conversation. . . . Conversation is in general the least premeditated and least rhythmical of human utterance; and it depends very heavily upon intonations and even gestures and facial expressions which are not at the disposal of the poet."[6]

It is obvious that Winters does not believe in either the conversational or communicative norms. Apparently, neither does he believe in the oral interpretation of poetry. (Nor, even in the acting of Shakespeare.) To him, human performers spoil poetry.

Now, where are we? (Ambiguous question here.)

∿

RESPONSE

Janet Bolton

I fear that my reaction to the application of the "conversational norm" to oral interpretation duplicates Elbert Bowen's initial response except that I am going to stick to his guns! The idea is

[6] Yvor Winters, "The Audible Reading of Poetry," *The Structure of Verse; Modern Essays on Prosody,* ed. Harvey Gross, (Greenwich, Conn.: Fawcett Publications, 1966), 134.

not worth discussing further. The "conversational norm" was never an "issue" in oral interpretation (in spite of the earnest, albeit nonsensical, dialectic about it), because it has never been nor can it be a principle. Unless "oral interpretation" is a friendly informal discussion or an exchange of ideas about a literary text among a group of interested readers, the phenomenon of "conversation" is not relevant. As for "norm," which posits a standard or model generally based on medium achievement (the synonym for which is "average"), I reject the term totally. I reject likewise Dr. Bowen's premise: "Virtually everyone in the field of oral interpretation believes in the *communicative* norm." The oral interpreter indeed communicates, but the existence of a "norm" for aesthetic communication violates the untranslatable particularity (or ambiguity, if you will) that is its unique characteristic.

Yvor Winter's declaration of the poem or the reading of a poem as a "formal statement" seems to me eminently sound. Conversation ". . . .the least premeditated and least rhythmical of human utterance . . ." is antithetical to poetic utterance, written or oral.

Whether Mr. Winters (and many of us) decries oral presentation of literature on aesthetic grounds, or whether we extoll it as having aesthetic and/or educational value, the "conversational norm" offers nothing whatsoever to gratify any of us.

❦

RESPONSE

Elbert R. Bowen

It hurts to have one's ideas rejected, especially by one so qualified to reject them as my good friend Professor Bolton.

I should have used my dictionary first. It had not occurred to me that in these days a norm is considered to be only a median, average, or ever-fixèd mark. Such a notion, I had thought, was old hat. In this connection I recall reading fairly recently, in a bad but interesting magazine, an article proposing that we can now accept virginity to be not one condition but several: there are, the writer contended, several degrees or kinds of virginity available to the modern woman. I visualized the communicative norm to exist on a continuum similar to the new virginity. More particularly, the communicative spirit may manifest itself in many forms but is characterized by a common attitude, namely the attempt to communicate perceived literary significances to other human beings.

　　I *still* think most oral interpreters use the communicative norm in reading most forms of literature most of the time—that is, if such a thing exists, and I think it does; but I couldn't prove it if my life depended on it, which it doesn't. . . .

New criticism, with its emphasis on the poem as a complete object, is no longer new. In this next essay by Professor Don Geiger, the concept of new criticism is not the focus of the student's attention, but rather it offers a departure point to examine emotions, attitudes, and ideas of a poem. Geiger's position complements Bacon's contention that the study of interpretation requires more than a plus, suggesting that a reading rich in emotional display, responsive voice and body, still can be a bad interpretation.

This essay views literature as a complex of attitudes, and the interpreter as translator with an obligation to transport the poem from a written to an oral construct, while retaining the original complexity. Geiger cautions the student against confusing attitudes he has extracted with the complete poetic object, reminding us that it is never what the poem *says* as much as what it *is*. The importance of interpreting emotions in literature—which we have observed in essays—is reinforced in Geiger's new-critical frame, providing illumination from a new perspective. In the words of I. A. Richards: "Emotions are what the reaction, with its reverberation in bodily changes, feels like. Attitudes are the impulses towards one kind of behavior or another which are set ready by the response."[1]

The interpreter's efforts toward discovering "what the reaction . . . feels like" lead him not to a "naming" process, but rather to the appropriate response names. Geiger ends his essay with the poignant difference between the intelligent man, who knows the names of things, and the wise man who has developed a proper attitude toward the thing. Again, we are reminded of Richards's words: "And though his intellect is what is distinctive in man, he is not primarily an intelligence; he is a system of interests. Intelligence helps man but does not run him."[2]

[1] I. A. Richards, *Poetics and Sciences.* (London: Routledge & Kegan Paul, 1970), 28.

[2] Richards, p. 30.

DON GEIGER

Oral Interpretation and the "New Criticism"

What I would like to do in this article is to suggest the way in which the practice of orally interpreting literature verifies a basic insight of the "new criticism" into the nature of literary structure, and further, to show how the nature of oral interpretation suggests ways to enlarge (or make more precise) what this insight (or definition) means to the oral interpretation teacher's evaluation of his own function.

It is necessary to the above-listed purposes to think of the term *interpret* in the sense of *translate*. If this seems an unusual concept, still we know there is a way in which we may meaningfully say that the oral interpreter of literature is a translator in the sense that a man transferring a statement made in Spanish into English is a translator. He must preserve in the "language of lips and eyes" the meanings of the printed page.

❧

In an urge to teach or to practice "creative" interpretations we may possibly forget this translative aspect of the term *interpret*. We tend to think of differences in interpretation as "additions to" or "subtractions from." Take the evidence of a common phrase: "See what Olivier *did with* 'Hamlet,' " or, "I prefer Barrymore's 'Hamlet' to Olivier's." These phrases so emphasize the creative aspect of the interpretation as to make the concept of translation seem off the point.

But a skilled debater might argue that differences in interpretation, however significant, only call attention to the difficulty (even practical impossibility) of a *perfect* interpretation (that is, where all relationships of literary meaning are preserved in, or translated to, oral constructs). However this argument might be finally resolved, a less assumptive statement is sufficient to verify our proposition that, if it is not the only way in which interpretation may be considered, one valid meaning which may be got from it is that of translation. This lesser argument simply points to the fact that, though many interpretations may be more or less "right" and "good" it is also possible that many interpretations may be more or less "wrong" and "bad." Concretely, let us imagine a very *rich* oral interpretation: that is, rich in emotional displays, splendid carriage on the platform, beautiful voice, and so forth. Nevertheless, it is quite possible that this would be a very *bad* performance, simply because it was not true to the page read. The actor, fresh from a triumph in the role of "Hamlet," let us say, is not assured a triumph in "Macbeth" simply by repeating his performance of gesture and tone of voice, with different words accompanying.

The importance of this conception of the oral interpreter's job lies fundamentally, I think, in the implications it holds for a closer working between literary theory and oral reading. That is, literary theory has much to teach the oral reader, and perhaps something to learn from him. How this is so—in the sense of *interpreter* as *translator*—will be our purpose to trace.

Let us consider first the insight of new criticism which I have said the practice of oral interpretation verifies. Cleanth Brooks writes:

In each case, the unifying principle of the organization which is the poem is an attitude or complex of attitudes. We can discover, to be sure, propositions which seem to characterize, more or less accurately, the unifying attitude. But if we take such propositions to be the core of the poem we are contenting ourselves with reductions and substitutions. To do this, is to take the root or the blossoms of the tree for the tree itself.[1]

Now, if this is not a definition of literary nature which every modern critic would unqualifiedly affirm, it nevertheless has the advantage of emphasizing the one assumption around which the "new criticism" is organized (and which makes it, in a dialectical sense, "new"): that the proper study of literature is, in the first instance, the literary work itself.

The teacher of oral interpretation might say (with the appropriately malicious twinkle for his city cousins in the English department) that the proper practice of his art has always implied this idea. And this is what the new criticism takes for its dialectical starting point. That is, like the best of the new critics, the oral interpreter of literature has not decried the study of literary history as such, but he sees it as subsidiary to, and probably only relevant to, the study of literary work per se. Publishing the unpublished Wordsworth letters is of no help in communicating the meanings of "Composed upon Westminster Bridge, September 3, 1802" to an audience; or, to say it more accurately, the letters are of use to the interpreter only to the extent that they contribute to his knowledge of communicable structure.

Now if we are right in saying that meanings of the literary-construct may be preserved in the oral-construct, and Mr. Brooks is right in saying that meanings of the literary-construct is that it's a complex of attitudes, then it is clearly the job of the oral interpreter to communicate attitudes. These attitudes, or effects of them, may be called *moods* or *sentiments,* or something else, in one context or another; they may be approved or disliked, but they are, in the first instance, *attitudes,* or in the language of psychology, *sets* or *dispositions* to *respond.*[2]

I think the experience of every interpreter confirms this as-

[1] Cleanth Brooks, *The Well Wrought Urn* (New York: Reynal and Hitchcock, 1947), 174–175.

[2] John J. B. Morgan, *The Psychology of Abnormal People* (New York: Longmans, Green, 1928), 185.

sertion of Mr. Brooks. On a given word or line, the interpreter must be more or less sad, pensive, glad, and so on ad infinitum, through the immense range of attitudes possible to the human being. This is what he can (and what Mr. Brooks says in effect he must, if he is to communicate literary meanings) communicate. His experience confirms too the irreducibility of his communication. A statement about the oral interpretation falls neccessarily short of the complexity of the interpretation itself, where the delivery of each word subtly changes the nature of the total communication. I shall elaborate this point shortly.

However, if the interpreter's job in the first instance is to communicate attitudes, it is also true that his job is to do something more than this (or, if you will, this must be done in a larger context than Mr. Brooks states); what he does has bearing on Mr. Brooks's literary theory, I think, though to explain this we must first consider at greater length our conception of *translation*.

Translation may be effective to the extent that two different systems of meanings are congruent. Therefore, obviously, the nature of the language into which meaning is to be translated may provide very strict limits on the effectiveness of translation. For example suppose I wish to translate a Spanish editorial into English, but discover that there are no nouns, or noun-substitutes in English—I think that we can agree translation would be impossible, or only roughly approximate.

We may then, if we are not sure whether or not a given system of meanings may be translated into another given system, direct our attention to the system of meanings into which the translation is to take place. That is, thinking of an oral-construct as a system of meanings into which a literary-construct is to be translated, we might study the resources of the oral-construct, knowing that *its* limits would largely determine the effectiveness of a translation from literature.

To ask that question, however, would be to ask a question whose answer is already well known: the practice of good oral interpreters and actors since the dawn of our civilization testifies that the meanings of the printed page of literature may be communicated orally. Our real question then is—in a time when the meaning of literature is under constant examination—whether or not our knowledge of the oral-construct is precise enough to tell us something of the literature. To refer to our earlier analogy, it is somewhat as if we knew: (1) the nature of English; (2) that the English system of meanings was congruent with the Spanish system (i.e., effective translation was possible); and (3) wondered what was the nature of Spanish. To change the analogical terms, I shall assume (2) that literature can be translated effectively into oral-constructs; and direct the rest of my attention in this paper to showing (1) the nature of the oral-construct; assuming that it will imply certain characteristics of (3) the nature of the literary construct.

Let us investigate the medium of the oral-construct by asking what the translating agent, the *interpreter,* can do with it. I shall suggest that he can follow essentially three courses: the first is that which Mr. Brooks declares to be at the heart of literature—to communicate attitudes, descriptions, or paraphrases which (as I have already briefly remarked) are always "reductions."

An anecdote may perhaps most graphically illustrate this. I recall once having met in the lobby during an intermission of a ballet a friend of mine who was considerably agitated. He professed to having been moved "to tears" by the way the ballerina had "wiggled her foot" at a certain point in the performance. I had not been similarly moved, and though he spent some time attempting to persuade me to his emotion, we were at loggerheads: all his words were propositions which were "reductions" of the attitude communicated, and—though I thought for a time he was going to try—he was unable to "wiggle" his own foot in a way effective enough to permit me an immediate apprehension of his point.

Whatever may be adventitious in this illustration, it tells a basic truth. As a synecdoche leading into the field of oral interpretation, it probably makes clear why so-called mechanical methods of oral interpretation must always fail: no system for transferences, however comprehensive, is large enough to embrace the total number of attitudes of which the human being (and literary meaning) is capable.

However, an interpreter can do something else with his medium than be "sad" or "happy" or "jocular" in various levels of intensity. In fact, his ability to make something else of his oral-construct (implying a sensitivity to aspects of literature other than its "attitudes") is that which permits him to convey properly the attitudes themselves.

The second course an interpreter can take is, in a lesser or greater extent, to communicate notions of the properties of objects.

Let us consider a phrase, "gingerbread is preferable to hardtack." It is possible, as we have seen, for the oral reader, to indicate *preference,* that is to take an attitude toward "gingerbread and hardtack"—a smile on uttering "gingerbread," a look of disdain, a sneer in the voice uttering "hardtack." (I hope the reader maintains a proper "skeptical poise" on reading these "reductions," done in a comic "wiggle-the-foot" descriptive manner.) But as well as *taking an attitude,* the reader may suggest (though unquestionably in thin strokes or, in Korzybski's useful metaphorical phrase, by a "high order" of abstraction) properties of the object. Perhaps the significant properties which could be suggested here would be properties of *texture* (the softness of gingerbread the hardness of hardtack): a soft, luxurious quality of voice, let us say, for "gingerbread," a clipped, shorter articulation of "hardtack."

This suggestion of properties is, to be sure, so fused with *attitudes* taken toward these objects that they hardly can be separated, if at all, critically. But any reader can prove the point quickly enough to his own satisfaction simply by reading the statement, once attempting to communicate some idea of *preference,* and the second time attempting to communicate a notion of *preference* for a *soft* object, a *hard* object (the notion of preference for a *tasty* object to an *untasty* object is still fundamentally a matter of attitude; that is, we know it is *tasty* because of the *attitude* taken toward it: some variation of stomach-rubbing and lip-licking).

Now the importance of this second dimension of the reader's oral-construct is this; it permits him to know what *intensity* or *level* of attitude is proper. Let us imagine I do indeed say, "gingerbread is preferable to hardtack" with wide smiles, stomach-rubbings, and, before I am through with the phrase, wide, wide sneers and bitter growls. Something is rotten, this side of the gingerbread. Very simply, I know what attitude to take, in its exact degree or intensity, because I know now toward *what* the attitude is taken. With another phrase, let us say, "Thomism is preferable to presentationalism," I probably cannot say with much confidence whether any given intensity of the attitude of *preference* is right or wrong, good or bad, since, if any relationship involving preferences actually exists between these names-for-somethings, I don't know what it is.

A third course which may be taken by the interpreter with his oral-construct is to suggest the nature of action. We may relate this to the previous dimension of his medium by saying that he can denote *dynamic* properties of objects, or events. A good example of this might be found in a phrase of Arnold's where he talks of the sea's "melancholy, long, withdrawing roar," which the reader can communicate by suggesting in the context of briefer vocal signs, this "long" withdrawingness. If it is thought this overlaps too much with the above function, as an illustration of ways in which properties of an object may be suggested, a better example might be taken from Shakespeare. "How shall summer's honey breath hold out/ Against the wreckful siege of battering days?" I submit that one effective way of communicating this line would be to suggest, among other things, the nature of the action. "Days" are compared to the relentless, inexorable battering-rams of a feudal siege, so in reading the line, we could emphasize the regularity in meter until "battering," which could be, in effect, "spattered" against "days." That is, it would be possible to suggest something of the slow, regular, methodical way in which the soldiers lift the heavy ram, swing it regularly back and forth, and smash it into the gate (though my word "spattering" is certainly a "reduction" or "substitution" for what the oral reading could much more accurately suggest).

Now, I do not mean to say that these are necessarily the only ideas that an oral interpreter can communicate, or that this is the only way in which the oral-construct can be viewed. But when our purpose is to think of the oral interpretation of literature where literature itself is thought of as a "complex of attitudes," I think we may agree that something has been done to "fill out" Mr. Brooks's definition. That is, we might now say of the literary-construct as we may say of the oral-construct, that it is the non-paraphrasable communication of attitudes appropriate to the objects and events named.

I am sure that this would not meet with Mr. Brooks's dis-approval, since he evidently feels that attitudes must be taken *toward* something. Perhaps his feeling that this was self-evident kept him from making any special point of in the phrases I chose to quote. Actually, it is knowing toward what they are taken, which, as we have seen, makes it possible (and alone makes it possible) for us to know exactly what attitudes are (or should be) com-municated.

Since this is true, we might better say that the literary-construct and the congruent oral-construct are non-paraphrasable communications of attitudes appropriate to the *named* objects and events. The new position of *named* in our definition calls our at-tention to the fact that it is to the *name* rather than to the object or event, per se, that we respond. That is, I may *name* (give prop-erties to) "gingerbread," that spicy smelling, delicious, tangy stuff— or that mushy, foul-odored, swill-ish stuff—and though the *stuff* remains the same, my attitude toward it will differ.

This does not mean that the interpreter (or the writer before him) is to be lined up with other enemies of a psychologically sound "semantic." The facts are that, whatever else the "stuff" remains—the "gingerbread," the "hardtack," the sandpile, the for-est—and that human beings not only will, but must, take attitudes toward these items of the world. The solution, then, is not to refrain from *naming* them, but to name them so that we may know what attitudes should be taken toward them.

❧

We have come, I think, to the most important implication for the teacher of interpretation in this brief study of a coordinate theory of literature and oral interpretation. It is that the oral reader, like the writer before him, if at one remove, is engaged in the great task of *naming* the world.

Literary meaning assuredly does not *name* the world as science names the world. The world is named, in literature, in terms of the human interest. Science attempts to name "gingerbread" (assign properties to it) so that, were they conscious, trees and stars would find the name as satisfactory as a human being finds it; but literature must always name the gingerbread so as to recommend it to one kind of human use or another.

The point may receive clearer illustration when we notice that a fundamental difference between the *frames* in which scientific and literary naming occur may lie at the root of all to differentiate a "wise" man from a "knowledgeable" or "intellectual" man. To the extent that such attempts actually point to differences in educational adjustment (they are, of course, always partly arbitrary: surely a man may be both "intelligent" and "wise"), we might attempt a volitional definition to codify the differences. The "wise" man is he who has, in the first instance, learned the names of the items of the world with the *ultimate aim of taking attitudes toward these items;* and second, is one who has—from this point of view—named these items accurately. The "intelligent" man might also have named the universe correctly, but within a frame different from the "wise" man's interest. More briefly, the "intelligent" man and the "wise" man may ask different questions of the universe, and receive correspondingly different answers. It is enough for "intelligence"—in this scheme—to learn from the world that there is something meaningful occurring to which $E = mc^2$ may be accurately referred; but this name alone does not satisfy the search for wisdom which asks, "What does $E = mc^2$ demand of me?"

❧

This way of looking at his job places obvious and overwhelming responsibilities on the teacher of oral interpretation. Once he feels that he is engaged in a process of *naming* the world for the human interest, he knows that he is engaged in a process that is humanly significant, involving *accuracy*. Whether or not we will eat the gingerbread makes a difference to us, and how the gingerbread is *named* will help determine whether or not we eat it.

Very simply, Keats may have been far wiser in writing that "beauty is truth" than the positivists will admit; and once the teacher of interpretation sees his task involving him in this equation, new demands are made on his integrity, intelligence, and humility, as he sees more clearly his responsibility to the educating of that ideal creature of the educational process, the "wise" man.

In a brief but excellent resumé of New Criticism, Cleanth Brooks comments that "the 'new critics' have characteristically attempted to deal with the literary object itself rather than with its origins and effects—to give a formal rather than a genetic or an affective account of literature." (See *Encyclopedia of Poetry and Poetics,* Princeton, 1965, p. 568.) This general orientation in approach is probably the characteristic most certainly linking the highly individualistic writers to whom we refer as New Critics (or sometimes formalist critics). Major emphases frequently associated with New Criticism include assertion of the organic unity of poetic form and meaning, treatment of poems as dramatized enactments of attitudes, and defense of poetry as a unique form of knowledge.

Selected Readings

Geiger, Don. "Modern Literary Thought: The Consciousness of Abstracting," *Speech Monographs* XX (March 1953), 1–22.
———. "Pluralism in the Interpreter's Search for Sanctions," *The Quarterly Journal of Speech* XLI (February 1955), 43–56.
Ostroff, Anthony. "New Criticism and Oral Interpretation," *Western Speech* XVIII (January 1954), 37–44.
Watkins, Dwight E. "The Relation of the Speaker to his Literature," *The Quarterly Journal of Public Speaking* I (January 1916), 46–51.

The editors asked Professor Geiger if he would care to comment or go beyond what he says in "Oral Interpretation and the 'New Criticism.'" He does so in the next essay, "Interpretation and the Locus of Poetic Meaning." He takes on the crucial question of meaning in the poem. In his previous essay, Professor Geiger suggests we have much to learn from literary theory. After reading this one, we feel literary theorists have much to learn from interpreters. With so many schools of literary analysis today, it is a good feeling to know we are involved in primary criticism, the performance of the poem. It is also exhilarating to know that literary theorists support our kind of criticism. C. S. Lewis certainly does when he says: "The all-important conjunction (Reader Meets Text) never seems to have been allowed to occur of itself and develop spontaneously. Here, plainly, are young people drenched, dizzied, and bedeviled by criticism to a point at which primary experience is no longer possible."*

The last point developed by Professor Geiger becomes crucial. The interpreter's quest is to find the right reading. The poem is the score which the interpreter performs. Different readings are admissible; the question is not which is the *right* reading but which is the *best*.

* C. S. Lewis, *An Experiment in Criticism* (London: Cambridge University Press, 1961), 128–129.

Interpretation and the Locus of Poetic Meaning

In 1950 I referred to the emphasis of New Criticism on "the literary work itself."[1] A less ambiguous reference would have been to "the text itself"; Louise Rosenblatt remarks correctly that for New Criticism "the text is assumed to be the poem."[2] Broadly, the poem is held to be coterminous with the text; the poem's meaning is to be discovered by analysis of the "self-limited verbal context" of the poetic text.[3] There is much good sense in this critical approach, but in solving some problems it awakened attention to others, as we shall see.

For New Criticism, emphasis on the text itself was fundamental, grounding the possibility for an "objective" criticism in contrast to a Romantic "psychological" criticism which located the essential poem either in the privacy of the poet's prior vision and intentions or in the vagaries of individual reader response.[4] Today

[1] Don Geiger, "Oral Interpretation and the 'New Criticism,' " *The Quarterly Journal of Speech,* 36 (1950), 509.

[2] Louise M. Rosenblatt, "The Poem as Event," *College English,* 26 (1964), 127.

[3] See, e.g., John Oliver Perry, "Analysis and Interpretation of Poems by Varied Means," *Approaches to the Poem,* ed. Perry (San Francisco: Chandler, 1965), 13–14.

[4] See W. K. Wimsatt, Jr., *The Verbal Icon* (Lexington: University of Kentucky Press, 1954), 3–39.

most critics grant that the practice of New Criticism did much to correct certain critical excesses associated with Romanticism. But it is widely doubted that New Criticism established sound theoretical grounds for objective criticism—or what here amounts to the same thing, objective interpretation. Reservations have been entered on behalf of the author or the reader, or both author and reader, who are seen by many critics as "cut off" by New Criticism from the poem.[5] The upshot of various objections is to suggest, at the least, that on its honorable retirement as a literary movement New Criticism left the question of the locus of poetic meaning curiously unsettled. It is easier to note the difficulty than to solve it, whether in this or larger space. Hence I shall offer a provisional opinion which, though incompletely argued, may be a useful point of departure for observing some major aspects of the problem.

The position suggested here, with its obvious bearings on the character of reliable interpretation, is roughly this. A poet means what he says in his text, but he has no special province to explain his text's meaning. However it does not follow that the meaning of a poem is a self-contained entity, somehow perfectly lodged only in the text itself apart from its existence as a poet's utterance which may be understood by readers. Instead the locus of poetic meaning is in the communicative process which is completed, as I shall discuss, in reading performance, whether silent or oral. The meaning of a text is fully demonstrated in the responses of readers; but this position does not preclude our thinking that some responses are misleading or in error, or that, among right responses, some of them may be preferable, or qualitatively superior to others.

In considering this perspective, let us first observe the author's relation to his text. E. D. Hirsch, Jr., registers a significant objection to New Criticism on behalf of the author: "What had not been noticed in the earliest enthusiasm for going back 'to what the text says' was that the text had to represent *somebody's* meaning— if not the author's, then the critic's."[6] In Hirsch's opinion New

---

[5] See, e.g., Murray Krieger, *The Tragic Vision* (New York: Holt, Rinehart and Winston, 1960), 229–241, esp. 232.

[6] E. D. Hirsch, Jr., *Validity in Interpretation* (New Haven: Yale University Press, 1967), 3–4.

Criticism failed to recognize that "meaning requires a meaner," thus undermining the possibility for objective interpretation by making a poem's meaning the function of the individual critic's invention.[7]

The objection is a sound one as far as it goes, for surely poetic texts are written by poets, not critics. However to concentrate on "what the text says" need not be understood as an argument to the contrary but rather as an argument that the "meaner" or poet is not a privileged interpreter of his completed text. The proposition is not uniquely applicable to poets. Frequently enough we think that writers or speakers of nonpoetic discourse are not privileged interpreters of their own statements. Monroe Beardsley provides an example in the case of a puzzling sentence uttered by a person explaining something to us: "We ask him what he meant, and after awhile he tells us in different words. Now we can reply, 'Maybe that's what you meant, but that's not what you said,' that is, it's not what the sentence meant."[8] We may easily imagine parallel situations involving poets. For example, an obliging poet might say that he intended a certain puzzling passage to imply such-and-such. Surely we would be interested in his comment and perhaps it would affect our understanding of the doubtful passage. Yet the poet's comment would not preclude our saying, "O thank you, but despite your intention the passage does not imply such-and-such." A large part of creative writing courses and poetry workshops seems to be given over to this kind of exchange: "I didn't intend it, but following our discussion, I see that I achieved this confused expression." In such exchanges we are treating the poet's "intention" as his opinion of what he has actually said. He may be right, but his text is the court of final appeal which he attends as one judge among many.

These examples can scarcely be taken to mean that we are never privileged interpreters of our own utterances. Perhaps in fact we are not: decision on the question awaits a thoroughly satisfactory account of complicated and problematic relations among *thought,*

[7] Hirsch, 234.

[8] Monroe Beardsley, *Aesthetics: Problems in the Philosophy of Criticism* (New York: Harcourt Brace Jovanovich, 1958), 25.

language, forms of discourse, and *meaning.* Meantime we continue to believe that speakers or writers often know what they mean when they say something, and are privileged interpreters of their own statements; that is why, when we are in doubt and they are available to answer, we ask them what they mean.

However, we may detect at least two different major meanings of the notion of the privileged interpreter, depending on whether the speaker thinks that he did not, or on the contrary thinks that he did, state something clearly. (My discussion assumes that he is right in these assumptions.) The first of these cases requires that we modify our belief that a speaker is a privileged interpreter of his utterance; the second seems not very well applicable to poets.

In the first case, explaining my statement to a puzzled listener, I may assume: "I have a clear idea of what I wanted to say without quite yet having said it." This assumption or feeling, though natural, is probably delusory. My more certainly supportable assumption would seem to be something like this: "I am dissatisfied with what I have said, see that there is something wrong with it, and am now busily sorting my mental events in hope of saying something that both other people and I understand." In this situation the speaker's interpretive privilege amounts to the right to make his own revisions. Of course it is not unusual for us to pre-empt even this privilege of the speaker. When we are puzzled by a statement, we may say, "O you mean such-and-such," thereby trying to relieve the speaker from figuring out for himself what he would have liked to mean. Sometimes we are even successful in accomplishing this.

But there is another kind of situation in which we can reasonably think that the speaker is less equivocally a privileged interpreter of his utterance. In this situation the speaker in effect supposes, "I have already said what I mean; since you didn't understand it I will say something else which you and I can agree means the 'same thing' that I stated originally." There are many situations in which this supposition of the speaker is applicable; these are the situations in which we may most certainly consider a speaker a privileged interpreter of his meaning. But the viewpoint depends on the speaker's ability to say the "same thing" the second time around. Consequently, the view seems either inapplicable or only awkwardly applicable to poets. Even were the poet to offer an explanation of his text, neither he nor his reader would be likely to think it the "same thing" as his poem. This position should be a point of doctrine for critics spurning the "heresy of paraphrase"; the poet's paraphrase of his poem is no more likely than the critic's paraphrase to mean the "same thing" as his poem. But even critics who believe that a poem's meaning can be restated in paraphrase do not argue that a paraphrase offers the same content as the poem. Their argument is rather that what they can paraphrase shall be termed the poem's "meaning." But neither the critic who believes that meaning cannot be paraphrased nor the critic who believes that it can be, argues that the poet, already having put in his poem "the best words in the best order,"[9] can put the "same thing" in some other words in some other order.

With this observation we notice still another serious difficulty in treating a poem's meaning as "in" the text itself. Apparently the position can accommodate the poet's ability to mean in his poems what poems can mean, but it puts in jeopardy the critic's claim that he can read them. Presumably we intuit enough of the poem's "total" meaning to assert that our paraphrases and explanations do not reproduce the same thing. We may conclude then that the poem itself is an abstract or ideal entity of which any given interpretation or explanation can at best offer a partial view. Here I can only assert without demonstrating that there is much in New Criticism to suggest that we regard the poem itself, or "real" poem, as an ideal entity.[10] The notion confronts the reader with something of a dilemma. If the "real" poem is an ideal entity, thus presumably having one and only one "total" meaning,

---

[9] The phrase is Coleridge's; as a general view, no critic of poetry is inclined to dispute it.

[10] "Demonstration" would involve analysis of such discussions as those in Rene Wellek and Austin Warren, *Theory of Literature* (New York: Harcourt Brace Jovanovich, 1956), 129–145, and Cleanth Brooks, *The Well Wrought Urn* (New York: Harcourt Brace Jovanovich, 1947), 176–196, esp. 180.

there should be, finally, one and only one correct interpretation of it. But since no explanation can exhaustively reproduce the "real" poem, we cannot say what this correct interpretation will be. Insofar as this is the dilemma of New Criticism, its search for the grounds of objective interpretation may be said to have concluded in the position that the "real" poem eludes our interpretations.

Various efforts have been made to resolve the problem, protecting both the poem's status as an objectively understandable somewhat and the reader's right to understand it. Probably chief among these attempts has been to rely on a variety of experiences or interpretations of individual works. Of this variety some interpretations may seem to us clumsy or merely incorrect, but still others may seem convincing or useful though differing among themselves in this or that feature. Surely there is much good sense in assuming that we may learn a great deal about a poetic text from a number of interpretations or from observations of it from various critical perspectives. But reliance on useful variety only deepens our sense of the theoretical dilemma. There is nothing in the position to establish a logical terminus to the number of experiences by which the "real" poem will be known, and nothing to deny the possibility that some new reading, or fresh critical perspective, however distant in the receding future, may catch new glimpses of the "real" poem.

In still another approach Professor Rosenblatt offers a usefully suggestive resolution of the dilemma. Like many other critics she finds intolerable a treatment of the poem as an "ideal entity," which "neglects the role of the reader," his own creativity and background of personal experience, and situates the poem "somewhere as an object, separate and complete like the moon, if only partially seen at any time by any one reader." In Professor Rosenblatt's opinion the error lies in the identification by New Criticism of the poem with the text, and to correct it she suggests that we distinguish between them. Thus the word "poem" should "designate an involvement of both reader and text"; the poem is a certain "event in time," a "compenetration of a reader and a text."[11]

---

[11] Rosenblatt, 127–128.

There are some obvious difficulties in this position, according to which one text may afford a number of poems; indeed, as many poems as there are readings which show appropriate attention to the text, which is to be considered as "a 'control,' a blueprint, a guide."[12] This is an unusual way to conceive of poems and of course we should want a compelling reason to forego our ordinary assumption, merely shared by New Critics, that one text yields one poem. But if our position entails calling every appropriate reading or interpretation of a text a poem, we must question whether we have drawn a true distinction or merely termed "poems" what most other critics call "reliable," "good" or "valid" interpretations. Furthermore, if a "poem" is the product of a reader's creative appropriation of a "text," it may be hard theoretically to account for maverick readings. We should expect an honest reader to believe that he has been "guided" or "controlled" by the text in rolling his own "poem," no matter how outlandish his product might seem to the generality of readers. The notion of the text as a control or guide is provocative; its suggestions at least are much to my liking. The problem of course is to explain, without falling back on a conception of the text's total meaning as a self-enclosed entity or thing-in-itself, how a text can control a reading.

Although Professor Rosenblatt does not seriously attempt such an explanation, there is much promise, I think, in her general insistence on the poem as a communicative expression. This emphasis touches on the point of genuine difficulty in attributing a poem's meaning to the text itself.

I believe that more certainly useful than Professor Rosenblatt's particular conclusions is her general insistence on the poem as a communicative expression. This emphasis touches on the point of genuine difficulty, brought out so clearly by Professor Rosenblatt, in attributing a poem's meaning to the text itself. What was "wrong" with New Criticism was not that it identified a poem with a text, but the "wrong" was in the implication, often permitted by such phrases as "in the text" or "intrinsic meaning," that the text's total meaning is an ideal entity, only some of which can get into

[12] Rosenblatt, 126.

a reader's understanding. But possibly we can avoid such theoretical embarrassments if we consider the meaning of a poetic text—to shift Professor Rosenblatt's emphasis into the more familiar identification of a text with a poem—as a function of its use or communicative status. In this view, broadly, the text itself (merely marks on paper until invested with meaning) is its author's utterance which means what readers can reasonably take it to mean. This is a rather vague proposition which I now hope to clarify, even though my discussion here can merely suggest without fully listing the "rules" of communication according to which we can agree whether or not a given interpretation is reasonable.

The position, as I should like it understood, derives from the particular analysis of language initiated in the later philosophical writings of Ludwig Wittgenstein.[13] Through a rich variety of examples, Wittgenstein shows the muddles we get into if we identify "meanings" with "such entities as physical objects, 'concepts' in the 'mind,' or 'states of affairs' in the physical world";[14] the way out of these muddles, he suggests, is to talk about the way in which words and sentences are "used."[15]

It is of more than passing interest to notice that some of the leading ideas of New Criticism reinforce this view. The attack on the "intentional fallacy," for example, is an argument that we cannot discover the meaning of a poem by reference to some concept in the "mind" of the poet prior to his composition. Again, the stress on contextual determination of the meaning of words, sentences and "parts" in a poem—so important an emphasis that, considered as a theory of poetry, New Criticism is sometimes referred to as "contextualism"[16]—bears significant similarities to discussion by Wittgenstein and his philosophic followers of the

[13] See esp. Ludwig Wittgenstein, *Philosophical Investigations,* Third Ed. G. E. M. Anscombe, tr. (New York: Macmillan, 1958).

[14] See John Lyons, *Introduction to Theoretical Linguistics* (London: Cambridge University Press, 1968) 411.

[15] See Lyons, 410–411.

[16] See Murray Krieger, "After the New Criticism," *The Massachusetts Review* IV (1962), 187.

"use" of words. Parallels like these suggest that in also forwarding a version of the poem as an abstract entity, New Criticism relied on traditional "signification" theories of meaning which their own insights into poetry rendered suspect. But here I will not speculate further on the point. Rather, I shall discuss briefly a few aspects of "meaning" which seem to me compatible with Wittgenstein's analysis, and probably the result of it—though I do not insist that either Wittgenstein or philosophers influenced by him would approve my conclusions. Certainly they would think, as I do, that the points I mention concerning "meaning" are impoverished outside the context of Wittgenstein's own speculations. My justification is that the matters I mention seem to bear productively on our understanding the grounds of reliable interpretation of poetry. These matters may be put broadly into three propositions: "meaning" is indeterminate; "meaning" depends on "use"; "understanding" involves a correct or right response to meaning. As we shall see, these are closely related ideas.

Meaning is indeterminate in that each of us has a somewhat personal response to particular words and sentences. John Lyons suggests that if we were to say to someone something as apparently obvious as "Bring me the red book that is on the table upstairs," and examine him closely on his understanding, we should expect to reach a point "where something he did or said would show that his 'understanding' of these words is somewhat different from ours." However such variations, though factually descriptive of reactions to utterance, are largely irrelevant to efficient communication; "the speakers of the language in question are in sufficient agreement about the 'use' of words (what they refer to, what they imply, etc.) to prevent 'misunderstandings'."[17]

This "agreement" amounts to acknowledgment that various rules, principles, or conventions affecting the use of words and sentences govern the communication of meaning.[18] In effect, these rules

[17] Lyons, 411.

[18] See P. F. Strawson, "Review of Wittgenstein's *Philosophical Investigations*," *Wittgenstein: The Philosophical Investigations,* ed. George Pitcher (Garden City, N.Y.: Doubleday, 1966), 36–38.

are criteria for settling "misunderstandings." Without such rules the indeterminacy of meaning would be, logically, limitless; that is to say, communication would be impossible. Hence it is not an argument about communication—but a statement of its necessary condition—to say that conventions concerning use control the power of language-utterances to convey meaning.

One of the most important of these conventions or principles is, I think, that words and sentences derive central aspects of their meaning from the kinds of discourse in which they appear. Thus, considered as a command, our sentence about the red book on the table will mean one thing; as a request, it will mean something different. In a novel, the chief meaning of the same sentence might be what it suggests of the character of the speaker or his relation to the person to whom he is speaking.

In referring to kinds of discourse it is important to remember that we are speaking of characteristic tendencies rather than absolute differences. It is not a denial of the value of making broad distinctions such as those mentioned, to observe that a particular text or utterance of a given kind is likely to be a hybrid. In a closer analysis of utterance, Wittgenstein is surely right to suggest that "there are *countless* kinds and countless different kinds of use of what we call 'symbols,' 'words,' 'sentences.' And this multiplicity is not something fixed, given once for all, but new types of language, new language-games, as we may say, come into existence, and others become obsolete and get forgotten."[19] Thus it is scarcely surprising when we note that a certain informational report is tinged with "poetry" or that a particular poem forthrightly conveys information or offers instruction affecting behavior and the like.

In turning attention to what it means to "understand" utterance, we may be most forcibly struck by the usual ease with which we recognize the countless uses and kinds of use of language-utterances. We can only conclude that to know a given language is to know its uses. We do not make a conscious check-list of these uses; they are internalized as we learn the language. Presumably we know more about these uses than we can quickly explain. (Thus

[19] Wittgenstein, 11.

theory of meaning is the effort to make explicit what in significant ways we already "know.") In ordinary conversation, for example, we do not doubt in order to establish as fact that the noises we volley back and forth are invested with sharable meanings; we simply share meanings. As members of a given speech-community we typically take for granted that we "understand" one another's meanings. To generalize these ordinary cases we may say that "understanding" is a matter of correct or right response to a given use or uses of language-utterances.[20]

We find a suggestion of the value of this notion of "understanding" in Lyons's comment that "we have no direct evidence about the understanding of utterances, only about their *misunderstanding*—when something 'goes wrong' in the process of communication."[21] Let us apply this conclusion to our sentence about the red book on the table. Ordinarily we wouldn't expect much to "go wrong" in the communication of this sentence but we can invent a little trouble for illustrative purposes. The person to whom the sentence is directed is uncertain whether the table is in the north room, the south room, or the room in the attic; moreover he's not altogether sure whether what's wanted is the red book or the book he read recently. But after some discussion and "clarification" his questions cease. Our question is whether he has now "understood" the sentence; the answer is far from obvious. He may not act on the directive; still, that is not a certain proof that he does not "understand" the sentence. He may not act because he wishes to tease the speaker, or perhaps he becomes forgetful on his way upstairs. Also his reason for not acting may be that even though in one sense he "understands" the sentence, in another sense he does not; for example, other persons may think the sentence a polite request, but he may take it as an abrupt command demeaning his dignity. Even if he responds correctly to the sentence—that is, brings the book to the speaker—he may slam it down because he has mistaken an expression of legitimate need for lazy tyranny. There are many such possibilities which we need not proliferate

[20] See Strawson, 34–38.
[21] Lyons, 411.

to suggest the many ambiguities involved in the meaning of "understanding." In the case of the sentence mentioned, the most certain point seems to be that at least its "understanding" has *not* been demonstrated until the book is brought to the speaker; that is, until there has been a correct, right, or successful response to the particular language-utterance. We may say then, if with some caution, that although it may not be *all* that is involved in "understanding," correct response is its necessary component and final demonstration.[22]

"Understanding" as right response is most evident in cases where language is used imperatively: bring the book, pass the salt, shut the door. Other uses of language will of course require other kinds of response, often more subtle and complex. For example, we might demonstrate our understanding of a difficult philosophical text by paraphrase, adducing fresh examples, and the like. I do not of course insist on the soundness of that mode of response to philosophy, but the example suggests that right response or understanding will be adapted to particular uses of language.

Although this brief discussion of the relations of "use," "meaning" and "understanding" is scarcely conclusive, I shall hope it sufficient to suggest its possible value in application to interpreting the meaning of poems. We have touched on various difficulties in assuming that a poem's meaning is authorized by either the author or the reader or the text itself. These difficulties are of a sort not easily dispelled. Yet we may at least get a fresh grip on the question of the locus of poetic meaning, and perhaps solutions to some of the attendant problems, if we think of meaning as rooted in the communicative process. In this view a poem or poetic text, as an author's language-utterance, means what its "use" allows in its communication to his readers.

In exploring this view, with its implications for reliable interpretation of poetry, we will ask these questions: How is language used in the poem? How do we respond to it, when responding rightly? The questions do not predict the answers, and I will conclude by quickly sketching the broad outlines of only one position. Nevertheless it is, I think, a view that would be shared or at least

[22] See Strawson, 35.

accounted for in their personal perspectives by oral interpreters generally. My points, by no means novel, are these. In poetry, language is used dramatically; it yields dramatic meaning. Our correct or right response is to perform it; we demonstrate our understanding in performance. To reduce ambiguities, I take "performance" to include silent reading of a sort paralleling oral interpretation; also performance is intimately related to paraphrase rather than being a simple alternative to it.

In treating the foregoing position as that of the oral interpreter, I am not suggesting that it is his private possession. (Perhaps I need not add, Thank Heaven!) In commenting on poetry as well as its oral interpretation as a tissue of attitudes, actions, and properties of objects I was, in 1950, placing a dot on a map of poetic meaning already well charted by literary critics.[23] To recall the territory, we need only remind ourselves of the care with which modern critics, including many other than New Critics, have attended literary works (or in the extended sense of the term, poetry) as, variously, a complex of attitudes, gesture, symbolic action, verbal icon, dramatic discourse, imitation or analogue of life, presentational symbol and myth. Each of these general descriptions emphasizes the power of poetry to convey the sense of existential presence— of "characters" and "speakers" and what they say, perceive, do, and feel. To notice this emphasis should not mask the many differences, including crucial ones, in critical positions suggested by these several general descriptions and definitions. But even the differences enhance our appreciation of the deep fund of analysis from which we may come to think of poetic meaning as essentially dramatic, iconic, presentational, offering "a many-faceted reflection of the fullness of experience."[24]

It is scarcely remarkable that in a period stressing iconic aspects of poetry we might freshly appreciate the values of performance in interpreting poetic meaning. Insofar as poetry's meaning

[23] Geiger, 510–512.

[24] Murray Krieger, "Problem of Meaning," *Encyclopedia of Poetry and Poetics,* ed. Alex Preminger (Princeton: Princeton U. Press, 1965), 478.

is dramatic, we do well to perform it; if the job of an interpreter of a poem is to illuminate presentational meaning, a likely way of proceeding is to present it. With much justification we can see in oral interpretation a suggestive model for right reading of poetry, our correct response to it, though the usual reading is a private, silent performance. For some persons there may be an initial difficulty in thinking of silent reading of poetry as performance. But some introspection into their own most absorbed reading of poems —with its special savoring of details and alertness to tonal modulations deeply implicated in patterns of meaning and sound—should reveal an act of attention for which the term "performance" is aptly descriptive.

To insist on performance as the final, right response to poetic meaning may seem to thrust oral interpretation into competition as an interpretive mode with critiques or critical paraphrases of poems. The case is rather that they are intimately related activities. In one sense written and oral interpretation simply serve different, if complementary, functions in understanding poetry. In a critique or paraphrase we can indicate significant areas of implied meaning much more directly than in oral interpretation. Interpretation of almost any poem, randomly selected, serves as a typical illustration. In Henry Reed's "Naming of Parts," for example, the speaker's dizzy, almost hysterical sense of physical and spiritual frustration emerges implicitly from a set or cluster of "masturbational" images playing on "finger," "thumb," and "slide" in contrast to another cluster of images dominated by "gardens" and bees "fumbling" and "assaulting" the flowers. I but touch on a paraphrase which should indicate still more intricately connected layers of meaning in a poem revealing an instance of the conflict between the destructive sterility of war and the life-giving beauty and fecundity of nature. But the example is sufficient; obviously oral interpretation does not, as a good critical paraphrase would, spell out such matters. On the other hand oral interpretation can indicate what paraphrase "comes to"; oral interpretation can suggest more fully and with finer shades of implication than paraphrase the feeling or experience of the poem's dramatic speaker in meaning what he says in the words of the poem.

The latter observation suggests that we may best understand *paraphrase* and *performance* as aspects of a process in understanding poems. As Beardsley describes the "process of explication," its purpose is of course more adequate reading of the poem. For Beardsley, "to read a poem—that is, to sound the words, not necessarily aloud, and understand them—is to perform it;" and explication-statements are "about how, in the colloquial sense, the poem is to be performed." Thus, "the explicator is something like the music teacher or coach."[25] But relations between critique or paraphrase and performance are even more intimate than is suggested by the coach-player metaphor which indicates a linear movement from understanding to performance. In fact performance is involved in the process of coming to understand the poem as well as being the final demonstration of understanding.[26] We do not, for example, begin understanding a poem by paraphrasing but by reading it, and as we read we develop a sense of the whole in terms of which we may reread more fully and accurately. The oral interpreter preparing a poem for public performance is necessarily aware of the oscillatory movement, or interpretation, between thoughts about, and performance of, a piece. As he practices, the oral interpreter achieves effects according to what he "understands," but often enough as he hears or feels the effects he produces the oral interpreter revises his sense of the poem's meanings. Thus we may say that oral interpretation, like silent performance, is the final product of a "complex dialectical process" in which our understanding both "grasps the meaning of a sentence, and somehow in a reverse direction supplies the attitude and emphasis which alone can make the written word meaningful."[27]

I trust that in emphasizing the importance of performance in understanding poems, I have not suggested that ideally there should be one and only one right performance of a poem. Once we are

[25] Beardsley, 145.

[26] Cf. Geiger, *The Sound Sense and Performance of Literature* (Glenview, Ill.: Scott Foresman, 1963), 2–3.

[27] Richard E. Palmer, *Hermeneutics* (Evanston: Northwestern U. Press, 1969), 16.

satisfied that the "real" meaning of the poem does not lie some-where or another outside the communicative process, it becomes much more sensible for us to expect a range of permissible or right readings.[28] This does not mean that each of us should insulate himself in his own interpretation, even if it is a "permissible" one, from other opinion and performance of a poem. Of course we learn from one another about poems in discussing and performing them, and what we learn may well affect our own performances. But our possible growth in awareness is not, I think, of this or that aspect of an ideal entity forever beyond actual reproduction. Rather, we may learn from one another the meanings which a dramatic use of language can release into the communicative relation between poets saying their texts and readers reading them. We neither can, nor need to, predict how many right readings of a poem there can be; we will identify them if, as, and when they are presented. In the meantime we need not look beyond what we understand for "something else" somehow in the poem on principle, or concern ourselves with how the poem may be understood a century hence.

In closing I note that a reasoned tolerance for variation is perhaps a professional necessity for the oral interpreter. Over a period of years he will hear and produce not only some wrong or misleading performances of the same poem, but also some variety of right or successful performances. As he gratefully consigns his wrong performances to oblivion, the oral interpreter on occasion may need a little theory to sustain his memory of a few right ones.

Selected Readings

Ohmann, Richard. "Speech Arts and the Definition of Literature," *Philosophy and Rhetoric,* IV (Winter 1971), 1–19.

Parrish, W. M. "Getting the Meaning in Interpretation," *The Southern Speech Journal,* XXXIII (Spring 1968), 178–186.

Salper, Donald R. "The Sounding of a Poem," *The Quarterly Journal of Speech,* LVII (April 1971), 129–133.

[28] Cf. Geiger, "The Oral Interpreter as Creator," *The Speech Teacher,* III (1954), esp. 270–272.

A poem is made of words. For the most part, we know every word in the poem. But compressed and shoved around within the poem, the words grow unfamiliar as they sometimes attain a higher order of meaning. The interpreter encounters this special arrangement of words and discovers that some of them have become literary symbols. With some research, the interpreter can gain a particular manner of understanding the symbol, an understanding he can talk about or write about. It is not an easy task, but it is easier than meeting the responsibility of making the symbol meaningful in performance.

Professor Frances L. McCurdy deals with the complex problem of symbols in poetry. She speaks of a commitment that the interpreter must make when he puts himself in the position of the poem. Unlike the literary critic who talks about symbols, the interpreter must experience and reveal the symbol in performance. Professor McCurdy shows us how.

FRANCES L. McCURDY

The Ultimate Commitment

The position of this brief essay is that an ultimate commitment is required of the oral interpreter who would penetrate and share the complexities of poetic symbols. To be sure, much literature is complex, and, according to Robert Frost, "Every single poem written regular is a symbol small or great. . . ."[1] The present concern, however, is with a more limited definition of symbol[2] which excludes symbol as an act of language forming or as a synonym for metaphor, allegory, or image.[3]

Defining the symbol is somewhat like trying to define love. It can be better understood through encounter than by abstract definition. D. H. Lawrence asserts:

You can't give a great symbol a "meaning" any more than you can give a cat a "meaning." Symbols are organic units of consciousness with a life of their own, and you can never explain them away, because their value is dynamic, emotional, belonging to the sense-consciousness of the body and soul, and not simply mental.[4]

M. H. Abrams defines the symbol "as a word or phrase signifying an object which itself has significance."[5] This definition is adequate for the fraternity man's pin as an emblem of his group affiliation, for a flag as emblematic of a nation, and for the wedding band as

---

[1] Robert Frost, from the essay, "The Constant Symbol," *The Poems of Robert Frost* (New York: Modern Library, 1946). Reprinted in *Literary Criticism,* ed. Maurice Beebe (Belmont, Cal.: Wadsworth, 1960), 16.

[2] This article is a revision of an essay by the writer, "Reading Symbols of Poetry," *The Speech Teacher,* XV, 1 (January 1966), 42–48. The revised essay is printed by arrangement with the Speech Communication Association.

[3] The Symbolists of the nineteenth century wished poetry to be true to the world of ideal beauty. They hoped to take back from music what had been lost to it. For a history of the Symbolists and its relation to poetic symbols see C. M. Bowra, *The Heritage of Symbolism* (London: Macmillan, 1943).

[4] D. H. Lawrence, from "The Dragon of the Apocalypse" (1930) in his *Selected Literary Criticism,* ed. Anthony Beal (London: William Heinemann, 1955). Beebe, 31.

[5] M. H. Abrams, *A Glossary of Literary Terms* (New York: Holt, Rinehart and Winston, 1958), 95.

signifying an unending circle. It hardly accounts for the extension of associations aroused by great symbols in poetry. With a poetic symbol, associations go beyond a particular attitude or experience to connote the universal in the particular. An assertion about loneliness or grief does not recreate the experience of loneliness or grief, but through the symbol the poet may evoke a response to the unsayable complex of the experience. A symbol may be crudely defined as something that means itself and more than itself. William Blake's rose and invisible worm are obviously more than, as well as, their referents. Andrew Marvell's drop of dew is dew, but it is also soul, a vision of life, and perhaps an intimation of immortality.

The symbol is distinguished from metaphor in its recurrence and persistence. Metaphor invokes a single association; the symbol recurs as presentation and representation. Limited to its function as an unstated analogy, metaphor can be removed, or substituted for, without destroying the poem, although a successful metaphor is also an integral part of the poetic experience. In Robert Lowell's "Skunk Hour," the love cars that "lay together, hull to hull" form a vivid metaphor of mechanical and hollow seduction.[6] For his metaphor of the cars—though the substitutions are less effective— skeletons in embrace or mannequins flung together in a dark corner could be substituted. The mother skunk with her column of kittens is, on the other hand, an indispensable symbol. Like Ezra Pound's "meaning," it comes up with roots and associations.[7] Evoking both feelings and thoughts, the march of the skunks is the point of the poem; that march symbolizes the defiance of the persona who also refuses to scare in the midst of madness and decay.

The symbol not only evokes emotional response, it can act as an intellectual stimulus. William Butler Yeats, who has written more and more clearly about the symbol than any other poet, asserts that, "all sounds, all colours, all forms, either because of their pre-

[6] Robert Lowell, "Skunk Hour," *The Contemporary Poet as Artist and Critic,* ed. Anthony Ostroff (Boston: Little, Brown, 1964), 82–83.

[7] Ezra Pound, *ABC of Reading* (New York: New Directions, 1960), 36.

ordained energies or because of long association, evoke indefinable and yet precise emotions . . ." and illustrates:

> If I say 'white' or 'purple' in an ordinary line of poetry, they evoke emotions so exclusively that I cannot say why they move me; but if I bring them into the same sentence with such obvious intellectual symbols as a cross or a crown of thorns, I think of purity and sovereignty. Furthermore, innumerable meanings, which are held to 'white' or 'purple' by bonds of subtle suggestion, and alike in the emotions and in the intellect, move visibly through my mind. . . .[8]

An example of a symbol that is both intellectual and emotional is Percy Bysshe Shelley's "Ozymandias." The sneer of cold command stamped on the shattered visage arouses dislike, but the dominant response is the intellectual recognition of the irony in the situation. The emotions are less significant than the thoughts evoked by the symbol of the impermanence of power held by the mightiest ruler and, by association, the mightiest nation.

In Shelley's poem the symbol is obvious, yet even that obvious meaning is working beneath the surface. John Ciardi, in his analysis of Robert Frost's "Stopping by Woods on a Snowy Evening," notes that "even the TV audience" can see that the poem suggests meanings far beyond anything specifically referred to in the narrative.[9] Interpretation of the symbol demands of the reader more sensitivity than William Wordsworth ascribed to Peter Bell to whom:

> A primrose on the river's brim
> A yellow primrose was to him
> And it was nothing more.

In this age of introspection, however, we are more likely to be over-preoccupied by symbols than to be unaware of them. We may

---

[8] William Butler Yeats, "The Symbolism of Poetry" (1900), *Essays* (New York: Macmillan, 1924), 188–202. Beebe, 28–29.

[9] John Ciardi, "Robert Frost: The Way to the Poem," *The Saturday Review* (April 12, 1958), 13.

make symbols out of primroses where none exist. A morbid pre-occupation with the subliminal that leads a reader to see a tree as the cross and a billboard as man's enslavement to machines in the lines "I think that I shall never see/ A billboard lovely as a tree" is absurd. We can enjoy Ogden Nash's "Song of the Open Road" for its light irony, just as we can enjoy many other poems for their suspense, wry humor, or individual charm without searching for non-existent symbolic meanings. Not all stories or poems are designed for exploration of multiple levels of meaning. In his preface to *Adventures of Huckleberry Finn,* Samuel Clemens warned, "Persons attempting to find a motive in this narrative will be prosecuted; persons attempting to find a moral in it will be banished; persons attempting to find a plot in it will be shot."[10]

Despite the threat, readers find plot, moral, and symbol in *Huckleberry Finn.* Northrop Frye points out that it is impossible for any reader today to respond to a work of art with complete or genuine naiveté.[11] We cannot forget all that we have previously read and learned when we pick up a new novel or poem, and we do not suffer from this condition. Literature with enduring appeal is likely to offer multiple levels. Below the surface of plot and direct statement, roots and associations are working. Commitment to the full experience of a work of art does not lessen but rather expands enjoyment of it.

Interpretation of such generally accepted symbols as the seasons, roads, clouds, and shadows is a part of the speech of every day. Symbols that allude to people, places, myths, such as Molly Bloom, Babbitt, Byzantium, or the Phoenix are also generally familiar or readily yield their significance after a little search. But when a poet presents his vision in symbols private to himself, difficulties arise. When his symbols are evoked from his own ex-

[10] Mark Twain, *The Adventures of Huckleberry Finn* (New York: The New American Library, A Signet Classic, Eighth Ed., 1963), Preface.

[11] Northrop Frye, "The Road of Excess," *Myth and Symbol: Critical Approaches and Applications,* ed. Bernice Slote (Lincoln: University of Nebraska Press, 1963), 10.

periences and his readers are remote from those experiences, they must retrace the poet's associations in order to interpret his work. The kind of retracing necessary for such symbols can be demonstrated through a study of Yeats's "The Song of Wandering Aengus," quoted in full in the following lines:

> I went out to the hazel wood,
> Because a fire was in my head,
> And cut and peeled a hazel wand,
> And hooked a berry to a thread:
> And when white moths were on the wing,
> And moth-like stars were flickering out
> I dropped the berry in a stream
> And caught a little silver trout.
>
> When I had laid it on the floor
> I went to blow the fire aflame,
> But something rustled on the floor,
> And someone called me by my name;
> It had become a glimmering girl
> With apple blossoms in her hair
> Who called me by my name and ran
> And faded through the brightening air.
>
> Though I am old with wandering
> Through hollow lands and hilly lands,
> I will find out where she has gone,
> And kiss her lips and take her hands;
> And walk among long dappled grass,
> And pluck till time and times are done
> The silver apples of the moon,
> The golden apples of the sun.[12]

On the surface level the poem is a story told by the minstrel Aengus of his never ending search for the glimmering girl who

[12] W. B. Yeats, "The Song of Wandering Aengus" from *Collected Poems* (New York: Macmillan © 1950), 57–58, quoted by permission of The Macmillan Company. I have chosen this example because it seems to offer difficulty in its use of mythology.

had been magically transformed from a little silver trout. Though his search has continued for many years, he remains strong in his determination to find the girl and claim her for his own in that timeless land where apples of silver and gold are to be had for the picking.

The poem is obviously more than that; and since at the time this poem was written Yeats commonly used symbols from Irish mythology to present his poetic visions, we can expect to find the key to his symbols in that lore. Not all readers are familiar with Celtic mythology but the symbols do not present too much difficulty since they are taken from a common stock and are mutually related. In Celtic legends Aengus is the master of love and the hazel wand is his emblem, but if we read the poem simply as a romance we will be misled; we must search further. The hazel has other associations. It bears after nine years, and nine is the number sacred to the muses. The nut in Celtic language is a symbol of wisdom; hazel nuts are associated with knowledge of the arts and sciences. (Robert Graves in *The White Goddess* points out the vitality of the nut as a symbol of concentrated logic in our modern reference to "putting the matter in a nutshell.") Traditionally, the hazel nut is associated with poetic knowledge and inspiration. *The Rennes Dinnesenchas,* an early Irish treatise, describes a fountain over which hung nine hazel trees, sacred to the poetic arts. These trees simultaneously produced flowers and nuts, signifying beauty and wisdom.[13]

Both the hazel and the apple are sacred trees in Irish mythology. The hazel is the poet's tree; the apple has multiple associations with immortality. An old Welsh legend suggests the nature of poetry in the story of a bard who saved himself from being carried off to the infernal regions by catching hold of an apple tree and clinging to it. Being too sinful for heaven, yet safe from hell, he gained immortality, ever after haunting the earth as a will-of-the-wisp.[14] The apple, mentioned three times in Yeats's poem —first as blossoms in the hair of the glimmering girl and later as

---

[13] Robert Graves, *The White Goddess* (New York: Vintage Books, 1959), 68, 187–189.

[14] *Ibid.,* pp. 263 and 271.

the fruit of both the moon and the sun—is an ancient and wide-spread symbol of immortality. When the apple is cut in half, the position of the seeds gives to each half the appearance of a five pointed star, an emblem of immortality. Graves suggests additional associations with the apple. The word *apol* may be a chance approximation to Apollo, god of the sun and poetry; further, the apples given to Hercules by the Three Daughters of the West made him immortal.[15]

The glimmering girl clearly suggests the White Goddess of poetry. Her Aegean prototype was a Moon Goddess, the moon being associated with poetry. But Apollo, god of the sun, is also traditionally a god of poetry and the nine muses are his ladies-in-waiting. The confusion over the relative authority of the feminine or masculine influence is clarified by an examination of the concept of fatherhood in myth. In early mythology, one triple goddess ruled. She was goddess of the muse, goddess of the earth and goddess of the moon and sky. As goddess of the moon, her Star-Son and the Serpent alternately enjoyed her favors, symbolizing the dying and rebirth of the year. Poets derived their power from this Moon Goddess. Gradually, however, as the concept of fatherhood was introduced into mythology the Thunder-Child superseded both the Star-Son and the Serpent, and marrying his mother, begot sons and daughters. Among the sons was a god of poetry, music, art and science, who was eventually recognized as the Sun-God.[16] Yet, the ascendancy of the Sun-God did not erase the association by poets of the moon with magic and romance.

The transformation by enchantment of an animal into human form, or the reverse, is a familiar device in fable and myth. For example, an allusion to the frog prince is immediately understood. Less well known is the narrative of the early poet, Callimachus, who sang of a maiden pursued through the changing seasons until she escaped her would-be captor by transforming herself into a trout.[17] No evidence exists to directly link Callimachus's narrative

---

[15] *Ibid.*, p. 276.
[16] *Ibid.*, pp. 424–454.
[17] *Ibid.*, p. 447.

to the experience of Aengus, but Yeats's poem bears a strong similarity to it in its reversed transformation and in the long pursuit with the goal of physical and spiritual union voiced in the desire to "kiss her lips and take her hands."

The metaphoric fire in the head of Aengus does not require a search into legend; it connotes the fever of creative energy, perhaps the Promethean fire. The moth-like stars reinforce the earlier image of white moths on the wing and forecast the flight of the girl who fades into the distance like a will-of-the-wisp.

The symbols in the poem clarify and expand the experience. They can not be too tightly tied to a one-to-one allegorical relationship, but must be permitted as much freedom of association as their context allows. The poem is obviously about the quest of a poet. The quest is the recurring and persistent symbol. It governs and ties together all the other symbols. The persona of the poem is a minstrel singing of his long search for the poetic muse and of his certainty that he will someday find her and know immortality. The apples are no ordinary fruit to satisfy physical hunger; they are the gift of immortality from the gods of the sun and the moon. Through the interpretation of the symbols, Yeats's vision emerges as the poet's never ending pursuit of the poetic ideal. It is a search begun in wonder and pursued with constancy. The meaning is universalized as the dream of all men who pursue the unattainable.

Discovery of the meaning is not the end, however, for the oral interpreter, but the means to the end of performance. Prior to any discussion of the process of sharing through performance, the question of the wisdom of attempting to share complex poems through oral reading should be raised. The view of the writer is that the performance of any poem, either complex or simple, completes imaginatively the total act of the poem. Performance requires the reader to place himself in the position of the poem, identifying himself with it and responding to its complexities. The performer seeks the same kind of cooperation with the poem that the social psychologist describes when he says that cooperation is possible only when each acting individual ascertains the intention of the acts of others and makes his response on the basis of that intention.

The performance tests the reader's ability to ascertain the intention of the act that is the poem and to respond visually and audibly in conformity with it.

The symbol is generally considered the richest of the poetical figures. It suggests more than it says. Through it the poet can evoke multiple meanings and feelings. He can create patterns of thought and feeling that did not previously exist. The resulting complexity should not, however, be an insurmountable barrier to performance. The symbol is there to be experienced rather than talked about. Suggesting its multiple meanings through the language of the poem is a challenge to the reader to penetrate the symbols, to feel and think himself into them, and to recreate them for the listener. The audience of the oral interpreter may be only himself; oral reading assists most people in imaginative completion of the symbolic action, and sharing the experience with the poem is sufficient reason for an oral reading. But "audience" generally implies listeners other than the single reader, and I shall use the word in that sense.

Although each poem presents individual problems for the reader, an illustration of the way in which one poem can be shared may be applicable to others. Since the "Song of Wandering Aengus" was used to illustrate penetration of symbols, the same poem will be used as an example for performance.

The reader should probably assume that his listeners are unfamiliar with Celtic mythology and aid them by identifying Aengus and the White Goddess of poetry. His reading will no doubt gain if he also explains some of the associations with the hazel and the apple, but for the most part, the performance of the poem itself will evoke feelings and thoughts without extended explanations.

Tone, important in all poems, is especially important in this poem. The teller of this tale is sharing an experience that has changed his life. He begins in a relaxed, rather matter-of-fact tone to tell how he went out to fish. Though the experience is commonplace, no ordinary man is telling the story. He is a man with "a fire in his head," sensitive to the elfin quality of the scene. The first two lines of the second stanza shift the scene from the hazel wood to the singer's cottage (he speaks of the floor), but the tone is unchanged. The excitement heightens with lines three and four of stanza two. A note of puzzlement is heard, then wonder, desire and longing as the lines rush headlong forward (with no end punctuation) to the fulcrum at the end of the second stanza.

A pause before the third stanza and a slower rate of reading the final eight lines are indicated by the sense as well as the rhythm of the poem. The mood has shifted. The singer, who had almost forgotten his fictive audience in the second stanza, once more becomes aware of it. Though he has grown old, he is neither depressed nor feeble. He remains ardent in his pursuit of the goddess of poetry and the apples of immortality. The final lines carry a tone of affirmation as he savors the joys awaiting him. Despite the reduced tension at the beginning of the final stanza, the climax again builds as the poet envisions the fulfillment of his quest.

The rhythm of the poem also demands the attention of the sharer. Yeats said of rhythm, "the purpose . . . it has always seemed to me, is to prolong the moment of contemplation . . . by hushing us with an alluring monotony while it holds us waking by variety. . . ."[18] Aengus's tale has the dominant rhythm of a William Morris song. It is a simple melody. The pattern is iambic with anapests to quicken and give variety. The phrases "White moths" and "moth-like stars" demand attention by introducing two and three stressed words together. The regularity of the iambs and anapests in the last four lines of the second stanza and the last five lines of the last stanza require the reader to compensate by slowing his rate and increasing stress on the key words. The lack of variety in rhythm is compensated for to a considerable degree by the alliteration in such phrases as "glimmering girl" and the long vowels in "name," "faded," "though" and "brightening" and by the repetition of the key words "time" and "apples" in the final stanza.

Sound reinforces sense in "wandering," the only word at the end of a line to end in an unstressed syllable, and in such other words as "flickering," "rustled," and "faded." Sounds are generally grouped to create a smooth, almost singing effect. The poem is obviously a song.

Since a primary value of the symbol is its multiple meaning,

18 Yeats, "From the Symbolism of Poetry," Beebe, p. 28.

the performance should retain some of the ambiguities. Though the quest symbol is in itself unambiguous, it may evoke different responses from varying listeners. Katherine Loesch has demonstrated that the oral reader is not forced to clarify every object and attitude within the poem.[19] Shifts of pitch, stress and juncture in the lines "Someone called me by my name," can heighten the ambiguity rather than remove it. For example,

> And someone / called me / by my name;
> . . . .
> . . . . and ran //
> And faded // through the brightening air.[20]

with its rising inflection on *someone* increases the possibilities of the identity of the caller just as the sustained ending suggests possible anticipation of fulfillment or perhaps disappointment at her retreat.

Virtually all symbolic poems can be shared if the reader commits himself to penetrating the symbols, feeling and thinking his way into the poem, and completing the gesture of the language in the poem. Listeners, who have varied imaginations and experiences, have varied abilities and willingness to commit themselves; but even if all the richness of the poem is not shared, much can be revealed through a good oral reading, and the listener may receive what his abilities allow.

[19] Katherine T. Loesch, "Literary Ambiguity and Oral Performance," *The Quarterly Journal of Speech,* LI, 3 (October 1965), 258–267.

[20] The symbols are from George L. Trager and Henry Lee Smith, Jr., *An Outline of English Literature Studies in Linguistics: Occasional Papers,* No. 3 (Norman, Okla.: Battenbeurg Press, 1951). The four stresses are primary /´/; secondary /^/; tertiary /`/; and weak /ˇ/. Pitches are from highest to lowest as /1/; /2/; /3/; and /4/. Junctures are in order of length /1/; /11/; and /#/. I omit weak stresses and pitch notations.

A poem, as well as the poetic play about which T. S. Eliot was speaking, provides " 'several levels of significance,' plot for the simple, character for the thoughtful, words and phrases for the literate, and for those with sensibility 'a meaning that gradually reveals itself according to different degrees of consciousness.' "[21] Not one or twenty readings exhaust a rich poem any more than twenty repetitions exhaust a great drama, but enough of the experience can be conveyed in a single reading to make performance stimulating and pleasurable.

Selected Readings

Burkland, Carl E. "The Presentation of Figurative Language," *The Quarterly Journal of Speech* XLI (December 1955), 383–390.
Gordon, Edward J. "Teaching Students to Read Verse," *The English Journal* XXXIX (March 1950), 149–154.
Horan, Robert. "The Uniquity of Poetic Language," *Western Speech* XIX (October 1955), 231–244.
Newcomb, Charles M. "How to Stimulate the Imagination in Interpretative Reading," *The Quarterly Journal of Speech Education* IV (March 1918), 135–149.

[21] Eliot quoted in William York Tindall, *The Literary Symbol* (New York: Columbia University Press, 1955), 123.

As with most dimensions of interpretative theory, the tone of literature evokes comment from modern theorists. Tone is central to the interests of oral interpreters in that the powers of a poem seem to center themselves in tone. Laurence Perrine has stated: "In interpreting literature the reader who understands the literal content of a poem but who mistakes its tone may be much further from understanding the poem than the reader who makes mistakes about its literal content but who understands the tone."[1]

Eric W. Carlson places his essay in perspective:

The following summary is a reconstruction, from my notes, of the lecture delivered on March 11, 1936, in the New Lecture Hall at Harvard, the second in the series of six Charles Eliot Norton Lectures by Frost. As Frost spoke without any manuscript, no attempt has been made to publish these lectures, nor is any likely to be.[2]

[1] Laurence Perrine, "The Importance of Tone in the Interpretation of Literature," *What to Say About a Poem . . . and other essays,* W. K. Wimsatt, Jr. and others (Champaign, Illinois: The National Council of Teachers of English, 1963), 389.

[2] From Carlson's introductory remarks in his essay.

Robert Frost on
"Vocal Imagination, the Merger
of Form and Content"

[II.   The Vocal Imagination]

In the first place, there is the question of reading poetry—the author's reading, etc. "A poem should be read as written; poetry is a writer's art, addressed to the mind's ear. I hear my poems better with my mind's ear. My vocal imagination gives the best coordination. One mad theorist" (Vachel Lindsay, presumably) gives reading directions with his poems. "When I say *poem,* tone is the main thing:

> When, in disgrace with fortune and men's eyes,
> I all alone beweep my outcast state,
> And trouble deaf heaven with my bootless cries,
> And look upon myself and curse my fate.

What do we hear in such a poem? We hear meter, rhyme, and vowel sounds." We should avoid Swinburne's overconcern with vowels, his "vowelling." Vowels should not receive too much attention, or we may fall into the error of loading the line with broad vowels.

[III. Dramatic Tone]

"A dramatic, expressive tone merges the form and content. I always feel that the great interest for me is the sensuous interest of the sounds, for instance, in Chaucer. I look for them in old languages." In Latin, the sounds (the dramatic tones) do not change with the mood of the speaker because we have lost the tone of the language and scansion is necessary.

Voice tones, which are limited in number, appear in ordinary conversation. For instance, "Well, I should say not!" Or, among children: "I do, too! You do, too!"

These tones are usually absent from written themes. The editorial tone is the simple declarative, with some variation in sentence structure.

The tone adds definitely to the meaning; it can change meaning entirely. The tone seems "to come to me with the vividness of hallucination, stinging the mind. When it comes, this dramatic seizure is better than using the imagination (i.e., the visual imagination). It is this that I live for."

When reference is made to "visitation of style," it must mean "a very hearing state and a great command of good concrete images of sound."

Poetry is largely a matter of sound, but there is more than meter, rhyme, alliteration, and assonance to consider. Poetry is like the letter *M,* its four strokes consisting of sound, visual images, metaphor and insight (psychological glimpses). The imagists made the mistake of insisting on visual images only. Ezra Pound called himself an imagist on being concerned with pictorial images only.

[IV. The Play of the Voice]

With "the play of the voice" will come "a set of sounds, a set of sentences." (These "sets" are groups of expressions in idiomatic harmony with each other, the peculiar idiomatic sound of which must be caught.) These "concrete images of sound" mark certain high spots in literature: "Come soon, soon!" (the last line of Shelley's "To Night"), "Yet myself in these thoughts almost despising"

(Shakespeare's Sonnet 29). From "The White-Tailed Hornet" a passage including these lines:

> He struck a second time. Another nailhead.
> "Those are just nailheads. Those are fastened down."
> Then disconcerted and not unannoyed,
> He stooped and struck a little huckleberry
> The way a player curls around a football.
>
> .   .   .   .
>
> How like a fly, how very like a fly.*

Inspiration comes from hearing objectively sounds of phrases like these. The greatest satisfaction comes from weaving intonations together to make a work of art. "The tone of bookish images is wrong. 'How very like a fly'—I stole that out of a book."

A directness of tone often goes with old sentiments the modernist cannot lend himself to, as in

> I know my life's a pain, and but a span;
> I know my sense is mock'd in everything:
> And, to conclude, I know myself a man,
> Which is a proud, and yet a wretched thing.

"I care least for the merger of meaning to tone" (i.e., for striving after it consciously). The tone is most important. "The tones are closest to the form, especially where we start and where we end a poem. I get hold of one end of the material . . . it becomes a gathering thing . . . I get all the material I can . . . the form comes later. The form is inside when you begin, and when you get through rolling it the material is inside and the form is outside."

---

* From "The White-Tailed Hornet" from *The Poetry of Robert Frost* edited by Edward Connery Lathem. Copyright 1936 by Robert Frost. Copyright © 1964 by Leslie Frost Ballantine. Copyright © 1969 by Holt, Rinehart and Winston, Inc. Reprinted by permission of Holt, Rinehart and Winston, Inc.

∾

RESPONSE

Frances L. McCurdy

Brief and inconclusive as are Mr. Carlson's notes, they touch on topics of great interest to the interpreter: the writer's act of creation and the reader's act of interpretation.

For Frost, the rhythms, tones, accents, and shapes of the words were the distinctive features of poetry. He once said, "When someone else says lightly that she writes to the ear, I should like to ask 'To what else did anyone ever write?' Poetry is just tones and syllables."* The speaking voice was the sound that Frost repeatedly advised poets to capture. He trained his own ear to hear the voices "fresh from talk" and reserved his highest praise for other poets who caught the sound of a spontaneous speech.

He explained dramatic tone as a "kind of acting up," an expressiveness that preceded words and sometimes superseded them. At times he likened it to the switch of a little girl's skirt as she talked; at other times he implied that it involved the strain of sense against the meter and the exploration of the moods of the poem. Sometimes he talked about dramatic tone as a "kind of catchiness" or a coming alive. Always dramatic quality was related to the voice tone.

An answer to the question whether the poet says the words of his poem aloud or hears them imaginatively in his mind's ear probably varies with the poet and does not alter the general agreement among poets that it is the full body of the words, their shape in the vocal organism and their sound in the ear, with which the poet works, rather than with the printed symbols.

It is also with the full body of the words that the interpreter works as he seeks to bring the poem alive in its rhythms, its sound of speech, its exploration of moods, and its dramatic quality. Mr. Carlson's notes raise a provocative question for the interpreter of a

* Robert Frost, "Can Poetry Be Taught?" *The English Journal* XXIV (February 1935), 141.

lyric poem. Whose is the voice that is speaking? In a drama the characters are assumed to be speaking. In a narrative poem the situation generally suggests a speaker, but whose is the voice in a lyric? Does the poem take on a voice of its own generated by the mood? Is the poet speaking? Is some speaker assumed? For instance, is a shrewd and wise materialist speaking in Frost's "Provide, Provide"? The question is not related to a rhetorical approach; the audience may be of little consequence; but the speaker is important in determining tone. Whose voice is heard in the lyric?

≈

RESPONSE

Alethea S. Mattingly

Because Robert Frost, a "master conversationalist," talked to so many small and large audiences and has been so often quoted, Mr. Carlson's notes about a 1936 lecture add little to what one already knows of Frost's *ars poetica*. Tantalizingly brief and thin, the notes do, however, touch upon a provocative but elusive term, *tone*. This metaphor, borrowed from music and made popular by I. A. Richards, appears frequently in analyses of a literary text and in critiques of an interpreter's performance. Moreover, paralinguistic features today concern linguists, anthropologists, behavioral scientists, and others. Like Frost, most of them relate the term to the human voice.

As a young poet Frost said that he tried to "entangle the speaking tone of voice" in the words of the poem. Carlson's notes repeat that notion. Later, Frost insisted that he *said* his poems, not that he read them for an audience. A sentence in a poem should, he felt, be "a thing caught whole by the ear as spoken." Such comments, together with those Carlson reports about "dramatic tone" and "the play of the voice," recognize the great oral tradition of all literature.

In his use of *tone* Frost refers chiefly to what is addressed to the mind's ear rather than to a listener's ear. Yet he indicates the basis of the auditory imagination as being actual voice tones. Despite the monotonous voices heard in our society, some of us would quarrel with the idea that voice tones are limited in number. Frost's two illustrations seem to equate tone with emphasis. Paralanguage, of course, includes much more, as Frost is aware when he says to consider aspects in addition to the meter, rhyme, alliteration, and assonance heard in a poem. (Padraic Colum likened Frost's own voice to "the barking of an eagle.")

Interpreters will quickly agree that tone adds to meaning and can change meaning entirely. Mindful of Frost's statement that, "poetry provides the one permissible way of saying one thing and meaning another," the interpreter seeks to let tone merge form and content, as Frost says it should, and to read the poem "as written."

᙮

RESPONSE

Wallace A. Bacon

Yes, Mr. Carlson's notes are thin enough. But there is a larger difficulty. Frost is no theorist, really, except with respect to his own aesthetic. Reading what Frost says is of interest because of Frost's poetry. Otherwise what he says is too elliptical, too spare, too ambiguous.

To say that a poem "should be read as written" is to beg all the vast problems interpreters face. Should a Shakespeare sonnet be read in Elizabethan English? Should a poem by Thomas Moore be read in Irish dialect? Should one read Marianne Moore the way Miss Moore does? Surely one mind's ear is not the same as another mind's ear.

Tone is a central consideration, surely; but others have written more illuminatingly about it. To say that tone merges form and content is to say something which I, at least, cannot find either very helpful or very true.[1] Nor can I feel that *my* great interest is "the sensuous interest of the sounds. . . ." The movement of the mind is not either in terms of sound apart from meaning or meaning apart from sound; it is a movement perhaps best thought of as felt sensing of the whole. When I hear Shakespeare's sonnet to which Frost refers ("When in disgrace with fortune and men's eyes") it is certainly not very *instructive* to say that what I hear is "meter, rhyme, and vowel sounds." Nor do I think for a sonnet that it describes very fully what Frost heard.

What Frost hears, and what Frost tries to capture in what he calls "a set of sounds, a set of sentences," is meaningless for Frost's poetry. He *does* catch local idioms. He does catch the flavor of real speech as *he* hears it.[2] That is why I like to listen to Frost's rather disconnected comments, here and elsewhere—they may illuminate Frost's own work for me. They do not help me a great deal with poetry in general.

Neither of the earlier commentators has mentioned Frost's statement about clarity. Here, it seems to me, is a generalization which illuminates much more significantly the totality of Frost's poetry, in which "stored-up combustibles are touched off against the night and the dark and the individual sees something against the universe." Much of Frost's feeling (meaning and tone as *one*) is of the dark and the night, and of the individual's finding his way in them, sensing the universe as he moves. It is Frost's whole perception, his hunger for clarity, which engages us; perception is not to be limited to a matter of tone, meter, rhyme, vowels, alliteration, assonance.

---

[1] Coleridge's discussion of tone and atmosphere in the working of the creative mind is of interest. See Chapter IV of *Biographia Literaria*. But for him tone clearly involves the whole expressive power of communicating what deep feeling and profound thought in *union* bring forth.

[2] See the unpublished doctoral dissertation (Northwestern University, 1970), by Kenneth Crannell, "A Prosodic Analysis of Selected Dramatic Narratives of Robert Frost." Mr. Crannell attempts in a stimulating way to document the means by which Frost achieves the quality of speech.

At the end of his notes, Mr. Carlson seems to quote Frost as saying that tone is more important than "meaning," that tones are closer to form than "meaning." If I follow what Frost is saying, I can only conclude that his notion of "meaning" and "form" represents a dichotomy which is for me hopeless.

∿

RESPONSE

Don Geiger

Professor Bacon astutely reminds us that Frost's critical comments are most certainly valuable in illuminating his own poetic practice. Yet Frost's emphasis on the importance of "voice" and "dramatic tone" in poetry seems to be widely applicable. In some respects he might have been even more emphatic without risk of becoming a mad theorist. Thus Professor Mattingly is surely right to remark the plenitude of possible voice tones. Frost himself later wrote: "The possibilities for tune from the dramatic tones of meaning struck across the rigidity of a limited meter are endless."[1] With appropriate substitutions for sound-patterns other than meter, the poet or critic defending "free" verse should welcome Frost's amended opinion of the range of intonational patterns, or "tunes."

At still another point in his lecture, when Frost comments on Ezra Pound and the imagist vers-librists, he probably minimizes unduly the role of dramatic voice in a kind of poetry much different from his own. Doubtless the typical imagist poem was but a slight poetic achievement. But Frost is too drastic in suggesting that imagists produced only soundless fractional parts of poems. For example, when we turn to Pound's little showcase poem of imagist practice, "In a Station of the Metro," we find Frost's whole

[1] Robert Frost, *Complete Poems of Robert Frost* (New York: Henry Holt, 1949), v.

big M of Poetry, carefully stocked with all of its strokes, sounds, visual images, metaphor and a psychological glimpse or two.

Frost (no doubt encouraged by the imagist's own pronouncements) seems to have been thinking of imagism as a kind of mute "pictorial" art. But in recognizing an emphasis he probably mistakes an analogical for a literal description. Poems are made of language, and "language is something that is spoken."[2] Recollection of this truism, on those occasions when we too find ourselves treating poems as literally "pictures" or "objects," may strike us as would an unexpected blow. Nevertheless it remains a truism: there are no unspoken poems. Consequently there is little profit for the critic in seeking to distinguish between sounded and unsounded poems. His more productive question is likely to be, as Professor McCurdy suggests, whose (what) voice am I hearing? Pursuing an answer, the "vocal imagination" does not require a photograph of the speaker. Thus we do not identify an imagist poem as the utterance of a highly particularized speaker, whether the poet or his persona, having such-and-such firmly suggested personality traits. But it does not follow that because a given poem is not uttered by a particular someone it is therefore uttered by no one. The voice of an imagist poem, and many another lyric, would seem to be a particular speech act or composite of speech acts (as the voice of the Pound poem both describes and appraises) which might be uttered by any reasonably adult person knowing the language in which the poem is written. We may then say that, from the perspective of the oral interpreter, the voice he hears is his own when he identifies and reproduces faithfully the particular speech acts that emerge from the words of the poem and govern their meaning.

[2] R. Rhees, "Can There Be a Private Language?" *Wittgenstein: The Philosophical Investigations,* ed. George Pitcher (Garden City, N.Y.: Doubleday, 1966), 285.

∾

RESPONSE

Richard Haas
and David A. Williams

At given moments, particularly after reading Carlson's notes on Frost's lecture and the responses by Professors McCurdy, Mattingly, Bacon, and Geiger, it seems that the tone of literature and the oral interpretation of literature are as inseparable a construct as form and content. And yet, at the same time, it is also evident that tone, despite its centrality of importance, is not the totality of a poem's meaning, and further, any statement regarding tone should be evaluated by the definition used to establish those opinions.

The preceding commentaries are helpful in expanding the realm of tone. Too often tone in a poem is immediately relegated to a particular speaker. As Professor McCurdy suggests, some poems tend to produce a tone, a speaking voice, apparently independent of a persona. Rather than advising the oral interpreter to assign the oral dimension of a poem to a particular persona, it seems wiser to suggest that the interpreter suspend the assignment of a speaker until he hears how the poem generates its own orality.

Tone is influenced by most every feature of a poem, "on sound as well as sense, on rhythm as well as grammar and sentence structure, even on spelling and punctuation. But the clearest clue to a writer's tone is his choice of words."[1] But it is simpler to say that anything in and of a poem can contribute to its tone. Additionally, tone is as expansive as the human condition and the emotions assignable to mankind. Tone is more than what is "said" in the poem and even more than speech. Brooks and Warren in *Modern Rhetoric* "find that we must 'read between the lines' in order to understand a letter, or that we must take into account the tone of

[1] William W. Watt and Robert W. Bradford, *An E. B. White Reader.* (New York: Harper & Row, 1966), 31.

voice and the facial expression if we are to understand fully a conversation with a friend."[2]

The great expanse of tone possibilities in literature are channeled through the oral interpreter in performance. Surely an ideal tone does not exist for a piece of literature. It may be ideal for a particular interpreter, but another interpreter could present an equally artistic and literarily accurate interpretation of the poem and present a tone that is similar to the first performance, but would have the shades of meaning appropriate to his personality and expressive skills. It is the interpreter's expressive skills that eventually determine the realization and presentation of tone in performance. The following essay explores various dimensions of expression and their influence upon oral interpretation.

Selected Readings

Bacon, Wallace A. "The Act of Literature and the Act of Interpretation," *Oral Interpretation & the Teaching of English,* ed. Thomas L. Fernandez (Champaign, Ill.: National Council of Teachers of English, 1969), 1–7.

Beloof, Robert. *The Performing Voice in Literature* (Boston: Little, Brown, 1966), 143–177.

Brower, Reuben. "The Speaking Voice (Dramatic Design)," *The Fields of Light* (Oxford, Eng.: Oxford University Press, 1951).

McCurdy, Frances L. "Oral Interpretation as an Approach to Literature," *Oral Interpretation & the Teaching of English,* pp. 9–16.

Ong, Walter J. "A Dialectic of Aural and Objective Correlatives," *Essays in Criticism* VIII (January 1958).

Richards, I. A. "The Four Kinds of Meaning," *Practical Criticism* (London: Routledge and Kegan Paul, 1929).

NOTE: The essays by Brower, Ong, and Richards are reprinted in John Oliver Perry's *Approaches to the Poem* (San Francisco: Chandler, 1965).

---

[2] Cleanth Brooks and Robert Penn Warren, *Modern Rhetoric,* Shorter edition. (New York: Harcourt, Brace and World), 291–299.

RICHARD HAAS

"To Say in Words
. . . To Read Aloud"

Professor Bacon is right in placing oral interpretation between two "dangerous shores." It should be recognized, however, that the expression *shore* is the dimension of interpretative study that makes our art *oral* interpretation. There is no question that literary study is the foundation of interpretation. It is just that expression, despite the pages devoted to it in textbooks, receives less attention than impression, and for no wonder after its half-century stigma as the speech field's pariah. Interpretation needs to recognize that a decrease of interest in delivery will lead "to the ultimate disservice of 'content'."[1]

Today, interpretation's problem is a mixture of not providing *enough* attention or the *proper* attention to vocal expression. The art of oral interpretation, the oral expression of literature, is far more involved and demanding than the general emphasis on delivery would indicate. Attention to expression must recognize the form/content relationships between printed literature and its oral form, the perceptual problems in the impression-expression relationship of interpretation theory, and the need for a proper training and understanding of interpretation's expressive shore. Without a proper un-

[1] Wallace A. Bacon, "The Dangerous Shores: From Elocution to Interpretation," *The Quarterly Journal of Speech* 46 (April 1960), 151. Printed elsewhere in this volume.

derstanding of expression in interpretation, the sole interest in performance can result in the display of expression techniques. In such a situation, the performance is not the text, but rather an elocutionary display, and that's all it can be, for the literature was used as an excuse for performance rather than "the interpreter's excuse for being."[2]

The basic problem lies in the form of oral interpretation itself. It must be understood that the oral interpretation of a poem is an alteration of the poem's printed form. Rather than thinking of oral interpretation as something added to the poem, consider that the printing is something added to the poem. Presently, we discuss the oral form in literary terms or in terms of delivery when, in fact, the oral form requires both sets of terms, or better, a new set of terms which properly identifies what we are doing when we interpret orally. The oral interpretation of literature is inextricably bound to the printed page, but it should not be limited by it. Our attention should be directed to how we are bound to the page and how we are not limited by it. Because the understanding of literature and the expression of it must be considered together, as they are in performance, this discussion of expression will be limited to matters that imply an understanding of literature as performance and the role of expression as a critical facet of interpretative study.

Before addressing the distinctions between the oral performance of literature and the printed poem, the basic form/content relationship should be clarified. If you take a simple word (hello) and present it aloud, you change the form of the word from a printed form to an oral form. Hopefully, you are not sure how to say it (in what oral form to perform the word). Is it a friendly greeting, simple chitchat, or possibly a humorous, slang interjection? Even if you and the entire class agreed that it was a friendly greeting, probably no two of you could say it in exactly the same way. The similarity of printed form is possible because of a similarity of typography; but the similarity of an oral form is impossible, owing to the individuality of each person's oral expression. If we take this example one step further and print the word differ-

[2] Bacon, p. 150.

ently (hell-o), would you read it differently? The visual, printed form has been changed and accordingly the content (what the word "means") has been changed.[3] The oral interpreter constructs the form of his presentation from the form of a poem, even from as minor a consideration of form as its typography. The oral interpreter must recognize that the printed form has its own meaning, its own organic life, its own manner of expression within its structure on the page, for it is the poem's printed structure that must be understood and penetrated in the search for the poem's oral form. But this alleged similarity of the two forms does not preclude that the two are indeed distinct.

The oral interpreter must recognize both the similarity and distinction in form, for it is the basis of his art. The art of oral interpretation is a compromise of the printed event on the page and the resurrection of its oral sense and impulse into an oral form. This compromise can create dimensions of the poem that may enhance the silent poem; but more importantly, it establishes the poem's oral form which, for the interpreter, is the poem's most appropriate language medium. Unfortunately, this opinion is not shared by all. We live in a society which is acclimated, academically toilet-trained if you will, to perceive language as printed words, as the product of one person's "spelling out / The patterned letters, not the meaning word."[4] The "patterned letters" are cold print; but they are treated as though they are the origins of language, which they are not. The interpreter resurrects the "meaning word" from

[3] The typographic arrangement of print is only one of many aspects of form in literature. X. J. Kennedy deals clearly and entertainingly with five meanings of form in *An Introduction to Poetry* (Boston: Little, Brown and Company, 1966). A more philosophical discussion can be found in Herbert Read's *Form in Modern Poetry* (New York: Sheed & Ward, 1933). Among many other discussions are John Ciardi's "Thing is the Form" in *The Nation* (April 1954) and Ralph Edward Fulsom's "An Investigation of the Structural Aspects of Free Verse As They Affect the Oral Reader" (Unpublished dissertation, Northwestern University, 1956).

[4] Elder Olson, "Children," *Collected Poems* (Chicago: The University of Chicago Press, 1963), 18. Printed by courtesy of the author.

the "printed letters" by perceiving the oral origin of language and the oral impulse of the printed poem.

If the oral interpreter says he gives sound *to* the printed form of literature, he is saying that print is more the origin of language than is speech. The history of printed language is, in part, an effort to notate the sounds of speech. It must not be overlooked "that written records give us only an imperfect and often distorted picture of past speech."[5] And if we consider modern writing, we find both the writer and the oral interpreter bound by a system of shared written symbols which is different than the oral speech pattern of either the writer or the interpreter. The oral interpreter must recognize the medium of print as an aboral form existing between two oral forms: the speech event potential of the literary structure and the oral performance of the literature. This is not easy to do or to appreciate, particularly when the modern literary condition tends to sanctify the printed word. When the Egyptian god Thoth explained his invention of writing to Thamus, the ruler of Egypt, Thamus replied, "O most ingenious Thoth, one man has the ability to develop a new skill, but another to judge whether it will be a curse or a blessing to its users."[6] Hopefully, the oral interpreter is the one who determines the varying degrees of Thoth's curse or blessing in each particular poem he addresses. For Scholes and Kellogg, "words in their printed forms have become more real for us than either the sounds on the lips of living men or the concepts they represent."[7] Literacy arranges our attention on literature as print, as though the writer's mouth were a typewriter; but "if it can be shown that a consequence of literacy is the turning of a poem into an object, it can also be shown that it has been the particular function of oral interpreters to retrieve poetry from that state—to insist that poetry be heard rather than seen, experi-

[5] Leonard Bloomfield, *Language History* ed. Harry Hoijer (New York: Holt, Rinehart and Winston, 1965), 293.

[6] Robert Scholes and Robert Kellogg, quoting Socrates in the *Phaedrus, The Nature of Narrative* (London: Oxford University Press, 1966), 19.

[7] Scholes, p. 19.

enced rather than contemplated, understood from a point *inside* the poem rather than at a critical remove."[8]

A further step in clarifying the distinction between the printed form and the oral form can be made by evaluating an observation of print as a medium of expression. In a McLuhanesque perspective, print on the page is considered to be an extension of the eye.[9] But if we remember that print comes from speech sounds, we change the point of contact that print makes upon us. Print then becomes an extension of the ear. And it is in this distinction that good oral interpreters are made: to know and feel the performance of literature as a speech event, as the dramatic utterance of the poem's oral expression of itself. An obvious example will help illustrate the possible stifling effects of print on literature. A ballad, such as "Lord Randall," existed for years as oral speech, as an event. Eventually, one version of the ballad was written down, printed, and declared to be the ballad "Lord Randall." When the oral interpreter reads "Lord Randall" with the intent of giving sound to the printed word, he is accepting the printed form of the ballad as the real ballad, when in fact, the real ballad preceded any written form of it and exists somewhere beyond or through the printed version. The interpreter's task is to transcend the printed word and to resurrect the sound of the ballad through the inaccurate "patterned letters" on the printed page.

The position taken so far is that the poem can dictate its oral form to us if we are ready to cope with the problems of printed forms, the "consequences of literacy," and the various attitudes regarding the dramatic nature of literature. There must be times in our quest for the oral form when we attend seriously to the printed object; there must also be those times when we recognize that the poem has an oral expressive nature which, if we will listen, will guide us to an awareness of how the two forms create the oral

[8] Thomas O. Sloan, "Oral Interpretation Before the Ages of Sheridan and Walker," A paper delivered at the Western Speech Association Convention in November 1970, p. 9.

[9] James H. Birdwell, "Marshall McLuhan: An Experience," *Central States Speech Journal* 21 (Fall 1970), 156.

form we are seeking. What has not been discussed is how the interpreter himself is a feature of the oral form.

~~

The critical analysis of literature, as an effort to discover the oral form of a poem, is no guarantee for a successful performance. Two problems are immediately evident: (1) did the interpreter perceive enough of the poem's expressive manner to substantiate a successful interpretation? and (2) if he did perceive sufficiently the poem's performance of itself, is he capable of expressing it? These questions are no more than the impression-expression relationship, but the relationship is far more complex than the simple dictum: Allow your impression to dictate your expression.

The perceptual limitations of the interpreter as student of literature impose restrictions on the interpreter as performing artist. It would be by accident only that an interpreter could present the expressive functioning of a poem in his oral reading if he did not perceive it in his analysis. One cannot express knowingly that which he does not perceive. But if it is assumed that the interpreter perceives the expressive interworkings of a poem, it remains for the interpreter to express these gestures of language in performance. If he cannot express in performance the expressive features he perceives in analysis, the performance cannot fulfill his own requirements. The performer himself would consider such a reading foreign to his understanding, or at least inadequate.

Interpretation might lean too securely on performance criticism which states that the performer either did not know enough or could not express it well enough. Consider first that it is common for a good oral performance to reveal dimensions of a poem's meaning which no silent analysis could reveal. Only a rigorous advocate of the print form of poetry would find that objectionable. Indeed, there are dimensions of a poem's meaning that are not there to be seen; they are there to be heard. But if we believe that the oral performance is decided upon by how the interpreter "hears" the poem in his analysis of it, then what influences how he "hears" the poem's performance of itself? Knowledge and sensitivity to the oral form is an acceptable answer; but what influences the interpreter's knowledge and sensitivity to oral forms? Aside from additional knowledge and greater sensitivity, the answer might lie in the dimension of the interpreter that most approximates the poem's oral expressive manner, the interpreter's expressive abilities.

One of literature's alleged functions is to expand the reader's perception of life, the experiences of the human condition.[10] But the interpreter might be satisfied to accept his perception of a piece of literature as adequate because it expands *to* his perceptual limits. The typical student response to a teacher who attempts to point out additional features of a poem, features that extend beyond the student's perceptual limits, is the stopper: "You're reading things into the poem that aren't there—even the poet doesn't know they're there." Or, as a student said to me when I was impressing myself with Frost's "Stopping by Woods on a Snowy Evening": "You're making me sick." My analysis of the remark, which helped me redeem my sinking morale, was that I had entered into a consideration of the poem which was beyond the student's perception. For the student, he had involved himself and analyzed *all* that the poem contained because he had exhausted *all* that he could perceive. One of the first steps in approaching any analysis of literature is to analyze our perceptual limitations, the way we respond to a perceptual field.

The problem of perception has many implications for the interpreter in analysis, but it is also a controller of expression. The obvious relationship, as already discussed, is that the performances of language in a poem must be perceived in analysis if they are to be a conscious part of the interpreter's oral performance. But perceptual limits might be restricted, to some degree, by the interpreter's own expressive abilities. Gary Cronkhite has explored many problems of perception for the interpreter.[11] In his discussion of Helson's perceptual theory of adaptation level, he questions whether

[10] See Robert M. Post's essay, "Perception Through Performance of Literature," *The Speech Teacher* 19 (September 1970), 168–172.

[11] Gary Cronkhite, "The Place of Aesthetics and Perception in a Paradigm of Interpretation," *Western Speech* 34 (fall 1970), 274–287.

or not people culturally accustomed to great physical activity during speaking would perceive less emotionality in a performance than people whose culture practiced subdued physical activity in speech. The question is based on an individual's residual stimuli, in this case, acts of emotionality which the individual has previously experienced. To carry this question on to a closer relationship with the oral interpreter, it is reasonable to question whether or not an individual's own expressive abilities contribute to his perceptual limits. In other words, might some of the expressive performances of language in a poem go unperceived by an interpreter because he does not possess equal expressive skills as residual stimuli? The immediate objection to this line of inquiry is that observing a performer who is exceptionally skilled in performing abilities can supply the residual stimuli necessary to extend one's perception beyond his own expressive abilities. While this objection is undoubtedly substantive, it could produce in the interpreter the impression that all his own performances are not equal to the expressive excellence of. the exceptionally skilled performing artist. In other words, his perception of his own performance would be inferior to his residual stimuli. However, if an interpreter, with a particular range of expressive abilities and with a relatively complete impression of a poem, had his range of expressive skills extended in power, flexibility, and nuance, it seems reasonable to assume that he would read the poem differently. The question is whether he would read the poem differently because he wanted to exercise his new expressive abilities or because his increased expressive skill had provided him with an increased perceptual capacity to discover additional expressive manifestations in the oral form of the poem. Admittedly, this empirical question is based more on feeling than on proof. But the important consideration is that expressive skills might be a factor in an interpreter's perception of a poem's oral form.

Another perceptual limitation associated with expression is the "pre-voicing" nature of interpreters. Our performance orientation as oral interpreters and our disposition to perceive poems as eventual performances often result in a "performance" upon a first reading. It isn't a fully formed performance, of course, and it may well be good advice to respond first to a poem orally, but "pre-voicing" can lead to premature and stylized decisions about the poem's oral form. The more mature interpreter runs less risk than the beginner, but he too can burn-in a perception of the poem's expressive manner which might warp additional investigations or even eliminate the need for them. "Pre-voicing" also can lead to a dismissal of all poems that do not "sound" appropriate for oral performance. Both perceptual problems of residual stimuli and "pre-voicing" indicate interpretation's need to better understand the performing shore of our art.

Expression, then, is a part of literature's oral form and the interpreter's perception of it; but expression is also the basis of interpretation's critical dictum: the performance is the text. If the dictum is to be realized, the interpreter's expressive skills must be equal to the literature.

The oral interpreter must be trained in expression, or at least, he must possess expressive abilities equal to the performing intensities inherent in the poem. If the interpreter has not penetrated to the oral form of the literature, or if he is incapable of expressing the subtleties that exist within the poem, he would do as well to ditto the poem, hand it to his audience, and discuss it as a group than to present only the surface features of it. A good interpretative reading should reveal the subtext of the oral form as well as the text. After all, the audience "can read the text at home"; the interpreter should give them more.[12]

Probably no system of expression is adequate or appropriate for all individuals. But all approaches should focus on technique; for the performing art of interpretation, like any other art, is based on technique. The techniques of expression must explore and reveal the meaning and emotional intensity of the literature, not compete with it.

[12] Constantin Stanislavski, as quoted by Sonia Moore, *The Stanislavski Method.* (New York: Pocket Books, 1967), 49.

The greatest weakness of our art springs from its greatest strength. . . . [Our voice] in its untrained condition, wants to be master instead of servant. Furthermore, it seems able to hypnotize one into mistaking its sensations and excitements for thoughts and emotions. . . . The true technique of any art can be defined as the most successful way of making the material instrument reflect the mind's message while at the same time calling the least attention to itself. Such a technique is a matter of slow growth . . . [but] is absolutely necessary. . . . Our mission is to interpret and that necessitates a well-mastered technique.[13]

The elocutionary, mechanical approach to expression, with all its bird calls, posing, and gymnastics, turned interpreters away from methods of expression training. Their disfavor with elocution was reactionary, and because of professional pressures, they abandoned a critical attention to expressive technique. They rested comfortably on a "think-the-thought" approach, but neglected Curry's requirement that the performer be a highly skilled performing instrument. Without a systematic expressive method, interpretation pursued a "natural" method of expression training. But one hundred and fifty years ago, Ebenezer Porter found the same fault with one concept of the natural method as many find today: It is useless to tell students to read naturally when they read poorly naturally.

Old bromides of expression training such as "the manner of expression exhibited in animated conversation" or "speak the words as though they were your own" are not accurate guidelines for the student. They are helpful in some instances and for some students, but generally they can lead to a distortion of the text in performance. If a poem were read in the manner of an animated conversation, it would make the poem an animated conversation when the poem's expression might not be conversational in style. Similarly, the advice to speak "the words as though they were your own" gives the interpreter license to limit the expressive forces of the literature by adjusting them to his own abilities. The best expression training is that which expands and sophisticates the expressive skills and range of the interpreter. The oral interpreter,

[13] Leland Powers and Carol Hoyt Powers, *Fundamentals of Expression.* (Boston: Thomas Groom, 1930), 12–15.

after all, must express *up to* the level of the poem's performance, not force the poem through his own expressive abilities. The reverse of this approach is also a problem for those poems that are subtle in their expressive force, complex and intricate in their thought, and that can bear less expressive energy than interpreters are inclined to give them.

The time devoted to settling or arguing the actor-interpreter distinction has contributed to the digression of interest in interpretative expression. Most interpreters insist that the attention of the audience should be focused on the literature, not on the interpreter. But to accomplish this feat, developing the images so vividly that the listener's attention is on the images and not on the interpreter, requires a mastery of expressive technique. Too many interpreters leave performances undeveloped for fear attention will be drawn to them. The problem is that one cannot know all that a poem can yield in performance until it is attempted. It is also true that a poem can be made to yield meanings that have more to do with the performer's expressive artistry than with the poem's oral form. But the problem here is that too often poems are read up to a certain degree of expressive intensity, vocal modulation, and physical movement which make them all sound a bit too much alike.

The presentation of a poem in its oral form is not a filtering process. The expressive techniques of oral interpretation should be equal to the expression of the poem's performing voice as indicated by the poem's own performance of language. This literary responsibility does not diminish the importance of the performer when the oral form is appreciated and understood, but it does make him subservient to the poem. The oral interpreter is like an instrument that plays the literary score. If the poem is "clarinetish," and the interpreter "trombonish," a distortion of the literary score can be produced. This is not to say that interesting, even valuable dimensions of the score cannot be presented, but the original score would be marred. A trombone, even if it has trumpet, bass, and saxophone qualities, can only produce an inventive reading of a clarinet score. By this instrument metaphor, I do not mean voice pitch, timbre, or quality, but rather the manipulations of expression inherent in the functioning of the instrument. And possibly what we need is more inventive readings. But the point remains that trombones do not sound like clarinets, or *as* clarinets sound.

Despite the restrictive nature of this expressive approach, it must be remembered that a good poem carries more reasonable expressive possibilities than any one oral reading can handle properly. Like Roethke's recollection of a woman, a poem moves "more ways than one" and contains more shapes than "a bright container can contain."[14] Additionally, much of a poem's "meaning" is left for the listener's involvement, and rightly so. There are times, I am sure, when a listener perceives more of a poem's subtext than is being presented in a performance. The listener can fill in the gaps left by the interpreter, expand images, and reach symbolic levels that the interpreter does not understand and that are not presented in his performance. In a manner of speaking, the listener might applaud, though unknowingly, his own listening abilities, the precision and depth of his literary perception, more than he is applauding the performance itself. I am not condemning this act; for the union of these two arts, interpretation and listening, can produce a greater product than either one can produce alone. In this sense oral interpretation, as an act of sharing, most fully realizes its role with literature. But the degree to which a poem needs to be communicated to a listener is questionable.

It is possible to alter the poem's performance of itself in an attempt to communicate it. The intent to communicate a poem to a listener (that is, a listener other than the interpreter himself) can lead to a levelling of the poem to suit the taste and expressive expectations of the audience. For instance, Parrish said the important consideration about expression is that it be "normal," that it conform "to the pattern that a cultivated audience is accustomed to hearing."[15] This is a worrisome statement if it means that the poem's performance should be altered to fit the delivery pattern

[14] Theodore Roethke, "I Knew a Woman," *The Distinctive Voice,* ed. William J. Martz (Glenview, Ill.: Scott, Foresman, 1966), 162.

[15] W. M. Parrish, "Elocution—A Definition and A Challenge," *The Quarterly Journal of Speech* 43 (February 1957), 3.

that an audience is accustomed to hearing. Just as the interpreter should come up to the level of a poem's "density of effects," so should an audience be expected to come up to the level of the performance.[16] The audience should not be neglected, nor should it be worshiped as the determiner of a successful performance. Possibly the interpreter should coax, guide, and encourage the audience to participate in the oral form of the literature. In any event, the audience and the integrity of the literary text are like another pair of dangerous shores for the interpreter.[17]

There is no one right way to read a poem. As explained before, different interpreters and listeners will perceive different features of a poem. The individual's personal relationship and involvement with a poem's language is his understanding; but as emphasized in this essay, his understanding might not be manifested in his performance. The poet W. D. Snodgrass accepts the individual oral interpretations of poetry, asking, "What would be the point of having more than one reader if we all read it the same?"[18] The freedoms of interpretation extended by Snodgrass do not diminish the importance of an accurate analysis of the poem or the requirement that the interpreter be a well-trained expressive instrument capable of presenting in performance all the reasonably expressible dimensions of literature.

The question of the interpreter's mastery of vocal and physical performing techniques is inescapable. Oral interpretation requires expressive skills. But where does the student gain this expressive skill? Currently, judging from pedagogical formats in speech departments, it is gained from limited voice and diction work for the fortunate few and from observing models for others. In 1957, Parrish called for more attention to elocution, even "a basic course

[16] "Density of effect" is a phrase from Don Geiger's *The Sound, Sense, and Performance of Literature* (Glenview, Ill.: Scott, Foresman, 1963), 89. For a further discussion of the interpreter's demands and relationships with the audience, see Robert Breen's essay, particularly the last paragraph, "Chamber Theatre," printed elsewhere in this volume.

[17] Bacon, p. 151.

[18] Letter to the author, June 18, 1968.

in elocution," as a prerequisite to many speech classes.[19] And Anderson, in 1967, urged a similar incorporation as a fundamental study to all speech department training.[20] The need exists, but who can teach elocution and by what method? Have we dismissed the task of objectifying, measuring, and sophisticating expressive technique so long that we do not know when or how to teach it? That may be the case.[21] Hopefully, expression will become a more important facet of an interpreter's training so that the interpreter will be able

> —To say
> In words the way
> . . . .
> To read aloud
> . . . .
> Yes, Yes, It was like this,
> This way—[22]

Selected Readings

Crocker, Lionel. "Techniques in Teaching Interpretation," *The Southern Speech Journal* XXII (Winter 1956), 95–101.

Woolbert, C. H. "Theories of Expression: Some Criticisms," *Quarterly Journal of Public Speaking* I (July 1915), 127–143.

[19] Parrish, p. 11.

[20] Robert G. Anderson, "James Rush—His Legacy to Interpretation," *Southern Speech Journal* 53 (Fall 1967), 20–28.

[21] The 1972 SCA Convention presented a short course in "Voice, Diction, and Body Behavior: For the Actor and Teacher" by Arthur Lessac (see also his essay, "A New Definition of Dramatic Training," *The Quarterly Journal of Speech* 55 (April 1969), 116–125, and a program by Bud Beyer on "The Art of Mime: Training for the Interpreter." Possibly these activities indicate a resurgence of interest in expression for interpretation.

[22] From Elder Olson, "Prologue to His Book."

An aspiring baseball player wouldn't go to Abner Doubleday to find out how to play baseball. The game has changed drastically since he first laid out the diamond and rules. We are not sure if Abner would be pleased with all the changes that have been made—he probably had something different in mind for baseball than the multi-million dollar spectacle it is today, a form of entertainment. There is, however, every reason to go to the developer of Chamber Theatre to ask what he thinks now, a couple of decades later. Chamber Theatre is not as old as baseball, yet the changes in the activity indicate that it must be as old as the steamboat, movable type, stone tools.

Some of the confusions are unnecessary: Chamber's Theatre instead of Chamber Theatre, as though a Mr. Chamber devised and defined the activity, or possibly that the first production was held in Mr. Chamber's chamber; a synonymous use with Readers Theatre which certainly has enough confusions of its own to contend with; an entertainment form for the delight of those playgoers who haven't a play to attend; and more distortions than we believe Professor Breen would like us to relate here, unless, perhaps, he knows more of them than we.

Allow us to backtrack slightly on the allegations made above. The purpose of this book is to foster theoretical development through commentary, controversy, and discussion. We do not intend to diminish controversial reaction to Breen's position, but we feel obliged to alert oral interpreters to compare their theory of Chamber Theatre and the productions they have seen to Breen's theory and implied production concepts. He is, after all, the man "who has most fully served to define and develop" Chamber Theatre.[1]

Bacon's discussion of Chamber Theatre is helpful to anyone interested in working with the form. From that which has been written about Chamber Theatre, which is surprisingly little considering its popularity, a few of its techniques stand out:

- It is a way of placing prose fiction on the stage, but "it is not a dramatization," nor "a stage adaptation of prose fiction."[2]

- It retains fidelity to the text, primarily in the manner of employing the narrator. The tense of the narrative form is not

[1] Wallace A. Bacon, *The Art of Interpretation* (New York: Holt, Rinehart and Winston, 1966), 319.

[2] Bacon, p. 319.

changed. The narrator establishes the scenes on stage as "seen through an intelligence not identical with the intelligence of the actors."[3]

It does not rearrange the text for performance, although it may be cut for length, but fidelity to the text is paramount. It does not turn fiction into drama. It allows the narrator to fulfill his role within the structure of the fiction.

Bacon reports a "further refinement" of Breen's, whereby Chamber Theatre "treats as direct discourse certain parts of the text which are written as indirect discourse, assigning such passages to characters as if they were spoken aloud."[4]

In the following essay, Breen responds to the failure of Chamber Theatre to establish its own identity. Though it may be employed entertainingly, Breen sees Chamber Theatre as a "critical tool," a means of illuminating the function and operation of the narrator, theme, plot, characters, and an appreciation of style. While Breen says the theatrical excitement and entertainment of Chamber Theatre are "fringe benefits," he is politely acknowledging the major misuse of the form. Too often the audience is not credited with the ability to perceive a critical illumination of literature as entertaining, to recognize "knowing" as reward.

[3] Bacon, p. 321.
[4] Bacon, p. 319.

ROBERT S. BREEN

Chamber Theatre

Chamber Theatre, under that name, is twenty-three years old, old enough to have established its identity, to have acquired well-defined characteristics. That it has not done so may be charged to its efforts to make the best of two worlds, the world of narrative literature and the world of dramatic literature. As long as Chamber Theatre tries to compete for the attention of silent readers on the one hand and of playgoers on the other there is little chance of success. But if it will settle for its value as a critical tool, a means of making manifest the structural dynamics of narrative literature, then Chamber Theatre has every possibility of succeeding.

The primary concern of Chamber Theatre is the presentation on the stage of narrative literature without sacrificing its narrative elements. Chamber Theatre may be and often is "entertaining" and "theatrically exciting," but these are fringe benefits. If they are too directly pursued, the critical function of Chamber Theatre may lose its centrality and suffer the fate of most novelties.

Chamber Theatre prospers best in the classroom. There it is free to expose the weaknesses of a literary text: its sentimentality, its awkward transitions, its false tone, its unrealized theme. Chamber Theatre is under no obligation, as it might be in a public theatre, to divert the audience from any recognition of aesthetic shortcomings by a display of theatrical virtuosity on the part of the actors or director. Chamber Theatre is no less successful in recognizing the strengths of a literary text. The viva voce presentation of literature provides those elements of paralanguage and kinesics that place a literary text more actively in the condition of life. The simultaneity of action and reaction that the stage allows makes the relationship of characters more immediate and perhaps more convincing.

Critics still honor Aristotle's modal distinctions in classifying literary forms as lyric, epic, and dramatic. Students still honor those critics. However, the fullest meaning of such distinctions is best understood when the student must stand upon the stage and speak the words of the text. If, for example, he says, "Once upon a time," he may recognize that he is a storyteller, but he will also become aware of the importance of the question, "To whom is the story being told?" If his remark is enclosed in quotation marks, he knows that he is addressing some character in the fiction; if there are no quotation marks, he must assume that he is addressing the reader or audience.

To be sure, "Once upon a time" tells the speaker very little about his own character, but if it happens to be the phrase that opens James Joyce's *Portrait of the Artist as a Young Man,* "Once upon a time . . . there was a moocow . . . met a nicens little boy," the speaker can tell that he is not a conventional narrator because his diction is too informal, too much like baby talk. Still there are no quotation marks at this point in Joyce's text, nothing to indicate that the speaker is addressing a character in the story. The statement that follows in the text of *Portrait* says, "His father told him that story." The student-speaker now knows that whoever spoke the opening phrase, "Once upon a time," was in fact a father and that the "him" is no doubt the "nicens little boy." However, quotation marks are still absent, which means that the narrator is neither the father, though he speaks with the father's diction, nor is he the little boy, since he is referred to in the third person.

The problems of establishing the point of view (who tells the story) in Joyce's novel and the exact modal condition of the opening chapter cannot be solved here, but enough has been said to indicate that the questions inevitably raised through the staging of the scene are pertinent to the solution of those problems.

The dramatic form of storytelling has the virtue of presenting simultaneous action which is in the condition of life, while the narrative form is privileged to interrupt the action, either to explore motivations at the moment of action or to shift the reader's attention from the foreground to the background. Chamber Theatre by its own laws seeks to combine the virtues of the acted drama with those of the written narrative. Whereas drama prides itself on being able to *show* its story, the novel and the short story must be content to *tell* their tale.

However, the nature of illusion is such that it is not always clear in our imaginations whether we are being told or shown. When Duncan stands before Macbeth's castle and says, "This castle hath a pleasant seat," the playgoer must take his word for it. Too often what the audience sees is a rather grim-looking, grey stone, castle wall, painted and lighted to inflict a heavy tragic mood. In any case, there is not likely to be any visible evidence of the "pleasant seat" on stage. Then Duncan adds, "the air nimbly and sweetly recommends itself unto our gentle senses." Now we are entirely at the mercy of his words for the stale conditioned air of the theatre will not "show" us the evidence that has convinced Duncan.

Unlike the acted drama, the novel offers us *only* words, and yet, where is the reader who can say, when he has finished *Pride and Prejudice,* that he has seen only words? Surely the words tell the reader what to see and hear and, often by subtle indirection, what to feel. It is true that he sees and hears and feels only in his imagination, but it would take a metaphysician to make a qualitative distinction between an imagined scene and a "real" scene.

One of the strongest contributions to the student's critical understanding of literature that Chamber Theatre provides is a palpable experience of style. It is never enough to characterize style by pointing to figures of speech, punctuation, the contours of balanced, or periodic sentences. The student must speak aloud what has been written if he would have a full appreciation of the rhythmic qualities inherent in style. But, best of all, the student should not only speak but "act" the style. In other words, the student should lend substance to the metaphors commonly used by critics to identify styles: "mellifluous," "graceful," "stilted," "wooden," "pomp-ous," "circular." He should move and speak with those qualities which the metaphors assign to the particular style.

The narrative element in Chamber Theatre tends to "alienate" the actor from his character; the actor tends to become a demon-strator rather than an impersonator. This condition is contrary to the traditions of an illusionistic or realistic theatre, and audiences often feel that Chamber Theatre performances are too self-conscious. It is true that Chamber Theatre makes an audience conscious of the art of storytelling even as it tells the story. In this sense it is reflexive, commenting on itself as it comments on life. But this is nothing new in the theatre. Many excellent plays, old and new, are reflexive in that they are theatre about theatre. Lionel Abel calls such plays Metatheatre.

Plays as widely separated in time as *The Balcony* and *Twelfth Night* are metatheatre in that they confirm the notion that all the world is a stage. As Irma in *The Balcony* says of her clients, "each arrives with his own scenario." Beckett's plays are metatheatre, too, in that life in his plays has been deliberately theatricalized (viz. *Endgame*). For Brecht, too, the world is a stage. He asks his actors to act out a feeling as if they were telling of how some other per-son felt. This distance or "alienation" is also a feature of Chamber Theatre and answers the literary condition of narrative forms even better than the dramatic forms of Brecht.

The contemporary theatre is concerned with experiments in "audience involvement" which complicates the relationship between the stage and the auditorium, the actors and the spectators. It is significant that these experiments frequently include the use of nar-rative devices in order to mediate between illusion and reality, be-tween art and life. The psychological reality of the theatre and the psychological illusion of life are explored in such experiments as The Living Theatre, Theatre of Encounter, Open Theatre, and the latest innovation under the direction of Paul Sills, Story Theatre.

Story Theatre is a narrative theatre, but it is more concerned with theatrical effects, acrobatic skills of the actors, and the supple-mental blandishments of music and dance than with getting on with the story. Sills's theatre has its own style to which all the stories in its repertoire must submit. Chamber Theatre, on the other hand, makes a serious effort to accommodate itself to the stylistic demands of each story it performs. Chamber Theatre promotes the audience's critical acumen and lets the entertainment values of its performances follow if they will.

Selected Readings

Breen, Robert S. "Chamber Theatre," Chap. V, *Suggestions for a Course of Study in Secondary School Theatre Arts* (Washington, D.C.: American Educational Theatre Association, 1963), 50–52.

King, Judy Yordon. "Chamber Theatre by Any Other Name . . . ?" *The Speech Teacher,* XXI (September 1972), 193–196.

Lorenz, Boyd. "Chamber Drama: Versatile Language Arts Tool," *Scholastic Teacher* (November 2, 1960), 14–15.

Kemp Malone was professor emeritus of English literature in the Johns Hopkins University. In this address, before teachers and scholars of English, he touched upon points of oral interpretation that he thought should be values in the study of literature. Since most of his speech is not important to this volume, we have edited it considerably. For your appreciation of the responses by Professors Floyd, Bolton, Bowen, Bacon, and Geiger, it will be helpful for you to know that Malone admitted that his eight years in retirement made him "a man behind the times, a relic of the past . . . a back number, not a prophet, and I am better fitted," he said, "to look backward than forward." Nevertheless, he recommended the use of tape recorders and speech laboratories to aid the student in his study of literature through oral interpretation. Malone's assertion that his youthful recitational activity was valuable to him is tempered somewhat by his pride in recalling his PhD requirements of Latin, Greek, Icelandic, and Gothic.

We delight in the mixture of attitudes the contributors reveal in their responses to "that other study of literature."

KEMP MALONE

The Next Decade

It may well come to pass that instead of "bootlegging literature under the pretext of teaching reading" we keep the spirit as well as the letter of the law by training our students in a modernized, up-to-date form of what used to be a highly esteemed skill, the art of declamation. As schoolboys my fellows and I had to learn many a poem and not a few purple passages by heart. Some of these we were expected to declaim, with all the oratorical stops pulled out, before audiences: usually teacher and schoolmates only but sometimes the general public, or whoever was minded to come. On these public occasions the families of the budding orators would flock to the performance and if need be were ready to prompt from the floor a young speaker stalled in his tracks, for the pieces we recited were familiar to the general public. One favorite was Mark Antony's oration at Caesar's funeral; another, the address of Spartacus to the gladiators. I still remember how Spartacus started his speech: "Ye call me chief and ye do well to call him chief who . . ." From this point my memory fails me; I have always been better at forgetting than at minding. But I like to think that the sonorous periods of the speech stirred my hearers in those days as they stirred me.

Other times, other tastes, and we cannot make dead bones live. Even in the theatre the oratorical tradition, so far as it survives at all, does so as a mere shadow of its old self. But good diction, as it is called, has always been highly thought of and always will be. A reader's diction is said to be good when he reads the lines aloud in such a way as to bring out clearly the words of the text and the meanings and feelings that the words are meant to impart. This skill is eminently worth having. Indeed, one may reasonably doubt that a reader really understands and appreciates his text when he does poorly at reading it aloud. In learning how to read a text aloud a student learns the text, comes to know it in depth. Sympathetic understanding comes out to the full thus and only thus. Silent reading, however strongly focused, remains passive and unfruitful in comparison. Until we have taught our students how to read aloud we have not taught them how to read.

Here is a task that comes within the scope of Project English and deserves all we are likely to put into it and more. I cannot say how much attention it will get in the next ten years but I hope it will be less neglected than it has been in the past. In my own teaching I have always made much of reading aloud. Instead of talking about a silent text, black marks on white paper, my students and I would try to make the words come alive on our lips and in our ears. We would talk about them too, of course, but primarily we would say them and hear them. In this matter the teacher must lead the way with a performance not unlike that of an actor on the stage. His reading serves also, of course, as his interpretation of the text, and in some cases (e.g., Shylock's speech in *The Merchant of Venice* I. iii. 104–127) he may wish to make two or more readings, each bringing out a particular interpretation. In the nature of the case his readings will become models which at first the students will try to imitate, but as they become proficient and win confidence in themselves they will develop styles of their own. It will often come out that a student read a given passage poorly because he did not understand the text. And sometimes the teacher will make the same discovery about himself.

∾

RESPONSE

Virginia H. Floyd

We are nearly past the "next decade" examined in 1964 by Professor Malone, looking backward and forward to assess the future by the light of the past. I respect his practice of reading aloud in his teachings. Aside from a modicum of appreciation for this testimonial and agreement with his conviction regarding values for teachers of a classical background and knowledge of other vehicles of our literary culture, I feel uneasiness on several grounds. Agreeing with the proverb that "he who would know the future must behold the past," I am concerned that the past he beholds includes the art of declamation on public occasions complete with "good diction"—when "sympathetic understanding comes out to the full." One would wish he had taken a much longer look that embraced our ancient oral backgrounds.

Looking forward Professor Malone could not surmise rapidity in developments far more sophisticated than tape recordings and speech laboratories. Teleworms and sonoworms outnumber the bookworms! Interest in the interface between technology and art finds its manifestations in uses of hardware in a world where many argue that linear literature is dead.

His position, finally, is not one I share. His position may very possibly be typical of persons with the credentials of a teacher of English. He wants words to come alive on lips and in the ears: the words would be said and heard, with the teacher leading the way. *What* something is, however, must affect the way we teach it and make predictions about it. Central in my response is disagreement over what it is each of us wishes to bring to life: for him—the literary object (black marks on white paper); for me—the literary object experienced by the reader in that unique moment when the reader is *empoigne* by his text.

~

RESPONSE

Janet Bolton

Professor Malone's commendation of reading aloud as a means of understanding literature with a heightened enjoyment and appreciation is, of course, welcome. Literature has been—and is—the academic property of scholars and teachers of English deeded to the next generation of students of English. So Dr. Malone's approval of the worth of oral study and the skills of speaking literature would seem a gracious inclusion of the disciplines of spoken communication within that domain.

I regret some aspects of his approval. His enthusiasm for reading literature aloud seems grounded in nostalgic memories of declaiming "Spartacus to the Gladiators" with "sonorous periods" and "oratorical stops pulled out." He recalls a charming tintype so limited and quaint that speaking literature is first established—

and diminished—as the learning of poems and "not a few purple passages by heart."

His justification is phrased in simple, even banal generalities. Silent reading is passive; oral reading actively engages the student. A text is not "black marks on a white page"; words must be made to "come alive." Such statements are geared to elementary pupils in the language arts.

As a man who would try to look both ways in time, Professor Malone appears nearsighted in his recognition of the oral tradition in literary history and of its technological potential in the future. Well before the advent of print, literary forms and strategies were established. Audiences are once more responding to the impact of the speaking of words, to the dimensions of tone and attitude, of resonance and action.

Professor Malone recognizes the efficacy of reading literature aloud as a method of exploring the text; the literary text is his objective. Is the behavioral engagement with a literary text perhaps better viewed as a means of exploring significant human experience?

∾

RESPONSE

Elbert R. Bowen

I find myself not very excited by Professor Malone's defense of oral reading in the teaching of literature. Of course, I agree with it. I find it consoling when a distinguished professor of literature extols the oral approach to literature as a dynamic way to get beyond the little black marks on the white page. Those of us who teach oral interpretation know this so well that when an occasional professor of English breaks into print in an English journal with the assertion, we are likely to feel only momentary satisfaction. The thrill of subversion, evangelism, or vindication does not last long when the speaker seems to be either only a weak prophet or merely a voice from the halcyon past.

Many others have promoted the same contentions and much earlier than Professor Malone. Take two. Hiram Corson, in 1896, wrote:

Reading must supply all the deficiencies of written or printed language. It must give life to the letter. How comparatively little is addressed to the eye, in print or manuscript, of what has to be addressed to the ear by a reader! There are no indications of tone, quality of voice, inflection, pitch, time, or any other of the vocal functions demanded for a full intellectual and spiritual interpretation.[1]

And, Algernon Tassin, in 1925, wrote:

Sympathetic reading aloud is a fine art, and it is the only fine art within the gifts and opportunities of every student. To many, it affords the only aesthetic and spiritual development they ever receive in college, or—in the realm of art—in their lives for that matter. To this end, lectures about literature are important, but they are not so important as reading literature. They will of themselves only inform the mind; they will not enrich the spirit.[2]

I am inclined to sympathize with Malone's longing look back to the cherished past of his own literary education, even with the memorization of purple passages, though it was not typical of my own training. I recall having felt some chagrin when my father could recite passages he had learned many years before he ever thought of me, at a time when I, a student, could not do so. He did it with enthusiastic appreciation and apparent understanding. My own training was too often concerned only with the facts of literature: schools, authors, periods, biographies, works. I also recall my daughter's fourth grade teacher saying to me: "Reading aloud is all right for third graders, but fourth graders must learn not to move their lips." A tragedy occurred at the moment some influential educator decided that in the literary experience lips should not twitch, voices should not speak, and bodies should not move.

[1] *The Voice and Spiritual Education,* pp. 29–30.
[2] *The Oral Study of Literature,* p. 19.

Although Malone harks back to a golden age when the oralizing of literature was considered important in literary instruction, he hardly shows any realization of what oral interpreters have accomplished in ever increasing numbers and with ever increasing scholarly rectitude, in the last quarter century in particular. We can only admit a failure to indoctrinate English teachers with our methods. We know that our former students are using oral techniques in the classroom; we sense that our students are more frequently acquainted with oral approaches; we hear of a few seminars and workshops in which successful communication with English teachers has taken place, with the result that they have returned to their classes with renewed enthusiasm for a "new-found" approach. Let us hope that we ourselves do more in the next decade to convince others that oral interpretation is not just a dynamic approach to literary experience but is, for most students, the only good one.

∾

RESPONSE

Wallace A. Bacon

I do not wish particularly to comment on Kemp Malone's remarks. They are fairly perfunctory. Miss Bolton, Mrs. Floyd, and Mr. Bowen have all said things with which I generally agree. It is clear that Malone's remarks, in 1964, were meant (among other things) to suggest the value of oral reading; and I, at least, am old enough to remember a very active pleasure in those occasions when one did have an opportunity to express one's "sympathetic understanding" before an audience—though *many* students hated it, and I should not like to see those particular days return!

There is no point, however, in berating Malone, in retirement, for being old-fashioned. He is not totally jocular in saying, "As I have already told you and as you know without the telling, I am a back number, not a prophet, and I am better fitted to look backward than forward." (We all come to this.) What we ought to do, instead, is to see what in fact *has* come of his "prophecy." It is clear that many English teachers (at least on the primary and secondary school levels) feel the need for oral interpretation. Some of this has come about as a result of the Dartmouth Conference a few years back. Some has been stirred up by the NCTE publication *Oral Interpretation and the Teaching of English.* As of the date of my writing, a newsletter to be called *Oral English* is proposed to stimulate interest in interpretation among English teachers *beyond* the secondary level. But why are these steps always hailed and looked upon as "revolutionary"? I respond keenly to Mr. Bowen's comment that "we can only admit a failure to indoctrinate English teachers with our methods." I agree. However exasperating we find our failure—and I am constantly exasperated by it—I think we must confess it, examine it, and seek to remove it. Miss Bolton and Mrs. Floyd are, I think, right—it isn't for us, the black marks on the white page, but the whole transaction in human terms (experience, behavioral engagement) which is for us the heart of the matter. That may not always be what the scholar wishes for the literary text, but I am persuaded that it is what the poet and the poem want for themselves. I'm not at all sure that Kemp Malone would disagree.

❦

RESPONSE

Don Geiger

Although I claim an equal share of the brooding irritation that settled early on our little colloquy, I remain grateful for Kemp Malone's speech. As the commentators have indicated, oral interpreters will find some grounds for uneasiness and little that is new in Professor Malone's message. But we are Malone's wire-tapping audience, a melancholy relation at best. I daresay that in his own bailiwick many of Malone's colleagues found nothing truistic in his flat assertion: "Until we have taught our students how to read aloud we have not taught them how to read." I quote the last of five (more exactly, seven) consecutive sentences that comprise the outline of a highly promising though scarcely incontrovertible case for oral interpretation of literature. Unfortunately before the reader can see the likely implications of Malone's case, much less prepare a refutation or modification, he must have a reasonably well disciplined and fairly extensive experience of reading literary texts aloud. Without such experience, sentences like those which I have treated as lightning-strokes are delivered in something of a void—smashing good blows but with nothing much there to ignite.

My colleagues have added to our shared regret over this situation a good deal of evidence of increasing interest in an oral approach to literature—by general audiences, in interdepartmental seminars and workshops, and among teachers of both high school and college English. I expect further happy developments of this sort. Meantime, central responsibility in colleges for the oral study rests directly with teachers and students of oral interpretation. I will not speculate grandly on how many persons are directly involved in studying, maintaining, and advancing the quality and meaningfulness of our approach, but there are many. And I am confident that we *are* advancing.

While such observations offer small reason for complacency, we may find in them a measure of reassurance. If such reassurance fails adequately to brace us, oral interpreters have still remaining one certain source of comfort. At least we have not yet been made responsible for enlistments in, among the subjects of Professor Malone's admiration, Latin, Greek, nor even Icelandic.

Selected Readings

Brooks, Keith. "Oral Interpretation in American Universities," *Western Speech,* XXIV (Summer 1960), 142–147.

Robb, Margaret. "Trends in the Teaching of Oral Interpretation," *Western Speech,* XIV (May 1950), 8–11.

We began our reading with Wallace Bacon's "The Dangerous Shores: From Elocution to Interpretation." Our purpose in the volume is to get the reader a little closer to the theory of interpretation. There is no one theory, but many. However, we feel there are strong common strands of theory on which we all agree. We feel the place to begin study is with our history; knowing the tradition, from whence we came hopefully makes it easier to see where we are and where we are going. We have introduced you to a variety of theorists because we think the more varied the input, the better the perspective. As you read Professor Bacon's final essay, consider it in light of the discussion of studying the history of interpretation as well as the "plus," "paradox," "norm," "locus," "tone," "symbols," "emotion," and "expression" of interpretation. Have we resolved the debate over impersonation? Have we learned anything about choral speaking? Are we text-centered or reader-centered? Does the dichotomy have to exist? Hopefully, you are better equipped to make comment on these questions. Answers will not come easily. We are dealing with theory—not theorem. We are dealing with lively organisms, literature, and people.

WALLACE A. BACON

The Dangerous Shores
A Decade Later

The basic view is unchanged: The challenge to the teacher of interpretation and to the interpretative artist himself is to find the tensive path between flattering and risky alternatives, to seek the narrow rather than the broad gate,[1] and to observe a certain humility in going about his art—an art which seems to me to take more and more as its primary object *enactment,* the bodying forth of "the whole complex structure which is the work of literature."[2] If there is a central modification to be made in the position taken in my earlier essay, it is perhaps a modification in the statement, "Interpretation today seems to be moving in the direction of the thing read, not in the direction of the person reading."

I think that statement was probably true ten years ago. I think the direction was clearly of real benefit to the development of interpretation, and it is to be hoped that the lessons learned from that direction will stay with us. Knowledge of the text is a requisite for the interpreter; but it is also a *pre*requisite. It is *food* for creative thought, for the interpreter is among other things a creative performer.

The pendulum always swings: that is what history, above all, illustrates. Some of our earlier preoccupations with text have been exactly that—*pre*occupations. There has been some point to the criticism occasionally leveled against interpretation that it has sometimes seemed to devote itself too simply to exposition and explication of text, to the exclusion of a balancing interest in performance.

I think the widespread interest in Readers Theatre and Chamber Theatre (however they are to be defined) has had something to do with an increased emphasis upon performance. It has certainly had something to do with a loosening of "rules" and a greater—and desirable—flexibility among teachers of the subject, though unhappily hidebound rules do still exist in some places. It has even led to the creation of new kinds of texts, along with the introduction of new media of performance.

---

[1] "I am for the house with the narrow gate," says Lavache in Shakespeare's *All's Well That Ends Well,* IV. v. 52–58 in the Neilson and Hill edition of the complete works.

[2] The phrase given in the original essay.

The concomitant breakdown of certain arbitrary distinctions between interpreter and actor, interpreter and speaker, has been to the good. The interpreter is now "permitted" not simply to suggest but to *do*. He is "permitted" to be a person in his own right, not simply a spokesman for someone else. There has been increased interest in his relationships with an audience. Linguists, psychologists, philosophers have been drawn upon to enhance our notions of what enters into the act of performance. Paralanguage, kinesics, phenomenology, communication theory, metalanguage—these and other fields of knowledge are helping us to understand the elements of which our art is composed. Research in creativity is still, perhaps, in its infancy, but enough is known to be of use to us.

But of course a loosening of bonds—freedom—carries with it obligations to be responsible. If we are blown every way by the winds of change, we may easily end up on one of the dangerous shores. On either side of the deep channel are shoals.

I have never freely shared Don Geiger's view that interpretation is an amalgam, though Mr. Geiger states the view in an appealing and helpful way. One might as well say that interpretation is the inclusive art, and that the speaker and actor are simply branches of it (a view that has some historical claim to truth). But I should prefer to think of speaking, acting, and interpreting as essentially distinct, however much they may sometimes overlap, just as I finally have to think of rhetoric and poetics as distinct, however much they overlap. I must believe that the history of distinctions has some basis in truth, and that we ought to seek for distinctions just as we ought to seek for parallels. Definition is not harmful so long as definitions are allowed (along with the rest of life) to change. There is in the human state—and especially in the creative human state—"an essential and continuing tension between the maintenance of environmental constancies and the interruption of such constancies in the interest of new possibilities of experience. The creative process itself embodies this tension, and individuals who distinguish themselves in artistic, scientific, and entrepreneurial creation exemplify vividly in their persons the incessant dialectic between integration and diffusion, convergence and divergence, thesis and antithesis."[3]

I am concerned that we avoid both *shores:* that we not, in the interest of constancy, run aground; that we not, in the interest of a healthy diffusion, break up. Whatever we may learn from communication theory (and we have not yet learned enough), we ought to avoid thinking of the interpreter as one who manipulates an audience for "effects." Whatever we may learn from rhetorical theory (and the rhetoricians are expanding their own definitions to the breaking point), we ought to avoid thinking of the interpreter as one who "speaks his piece" to persuade his auditors. Whatever we learn from the art of acting (and in many aspects of our art the interpreter and the actor are profitably viewed as coexistent), we ought to avoid thinking of the interpreter simply as one who characterizes.

I have repeatedly said "ought," and I recognize the dangers in *that* word. I argue from *an* aesthetic, *a* view of both literature and interpretation,[4] for I can scarcely do otherwise. Let me very briefly —too briefly—set it down here. The dangerous shores as I see them are shores seen from the particular channel where I sail.

Interpretation is an art of performance. It has as its primary text a work of literature (though there are other kinds of texts). It has as its primary object the enactment or embodiment of that text, the fullest possible realization of the potential experience symbolized by the text. The text is an *act,* with the usual aspects of an act: inception, acceleration, climax, cadence.[5] In this respect, it is like life forms; it is a form created by man but with parallels in

[3] Frank Barron, "The Relationship of Ego Diffusion to Creative Perception," *Widening Horizons in Creativity,* ed. Calvin W. Taylor, Proceedings of the Fifth Utah Creativity Research Conference (New York: John Wiley & Sons, 1964), 81.

[4] Explicated at greater length in my text, *The Art of Interpretation,* particularly the second edition (New York: Holt, Rinehart & Winston, 1972).

[5] Though I must not charge her with the application that I make of it, this view of the act is suggested by Susanne Langer's *Mind: An Essay on Human Feeling* (Baltimore: Johns Hopkins Press, 1967).

forms created by nature. There are resemblances between texts as there are resemblances between life forms, but no one form totally duplicates another. The words of the text are like the roots, stem, leaves of the plant—the "skin" whereby the text is separated from the environment and also makes contact with the environment. Any one reader of the text is, first of all, part of the poem's environment.

But the interpreter, as reader, becomes more than that. He is himself a living form, an act made up of acts and with a rhythm of his own. What he does as a performer is to bring the two forms (his own, the text) into congruence, to the fullest extent of which he is capable. This means that he must *know* (consciously or not) the text. Fitting together of forms means clear apprehension of the forms. This is the point of textual analysis—that it enlarges the reader's awareness of the form of the text; it makes form *significant* for him. If analysis does not do this for him, it is fruitless. (And in practice it often has been.)

But if the text is form, so is the reader, too, form. He must know (consciously or not) himself—his behavior, his speech, his energies, his other resources. To know *all* is an impossible ideal; to know as much as possible is the most one can hope for, for that, God knows, is hard enough. Both text and reader, insofar as they are alive, are flexible. Each "gives" in the matching process; each form is to some degree elastic. The experience of the text is modified in the apprehension of the individual reader, necessarily; the experience of the interpreter ought, too, to be modified by the experience of the text. This is the sense in which literature "teaches" us, and there is pleasure in the teaching. (But also, from time to time there are certain agonies, as any interpreter will testify.) No interpreter ought simply to obliterate the text, to hide it behind his own personality, though there are readers who tend to do this and to give us not the matching of forms but the single form of the reader, so that all poems from this reader sound alike. On the other hand, no reader can expect simply to vanish into a text. The performer is always there—but if the corporal body (the body *fact*) is the interpreter, the enactment (the body *act*) is neither poem alone nor interpreter alone but the matched forms. For the actor, this normally means that the performer (the body fact) becomes the character (the body act). For the interpreter, it is not a matter of character only but of states of mind, scenes, images, thoughts which may not exist in any clearly defined or describable human personality. As I. A. Richards says, ". . . some poems are more obviously dramatic than others. By some we are invited to identify their voices with their authors'; others lend a character to or take one from other spokesmen; yet others, transcending personality, seem utterable only by 'miracle, bird or golden handiwork.' "[6] This is why it is possible to say, at times, of an interpretation that it "over characterizes," and why some performances of lyric poems by actors fail fully to realize the poem's potential.

I do not know that a work of literature can kill off a reader, though I have known audiences to faint; but an interpreter can certainly kill a text. Murder in the classroom is not restricted to the acts of teachers. But creation occurs in the classroom, too, when the reader and the text come to significant matching, when the miraculism[7] occurs by which two forms create a third which is unique and which cannot therefore be precisely duplicated.

This, for me, is the basic fact of interpretation, that it (through a process which involves re-creation, too) creates experience— experience which is related to real life but which is not identical with it; experience which has the form of the act (inception, acceleration, climax, cadence) and which ultimately "dies," though it can be brought to life again, changed. All the movement, rhythms, thinking, imaging in the *act* result in *feeling.* What the interpreter does is to body forth the total *feel* (not to be confused with simple emotionality). As the text acts (thinks, does, says), it *feels,* in the performance of the interpreter. The more complex the text the

[6] I. A. Richards, "Coleridge On Imagination," *Modern Criticism,* eds. Walter Sutton and Richard Foster (Indianapolis: Odyssey, 1963), 170. The point is a valuable one, for often the structure of a piece works *against* identifying the language of the text as the words of a definable personality. We too often, and too simply, take the dramatic impulse to apply to all literature.

[7] The word is from John Crowe Ransom, who employs it in his discussion of the kinds of poetry in *World's Body* (Baton Rouge: Louisiana State U. Press, 1968).

greater the pleasurable task of matching, but even a simple text (matching even a simple reader) is complicated.

If the process of enactment, then, is basic, I must feel that all other aspects of the total art of interpretation are, for the classroom teacher, relative. And I do. There are special problems of the audience—important, surely, and the interpreter must cope with them, for what the interpreter wants, at the right time, is to bring the audience into the match. But the problem of communication is a *subsequent* problem; there is a sense in which the basic problem is not communication but communion (though the theological connotation in part interferes). Nor is it useful, beyond a certain point, to think of the work of literature as being in its nature and function rhetorical; the language of imaginative literature has an *imm*ediate rather than a mediate use. For the interpreter, the literary text lives, *is,* it does not only *say;* it shows, it does not only tell. If the interest in the audience is primary, or if the focus is primarily upon the matter of communication, the basic problem of matching is likely to suffer. This is not to say that the audience doesn't matter, nor to overlook the simple fact that if there is no communication in the classroom one cannot even discuss the success of the match. It is an attempt to put first things first, to avoid dangers that have arisen in the past when second things or third things have been put first. While literature communicates, communication is not what literature *is.* A poem lying in a desk drawer can be called a poem whether or not it is taken out of the desk drawer and read—but of course something happens when it is read. The solitary interpreter can be called an interpreter whether or not anyone else is listening—but of course something happens when he is heard.

I shall seem to have wandered afield, but this is the point: Interpretation today seems to me vitally concerned with the nature of the embodiment, and we are no longer so solely concerned with the nature of the text being embodied. We are beyond, I hope, the notion that interpretation can be taught by spending a certain number of weeks on textual analysis, a certain number on voice, a certain number on bodily activity. *From the outset,* interpretation demands emphasis upon the totality of the act of performance:

the whole *feeling* of the words being uttered—the complete tensive state which is life. Literary analysis exists as a way of pointing to aspects of the experience to be embodied; vocal drill, training in movement, study of qualities and kinds of behavior exist as ways of yielding the necessary techniques by which the experience is to be embodied. But from the outset, it is the total configuration that matters, the way in which the whole body (including "mind") of the performer *enacts*.

The direction seems to me a healthy sign. The danger is, of course, that we may once more take too single an interest in "effects," or too simple an interest in "communication," or that we may find the performer's behavior so fascinating that we minimize the significance of the text for which that behavior is trained. The "personality performer" may be a great commercial success—and in America he often is—but I doubt that our schools and colleges and universities ought to exist to train him. The goal of education is to lead the performer outside himself, to bring him to experiences other than his own, to create in him a sense of the otherness of the other, so that in the long run he can come back to himself truly educated. "Going away to school" involves more than walking.